Scholarly Journals at the Crossroads: A Subversive Proposal for Electronic Publishing

An Internet Discussion
about Scientific and
Scholarly Journals
and Their Future

Edited by

Ann Shumelda Okerson
Office of Scientific & Academic Publishing
Association of Research Libraries

James J. O'Donnell
Department of Classical Studies
University of Pennsylvania

Office of Scientific & Academic Publishing
Association of Research Libraries
June 1995

ISBN: 0-918006-26-0

Office of Scientific & Academic Publishing
Association of Research Libraries
21 Dupont Circle, NW, Suite 800
Washington, DC 20036
202-296-2296 (phone)
202-872-0884 (fax)
arlhq@cni.org

∞ The paper used in this publication meets the minimum requirements
of the American National Standard for Information Sciences--Permanence
of Paper for Printed Library Materials, ANSI Z39.48-1984.

Acknowledgments

A large part of the preliminary and not inconsiderable work of making the ftp archives of the "subversive discussion" was done by Colleen Wirth, Department of Mathematics, Princeton University, Princeton NJ 08540 (wirth@clarity.princeton.edu). Wirth is also one of the Assistant Editors of *Psycoloquy*, the Internet peer-reviewed journal edited by Stevan Harnad. The book originated from the ftp archives.

The glossary was prepared by Ethan Starr (ethan@cni.org), a Research Assistant and graduate student at the Catholic University of America.

CONTENTS

INTRODUCTION   1

I   Overture: The Subversive Proposal   11

II   The Discussion Begins   13

The first response to Harnad's proposal was swift, practical: an offer by a systems administrator to house a comprehensive scientific electronic publishing system. A brief exchange about level of support took place. For the reader, the discussion here emphasizes that the problems with enacting such a large-scale vision are not technical but social.

III.   Who is Responsible?   17

Does the responsibility for scientific and scholarly findings lie at the grass roots with individual scholars or should there be institutionalization and centralization -- or both? Nobel Prize Winner Joshua Lederberg, looking to the practical uses of more and better information that the scientist can use, introduces the idea of institutional rather than discipline-based archives. From the library community, encouragement to recover some control over the economic fate of faculty products; then discussion of the place of the large learned societies in the publishing landscape ensues.

IV.   What Does Electronic Publishing Cost?   23

Discourse by a leader from the American Chemical Society, one of today's largest and most electronically seasoned publishers, takes the discussion to a new level and adds specific detail of costs and economics to the conversation. Whether electronic publishing will be cheaper or more expensive than print on paper, at least in the near term, is an important underlying question.

V.   Suggestions and Strategies   30

Several scientists contribute. One is a long-time editor of a substantive electronic newsletter for computer scientists and shares his economic perspectives. Another volunteers to promote the Harnad proposal. Another, a creator of the World Wide Web, comments and offers encouragement for the future. Yet another sees a role for the European Community. Striking is the consensus of the proposal's proponents that practical actions can take precedence for the time being over broader considerations.

VI.   Reprise   42

Ginsparg and Harnad return to speculation about the practical elements of the proposal. The first of a series of responses from the library community follows.

VII.   E-Journal Publishing; Infrastructure Investments   49

The American Chemical Society's Lorrin Garson returns to the discussion with detailed comments about the significant planning and investment course the Society has already taken in moving into non-print publication. He makes the case that scaling up and sustaining production require considerable thought and infrastructure support. More numbers are introduced; Harnad differentiates esoteric publication from other sectors of the information market.

VIII.   A Researcher's Perspective   60

Andrew Odlyzko of AT&T Bell Labs, himself a proponent of similar enterprises, joins the discussion as a third strong voice after Harnad and Ginsparg and presents an essay about staging the transition to electronic scholarly journals.

IX.   A Librarian Speaks   74

One of the proponents insists that moving to electronic journals is a more simple process than other discussants believe to be the case. Richard Entlich, a librarian at Cornell, with substantial hands-on experience in implementing online journals for university researchers, shares his experience and points to the complexity of the publishing landscape and the interrelated nature of the various parts.

X.   Reprise -- *Prima Facie* Worries   87

For several years, Harnad has spoken out about objections to electronic publishing that he sees as ill-founded. Here he takes the opportunity of a contribution to this discussion to review those worrisome issues.

XI.   A Librarian's View from Europe   92

Bernard Naylor is the University Librarian at the University of Southhampton. He initially joined the discussion through a paper coincidentally written at about the moment the "subversive" discussion was beginning. This section begins his various contributions to the subversive proposal.

XII.   Graffiti, Esoterica or Scholarship?   110

A return to a question of distinguishing "publishing" from other forms of network-public discourse. What seemed fairly simple in the world of print (for example, knowing the difference between a publication and a private letter) begins to be more complicated in a medium where formal discourse and chit-chat flow in the same pipeline. Does "esoteric" do justice to the significance of scholarly publishing?

XIII.   E-Journal Costs and Editorial Costs   118

The question of costs returns to the fore, arising from a proposal for a specific project. The question is taken up of what and whether editors should be paid. A university press journals manager contributes some current, real-world information to the discourse on editors and editorial offices. One of the undoubted inefficiencies of the present journal system is the delay and redundancy introduced by a distributed and publication-linked practice of peer-review, re submission, and limited acceptances.

XIV.   Journal Publishing Systems and Models   140

Bernard Naylor, who entered the correspondence with a paper he wrote for another forum, now offers extended remarks that take up the issues of the whole series. His new contribution views the journals publishing system holistically and takes up issues such as prestige, pressure to publish, conservatism of authors and publishers, and the prognosis for acceptance of electronic publications by all the players in the current academic information chain.

XV.   Brief Discussions -- Format, Economics, Submissions   164

Several messages pick up various topical threads that arose earlier in the discussion.

XVI.   The Collapse of Traditional Journals   170

Frank Quinn, a mathematician at the Virginia Polytechnic Institute and State University and a member of various American Mathematical Society decision-making committees, adds a further voice foreseeing radical change to the discussion.

XVII.   Systemic and Structural Costs -- Networks & Connectivity   180

A wider context for costs is invoked. How cheap will the infrastructure be? How expensive is a good network? Will universities and scholars have to pay more? How much?

XVIII.   Citations and Citation Frequency   201

The measure of use that is most easily quantified on a national or international basis is "citation frequency." This group of messages began during the net-wide subversive proposal discussion and then some of the discussants picked up the topic about two months after the main body of the conversation ended, for further probing. Not every message in the sequence went to the public lists directly; there was more discussion among individuals, with some of those postings occasionally being referred to the wider audience. In this regard, a rudimentary kind of editing and peer review is already taking place.

XIX.   More on Costs -- of Digitization   218

Some new evidence is presented suggesting that the costs of digitization, or at least compression, may be shrinking. In order to prepare this book for publication, the editors artificially cut off a discussion that still continues at the time of final proofs (May 1995) and shows no likelihood of ending for a long time.

CONCLUSION   225

HYPERLINK   231

GLOSSARY   235

INTRODUCTION

Scholars and historians tell us that technological change is a powerful engine driving economic and social change. Invent the automobile, they argue, and suburbs are inevitable, not to mention a sexual revolution and jokes about the Yugo. This principle has penetrated the public consciousness so far that now every technical innovation is greeted with enthusiasm by those who see ways for *this* gadget to shape the world to suit their particular tastes.

But the distance between hope and realization is great, and there are plenty of opportunities for imagination and ineptitude to compete with each other to shape the details of a new landscape. This is a book about hope and imagination in one corner of the emerging landscape of cyberspace. It embraces passionate discussion of an idea for taking to the Internet to revolutionize one piece of the world of publishing.

"Publishing" is a business with many faces, held together in the mind's eye by the common technologies of printing and binding. Comic books, phone books, popular novels, and scientific texts all find their audiences through one facet or another of an industry whose business decisions are made on certain common grounds: costs of acquiring the content and preparing it for publication, costs of mechanical reproduction, and costs of distributing it effectively to the target audience. Those costs are recovered in many ways and even profits are sometimes made: advertisers pay most of the cost of newspapers, end users pay for best sellers, and university budgets pay for much scientific literature both by contributing "page charges" to get faculty articles published and by paying for the journals in which they are published. But despite those diversities, the common technology gives all such "publishing" a common language for evaluating continuing forms of publishing and proposed innovations.

Not every branch of "publishing" is equally healthy in the late twentieth century. The romance novel is robustly successful, but the scientific journal and the scholarly monograph are threatened by rising costs, rising output, and constrained academic budgets. The most painful paradox is that in the interests of science, the law of the market *cannot* be allowed to function. An item with a very small market may yet be the indispensable link in a chain of research that leads to a result of high social value. Worse, even that value may be -- at the moment of production of the small market item -- years or even decades away. The research libraries of the world have the unenviable task of seeking in common to acquire the totality of scientific and academic discourse for researchers to use, even as that totality explodes in size and cost.

Enter technology. The commonality of printing and binding is less and less necessary to transmit information to a wide audience. Some parts of print publishing have already been vulnerable to this, as newspapers have seen their markets erode under the impact of radio and television, even while odd synergies emerge and the newspaper becomes the place to find a print record of the coming week's television programs. No linear connection can be counted on: film and television entertain the eyes and occasionally the mind, but bookstores are fuller than ever of diverting books and magazines.

Accordingly, it is impossible to say with any confidence what the introduction and widespread use of networked electronic technology will do to "publishing". It is easy enough to look at the power of the World-Wide Web to transmit words far and wide and conclude that there will be some impact, but where that impact will be felt is another question. What will we read on-line? What will still need paper? To look ahead in this way is to begin to see a world in which things commonly thought of together begin to disresemble each other more than they do now. The telephone book, for example, is far less efficient than an on-line index (with yellow pages, cross-references, reverse indexes, searching-by-address, and especially a click-and-dial feature) would be, and we may confidently imagine not only that the annual massacre of trees to produce mountains of new phone books will end, but that soon we will even forget to think of the information as the phone "book" in any meaningful sense. Even as we are all reading our Jane Austen on a summer's day in a hammock twenty years from now, the "book" will have changed by virtue of the things that won't be in book form any longer. Where will the scholars and scientists be?

The pages that follow are a fragment of serious and urgent discussions that are going on at this moment in many parts of the world where people worry about the future of scholarship and science. If -- the instinctively framed argument goes -- traditional academic publishing is caught in a price spiral that threatens its stability and if a new, powerful technology that wipes out whole sectors of the costs of distributing information is now available, won't it make sense to transport as much as we can of what scholars and scientists publish to the new environment as rapidly as possible? Won't that solve the economic problems of publishing?

Perhaps, perhaps not. One thing that has emerged in the last four years or so of serious discussion on these topics is that there are various competing interests at stake. All profess to have the good of the higher educational and scientific mission in mind, but it cannot be denied that everyone seeks a future in which not *only* that mission but also their own economic and professional future is assured. Professors, researchers, librarians, commercial publishers, learned societies, and university presses have all emerged with distinctive points of view. The discussions are not empty of practical consequences, for strong ideas well expressed are the basis for the confidence people will place in experiments and projects that go beyond the experimental in bringing a vision of electronic publishing for the scientific and academic community to reality. Many such experiments are already well under way, and indeed we reach a moment at which people are not so much impatient to try things as fidgety that we are not yet moving past experiments to full-scale realization of ideas. Yet those fidgets may be premature, with both the results of the experiments and the convincing formulation of the theory still up in the air. The "killer application" of electronic publishing seems not to have emerged yet.

The discussions now under way are taking place in a variety of forums. They range from the informality of the departmental coffee room to full-scale conferences, some of which resemble summit meetings between mistrustful opponents. Books and articles appear apace, the traditional form of publication. But between all these is discussion facilitated by the new media of communication themselves. It is no accident that the Internet is a buzzword of this decade, for the land rush of settlers to that frontier of cyberspace has been of majestic proportions, far outstripping any recorded human settlement on planet earth. No one knows quite what to make of the numbers, but it is beyond denying that many millions of people have staked a claim to a little piece of this curious world where you can go to live without giving up the mortgage or the lease back in ordinary reality. And the one thing people do when they move to cyberspace is talk to each other.

They talk to each other there with the promiscuity and eagerness of -- well, of people. Those who read what they find on the Internet with the skeptical eye of a consumer of print publications are often dismayed, even appalled by what they see, forgetting that human beings as a rule speak to one another in ways raw, unpolished, even illogical, far below the standards of the written word. It is not so much that cyberspace is begetting trash as that it is giving a degree of publicity and visibility to our ordinary, everyday conversations, and we are -- as representatives of the species -- embarrassed by what we see.

But the caricature of Internet discussion must not blind us to the recognition that just as in everyday life, people do rise to higher levels of coherence and lucidity. The constant surprise for regular visitors to the Internet is just how many interesting people are found amid the dullards and how much stimulating and otherwise impossible conversation goes on there.

So this book is an intersection between the issues of the time and the media that make those issues arise. It is a discussion about using the networks to publish, and it is possible only because the network was there in the summer of 1994 to make this feasible.

It began with the "subversive proposal" of the title. The author of that provocative document is a pioneering veteran of network culture. Stevan Harnad, who took up a position as Professor of Psychology at the

University of Southampton (UK) in the fall of 1994 after many years as a researcher and editor in Princeton, New Jersey, knows the twin worlds of paper and electronic scholarly journals as few others. He has been the editor for many years of *Behavioral and Brain Sciences*, a journal published by Cambridge University Press, and in 1990 he introduced *Psycoloquy*, the first peer-reviewed scientific journal on the Internet. He is particularly known (apart from his substantial scientific work) for his interest in the mechanisms of "peer review", by which the quality of published scientific research is guaranteed. He has pioneered in cyberspace the technique practiced by some paper journals of "open peer review", whereby the experts consulted on an article's worthiness submit their comments for publication along with the article, thus stimulating discussion in a way the article alone could not. *Psycoloquy* has been a notable success in achieving and maintaining a high standard of quality *and* in its ability to assure its audience of that quality.

Harnad has been a strong proponent of the use of the electronic networks to extend the reach and power and accessibility of scientific information, and he has not been slow to point out the economic advantages as well. Crudely put, it seems that the publisher is superfluous. If the originating scientist who does the research has access to the network, then he or she can "publish" with a few keystrokes; and anyone with network access anywhere in the world can get the results in a matter of minutes. No money need change hands.

That oversimplifies the position Harnad takes in his "subversive proposal", but it catches the gist of the unspoken hope or assumption or dream of many who look at this new environment. Harnad fully recognizes that the network itself and the tools individuals use to access it do not come free of charge, but once we can assume the ubiquity of those tools (and in the scientific community they are very nearly ubiquitous) their use adds marginal costs that are at most trivial. (The best current guess about the cost for using the Internet superhighway itself is about a dollar a year per user: Hal Varian of the University of Michigan studies this topic in ARL's *Filling the Pipeline and Paying the Piper* [1995].) How can we take advantage of this?

The simplest answer is that the problem is not technical, but sociological. How do we get the right user community interested and committed to communicating in this way? The first step is to talk up the idea, talk it through, and talk it out to the point of practical application.

This vital step was taken in the summer of 1994 in the discussion presented here. Harnad began it all on June 27th by posting his "subversive proposal" to the discussion list VPIEJ-L. (In the alphabet soup of the Internet, that is the name of a discussion list based at Virginia Polytechnic Institute, a particularly venturesome and interesting academic base for network activity; the list is devoted to "electronic journals", of which there are already hundreds, many dozens of them quite scholarly. ARL's *Directory of Electronic Journals, Newsletters, and Academic Discussion*

Lists is appearing [1995] in its fifth edition.) A great deal of the conversatoin was also branched to SERIALST@uvmvm.uvm.edu, a discussion list for serials librarians and other members of the serials "chain." Some of it was also copied to other lists on the Internet, BITNET, and Usenet.

The response to Harnad's proposal (it is the opening section of this book) was quick, lively, and wide-ranging. As is often the case, the most enthusiastic discussants were those who shared much of Harnad's position. One principal discussant is Paul Ginsparg, research physicist at Los Alamos National Laboratory and a recognized innovator in electronic scientific preprint publishing as well. Ginsparg runs a service that provides, free of charge to users, the full text of "preprints" reporting the most current scientific activity in high energy physics to readers around the world. Such preprints have been in use as a paper artifact among scientists for many years; in high energy physics, the paper circulation of such things has ended, and Ginsparg's service is the faster, easier, more widely circulated result. That server exemplifies the "free" use of the Internet for high quality information distribution. To be sure, the field of high energy physics is well defined by the laboratories where work gets done, and there is a kind of quality control exercised by readers who note where given papers come from and choose how to apportion their reading time appropriately. That is a facility that would not be so easily obtained if the field were, say, nineteenth-century English literature, where a small state college may produce work as reliable as large, well-endowed institutions do.

Also contributing sympathetically to much of the discussion is Andrew Odlyzko, research scientist at AT&T Bell Labs and himself author of a forthcoming article reprinted here in abridged form that makes arguments similar to Harnad's.

But discussion was not one-sided. There are serious objections to be made and considered to what Harnad proposes. If a large and diverse body of authors produce material and a large and diverse body of readers come looking for it, it is far from obvious that the match of author to reader will be easy and transparent. The nagging question for many Internet services today is "Does it scale up?" If the whole world does this, can we still afford to do it so cheaply? What kind of editing, peer reviewing, cataloguing, and finding services will the reading public, however scholarly, find necessary? How expensive will they be? Will we migrate to a new environment, only to find that we have reinvented there all the things that cost so much in the old environment? If so, what will we have gained?

Representatives of these caution-giving points of view are strongly heard here. Two in particular deserve mention. Lorrin Garson manages the publishing operations of the American Chemical Society, a huge and vital link in the scientific information chain. He does not represent a profiteering private corporation seeking to maximize return on investment, but he has real payrolls to meet and real expenses. He speaks vigorously for the value of the middle-man's contribution to the process of scientific communication and hence for the costs that will still be incurred. Garson's viewpoint is seconded by Richard Entlich, a Librarian at Cornell University, whose libraries have cooperated with the ACS and other electronic publishing experimenters in making electronic informaiton available to users. From a European perspective, Bernard Naylor, University Librarian at the University of Southampton, weighs in from the vantage point of one who must manage the point of contact between a wider audience and the universe of scholarly and scientific discourse as a whole. The value of this whole discussion lies in the vigor and frankness with which these various participants make their cases, while maintaining a remarkably cordial and collegial tone. As is the way of the Internet, other participants came and went, making their contributions.

Here we should emphasize the point to which Harnad returns with most frequency. He speaks from the first lines of his proposal of "esoteric" publishing, that is to say, work done by the few for the few. While some participants worry over the appropriateness of the exact word Harnad prefers, all are agreed that the exchange of information among researchers working at a high level is a different matter from flooding the world with romance novels. It is central to this discussion to keep that restriction in mind and to see what difference it makes. If the "phone book" disappears from the world of "publishing" in one direction, it can be argued that the scientific journal, which few if any ever read in a hammock, will disappear in another direction, replaced by a better, faster, more reliable form of communication.

The bulk of the discussion lasted about two months. But it did not disappear. For months afterwards, conversations among real living breathing people face to face and by telephone as well as e-conversations on the more ethereal medium of the network continued to refer back to "the subversive proposal discussion". The principals in the discussion still continue to maintain the discussion among themselves, copying their messages to a few other people who have expressed the most interest in being involved. The final section of this book, on citations of articles, represents that portion of discussion which was continuing as this book went to press.

It became clear that significant issues had received here the canonical form of presentation by which they would be discussed for some time to come. A stage in the evolution of ideas about electronic publication had been set. This book recognizes that fact by presenting the discussion, still now in a timely enough fashion to affect debate, and as a record of how the argument was moving at a turning point in the network's history.

One way to present the material, of course, would have been to invite the participants in the conversation to write formal papers for an anthology. The book that resulted then would have been familiar to a fault, and easily enough understood. But first of all the participants are all busy scientists and professionals, whose own work continues to move on restlessly in search of the cutting edge. Not all would have been willing to go back and rehearse their arguments one more time. Second, much of substance would be lost by such a stereotyped presentation.

For the real value of networked discussion of this kind is in a flexibility that is impossible both in print and in real life. In real life, we may have conferences to discuss a subject, but if halfway through the conference some novel issue arises, expert testimony can be difficult to well-nigh impossible to summon in a timely way. But on the Internet, the next expert is only an e-mail message away, and more than once here that kind of "deus ex machina" arrives to stimulate and advance the discussion just in time.

In print, on the other hand, everybody is a monologist. A collaborative volume turns into a series of individual turns, where author A deals not with author B, but with an idiosyncratic version of author B, whereupon B deals not with A, but with a version of A. Examples of the consequent phenomenon of perfectly intelligent and responsible people arguing past each other are not far to seek. But the flow of e-mail makes high-minded neglect of the other's point of view impossible. The network facilitates dialogue. If that dialogue sometimes descends into "flaming", that is only a sign that real human beings are rubbing ideas together, a process as volatile in cyberspace as it is in real life. From a scientific point of view, the value lies in the give and take, which may either lead to agreement or to a nuanced and valuable expression of the irreducible conflicts. The latter is, if anything, more valuable than the former, for the way it reflects the honest truth about the world, that there are many many issues on which reasonable people do *not* agree with each other. Traditional print media, privileging one voice at a time, can make it seem as if the goal is to find the one authoritative voice speaking truth from on high, when a more rational sense of what we are as people would suggest that we are better served when we honestly admit our disagreements and try to make our world out of respect for the points where we cannot all march together.

Accordingly, we have elected to present the discussion as it happened, as a series of e-mail messages that flowed over the network through the summer of 1994. At first, this may be off-putting to those who do not know this culture, but within a page or two, readers will get used to the rhythm. In particular, note the fairness with which respondents quote their interlocutors by incorporating paragraphs of earlier messages in later ones, to put idea/response together for readers. If, after all, some hundreds of readers are seeing these messages separated by hours or days, they need some reminding of where the course of discussion has gone. This inevitably creates some repetition when the messages are brought together here, but the clarity is also welcome.

We have edited with a very light hand. Only tiny irrelevancies have been deleted, and occasionally we have "corrected" the sequence of messages to make the flow of thought more obvious. (Every message comes on the network with a date and time stamp, and that is the chronological order we have mainly followed, but those numbers can confuse when a message written in Europe is answered "before" it was written by a prompt respondent five or six time zones to the west.) We have left authors with their individual styles, including those who (in a practice common on the network but attracting very little comment that we have seen) follow the capitalization style of archy or e. e. cummings, but we have also corrected what were assuredly typos. We have broken the flow of the argument up into "chapters" and added a few explanatory notes to give readers of the print version all the advantages that contemporary readers of the original had. We have also provided a short glossary of netspeak.

The discussion itself had no formal conclusion: real life doesn't have many neat endings short of the pine box six feet under. The issues are not resolved. The last phase of the discussion was a lively look at the question of just how often scientific publications are read/cited, a topic of notorious difficulty. In retrospect, the discussion ended when people in other venues began speaking of it in the past tense. Stevan Harnad archived the e-mail in a long series of files stored on a networked server at Princeton University, which has been our authority for most of what is contained here (but we have supplemented it with some messages kept separately). It will have had some readers from that source, but few would have known where to look, much less how to interpret what they found there.

We have added a brief concluding essay that picks up some of the issues and ventures to outline some of the terms for the discussion that must now ensue, but we must emphasize that we do so without consultation with the participants. (Both editors appear in fleeting walk-on roles in these pages, but they had no influence over the shape of the discussion and were for the most part simply fascinated observers.)

And so this book you hold in your hands is a curious thing. It is a traditional print publication, freezing in time a series of fleeting e-mail messages that envision a future of publishing that goes well beyond print. Will print become obsolete? The fairest answer is that it will become as obsolete as speech was made obsolete by the written word, or as calligraphy was made obsolete by print. It is a mistake to speak of succession and replacement, and more important to think of a world in which available media grow more powerful and various and the interconnections more supple and useful. We would not publish this book if we did not think the networked discussion was important and interesting, but we would not *publish* this *book* if we did not think that the networked discussion has an importance and an interest that reach beyond the network's ability to disseminate it. We hope that the readers of these pages will agree.

One last point. Many readers will *dis*agree with the subversive proposal and its advocates, perhaps fiercely. Some of those readers will themselves be publishers or other participants in the scholarly publishing community. We hope that the unpersuaded readers will be stimulated to think through the issues the most acutely, identify the points of disagreement, and clarify the issues at stake. If this proposal is invalid, what does it mean for the present and future that it is so urgently pressed, so widely discussed, and so fiercely believed? Is that not in itself a new and important fact about the environment in which we work? What would a truly creative response to this challenge look like?

Ann Shumelda Okerson
Association of Research Libraries

James J. O'Donnell
University of Pennsylvania

NOTE ON PRESENTATION

We have retained the flavor and the form of e-mail conversation as it takes place on the net today. Each message has a header (here stripped of some technicalities that appear on-line) with date/time, author, and subject. One or two small apparent departures from chronological order restore the actual sequence of messages whose time-stamps are confused by different time zones of origin.

It is a common practice for authors to embed parts of other authors' messages in their own in order to respond or comment. On-line, these will typically be marked by angle brackets at the left margin, which sometimes get doubled or tripled as a message containing embedded text is embedded in another and then perhaps yet another. We have followed this practice with two enhancements: all such embedded messages and (more often) parts of messages are printed in slightly reduced type (they have mainly appeared already in full earlier in the discussion), and where quotations-within-quotations occur we have occasionally marked the doubled and tripled angle brackets at the left margin with the initials of the writer being quoted to help the reader follow the line of argument. Finally, in the limited typography of the net, it is conventional to use asterisks for *emphasis*, and we have mainly retained them in these messages.

That said, if the reader is unfamiliar with the conventions of e-mail it will take some slight patience to get a sense of the rhythm of such conversation, but one reason for publishing this book in this form is to display an example of serious conversations on urgent issues in a novel forum with its own idioms and conventions.

I. OVERTURE: The Subversive Proposal

esoteric   213 aj .es-o-'ter-ik
LL [italic esotericus], fr. Gk [italic es{o-}terikos], fr. [italic
es{o-}ter{o-}], compar. of [italic eis{o-}], [italic es{o-}] within,
fr. [italic eis] into, fr. [italic en] in -- more at [mini IN]
1 a aj designed for or understood by the specially initiated alone
1 b aj of or relating to knowledge that is restricted to a small
group
2 a aj limited to a small circle <~ pursuits>
2 b aj [mini PRIVATE], [mini CONFIDENTIAL] <an ~ purpose>
esoterically 21313 av -i-k(*-)l{e-}

*(From the networked Merriam Webster
Dictionary at Princeton University)*

We have heard many sanguine predictions about the demise of paper publishing, but life is short and the inevitable day still seems a long way off. This is a subversive proposal that could radically hasten that day. It is applicable only to ESOTERIC (non-trade, no-market) scientific and scholarly publication (but that is the lion's share of the academic corpus anyway), namely, that body of work for which the author does not and never has expected to SELL the words. The scholarly author wants only to PUBLISH them, that is, to reach the eyes and minds of peers, fellow esoteric scientists and scholars the world over, so that they can build on one another's contributions in that cumulative. collaborative enterprise called learned inquiry. For centuries, it was only out of reluctant necessity that authors of esoteric publications entered into the Faustian bargain of allowing a price-tag to be erected as a barrier between their work and its (tiny) intended readership, for that was the only way they could make their work public at all during the age when paper publication (and its substantial real expenses) was their only option.

But today there is another way, and that is PUBLIC FTP: If every esoteric author in the world this very day established a globally accessible local ftp archive for every piece of esoteric writing from this day forward, the long-heralded transition from paper publication to purely electronic publication (of esoteric research) would follow suit almost immediately. This is already beginning to happen in the physics community, thanks to Paul Ginsparg's HEP preprint network, with 20,000 users worldwide and 35,000 "hits" per day, and Paul Southworth's CICnet is ready to help follow suit in other disciplines. The only two factors standing in the way of this outcome at this moment are (1) quality control (i.e., peer review and editing), which today happens to be implemented almost exclusively by paper publishers, and (2) the patina of paper publishing, which results from this monopoly on quality control. If all scholars' preprints were universally available to all scholars by anonymous ftp (and gopher, and World-Wide Web, and the search/retrieval wonders of the future), NO scholar would ever consent to WITHDRAW any preprint of his from the public eye after the refereed version was accepted for paper "PUBLICation." Instead, everyone would, quite naturally, substitute the refereed, published reprint for the unrefereed preprint. Paper publishers will then either restructure themselves (with the cooperation of the scholarly community) so as to arrange for the much-reduced electronic-only page costs (which I estimate to be less than 25% of paper-page costs, contrary to the 75% figure that appears in most current publishers' estimates) to be paid out of advance subsidies (from authors' page charges, learned society dues, university publication budgets and/or governmental publication subsidies) or they will have to watch as the peer community spawns a brand new generation of electronic-only publishers who will.

The subversion will be complete, because the (esoteric -- no-market) peer-reviewed literature will have taken to the airwaves, where it always belonged, and those airwaves will be free (to the benefit of us all) because their true minimal expenses will be covered the optimal way for the unimpeded flow of esoteric knowledge to all: In advance.

Stevan Harnad
Cognitive Science Laboratory
Princeton University
Princeton NJ 08542
harnad@princeton.edu
June 27, 1994

II.   The Discussion Begins

The first response to Harnad's proposal was swift, practical: an offer by a systems administrator to house a comprehensive scientific electronic publishing system. A brief exchange about level of support took place. For the reader, the discussion here emphasizes that the problems with enacting such a large-scale vision are not technical but social.

Date: Mon, 27 Jun 1994 17:42:13 -0400 (EDT)
From: Paul Southworth <pauls@locust.cic.net>

On Mon, 27 Jun 1994, Stevan Harnad wrote:

> We have heard many predictions about the demise of paper publishing,
> but life is short and the inevitable day still seems a long way off.
> This is a subversive proposal that could radically hasten that day.

OK, let's do it. I'll provide archive space, network connectivity, and accounts for the maintainers/referees (I think I'm qualified to provide some technical advice, but it sounds like you should form a committee of delegates from various fields to actually handle the processing).

Let me know when you're ready. If you decide to launch a pilot, just let me know who I should give the accounts to and I will give them disk space on a server.

I see several avenues to pursue with regard to this proposal. First, these are resources that I can immediately bring to bear on the project (i.e., starting tomorrow or as soon as you would like to roll out...). I'm assuming that I will not personally be doing the archive maintenance, only the system maintenance.

1. An archive server dedicated to public-access to electronic text files.
2. Space on that server to be maintained by the various referees /archivists associated with this project. I can offer about one gigabyte of space to start, on an as-needed basis.
3. Accounts for the referees/archivists, unlimited usage, no fees. Accounts to be used for archive maintenance (and related email /Usenet /Internet exploration).
4. Mailing lists to support communication both with the public and between archivists.
5. Access via anonymous ftp, gopher, and world wide web.

6. Some support for the archivists -- I don't have vast quantities of time for this, but I can certainly resolve system problems and keep everything backed up to tape.
7. Some support for archive users (problems unrelated to content, which should be handled by the individuals to whom maintenance is delegated). I see myself as a participant in the support process, not taking sole responsibility for it.

In the longer term:

1. I know archivists who already maintain mirror image archives of my electronic text files in the UK and Australia -- we can approach them to discuss overseas propagation to provide fast access to users in Europe and the South Pacific.
2. We may be able to work this project in with CICNet's existing efforts to obtain NSF funding for our Wide Area Information System Resource Management project (WAIRM). This would include funding for development of technical solutions, and working with the LOC and major research libraries (and research library associations) to fold quality electronic publications into established library catalog systems (and ultimately full-text access in all libraries).
3. Domain registration (are you thinking of incorporating a not-for-profit entity to manage this?). I can handle the Internic paperwork and the domain name service.

Date: Mon, 27 Jun 94 20:42:16 -0600
From: Paul Ginsparg 505-667-7353 <ginsparg@qfwfq.lanl.gov>

stevan forwarded to me your message:
> Date: Mon, 27 Jun 1994 17:42:13 -0400 (EDT)
> From: Paul Southworth <pauls@locust.cic.net>

> ok, let's do it. I'll provide archive space, network connectivity, and
> accounts for the maintainers/referees (I think I'm qualified to provide
> some technical advice, but it sounds like you should form a committee of
> delegates from various fields to actually handle the processing).

it might be useful for you first to have a look at what is already running in physics (see http://xxx.lanl.gov/ and related archives), starting three years ago (and currently with over 20,000 users; processing over 35,000 transactions per day via ftp, www, gopher, and e-mail servers, with daily e-mail notification to "subscribers" of new submissions received, typically over 200 per month for more active archives) -- for a general overview that i wrote, see the blurb link http://xxx.lanl.gov/blurb/ near middle of frontpage.

> I can offer about one gigabyte of space to start, on an as-needed basis.
> 1. I know archivists who already maintain mirror image archives of my

archive on xxx is already somewhat larger, and mirrored in europe and japan. has recently expanded to areas such as economics and computation and language, and a number of math archives are about to start in conjunction with msri in berkeley.

> libraries (and research library associations) to fold quality electronic
> publications into established library catalog systems (and ultimately
> full-text access in all libraries).

this is what we have done as a model together with the slac library and its spires-hep index (see http://slacvm.slac.stanford.edu/FIND/hep)

> electronic text files in the UK and Australia --

which files are these?

let me know if i can provide further info.

Paul Ginsparg

Date: Tue, 28 Jun 1994 12:15:14 -0400 (EDT)
From: Paul Southworth <pauls@locust.cic.net>

On Mon, 27 Jun 1994, Paul Ginsparg 505-667-7353 wrote:

> it might be useful for you first to have a look at what is already running
> in physics (see http://xxx.lanl.gov/ and related archives), starting three
> years ago (and currently with over 20,000 users; processing over 35,000
> transactions per day via ftp, www, gopher, and e-mail servers,
> with daily e-mail notification to "subscribers" of new submissions
> received, typically over 200 per month for more active archives)

That sounds about like CICNet, with a bit more traffic. We don't do e-mail (which is clearly important to the success of Stevan's proposal) and we have not developed WWW at all (mostly since this is just raw ASCII text, compressed). Most of our traffic is via gopher.

ps> > I can offer about one gigabyte of space to start, on an as-needed basis.
ps> > 1. I know archivists who already maintain mirror image archives of my

>
> archive on xxx is already somewhat larger, and mirrored in europe and japan.
> has recently expanded to areas such as economics and computation and
> language, and a number of math archives are about to start in conjunction with
> msri in berkeley.

The 1Gb is what I have in free space currently mounted on the server and immediately available, not my preexisting archives, which are about 2Gb of GNU zipped text. But anyway, my purpose is not to get into a bidding war over hosting this project -- it sounds very much like your site is more appropriate for it, since you are already dead-on with regard to content. CICNet's archives are content-random with a large amount of low-quality material grabbed fairly haphazardly. My purpose with regard to Stevan's proposal was *not* to fold that into what I have running already, since I think it would be completely inappropriate, but rather to provide a separate facility on a server that is already a substantial magnet for people looking for text files on the net -- naturally the same function could be performed by a well-placed link on our server pointing at the LANL site. If you're prepared to put the resources on line to make it happen, that sounds great and I will try to provide other assistance.

I think that quality and reputation for high standards will be critical to attracting authors to the electronic medium, and it looks like the LANL web server is already much farther along that track than we are.

Perhaps we should think of other uses for free user-accounts at a well connected site that can be used for a variety of maintenance purposes, and we can just keep CICNet's server-side participation down to a link.

ps> > electronic text files in the UK and Australia --
>
> which files are these?

Mirrors are on info.anu.edu.au and src.doc.ic.ac.uk. I also have a chunk of political-only files mirrored on ftp.uu.net. Perhaps we can use some of these prior arrangements to build a strong distribution network with a sensible level of redundancy.

Paul Southworth
CICNet Archivist
pauls@cic.net

III.   Who is Responsible?

Does the responsibility for scientific and scholarly findings lie at the grass roots with individual scholars or should there be institutionalization and centralization -- or both? Nobel Prize Winner Joshua Lederberg, looking to the practical uses of more and better information that the scientist can use, introduces the idea of institutional rather than discipline-based archives. From the library community, encouragement to recover some control over the economic fate of faculty products; then discussion of the place of the large learned societies in the publishing landscape ensues.

Date: Tue, 28 Jun 94 11:53:03 EDT
From: "Stevan Harnad" <harnad@princeton.edu>

> Date: Tue, 28 Jun 94 00:26:17 -0400
> From: Joshua Lederberg <jsl@rockvax.rockefeller.edu>
>
> Dear Steve:
> Now we face some strategy decisions. The new wrinkle that I got from
> what (I thought) you said was to bypass waiting for the disciplines
> to organize themselves; instead let each institution set up its own
> ftp-able archives for all of its scholars. That way, each place can
> also set up its own ground rules. Let the disciplines then come into
> play ad lib with peer review and those embellishments at their own
> pace and microstructure. Physics was a fairly homogeneous ensemble:
> just look at the journal structure compared to biomedicine. For the
> latter, there is scarcely consensus how to classify its subjects.
>
> Institutions also compete with one another, so there is likely to
> be constructive emulation of the pioneers; and there is some tacit
> quality labelling just by the name of the institution.
>
> Josh

That is exactly right. The grass-roots initiative should be at the individual scholars' end: everyone should establish a personal ftp archive, starting now...

But there's no harm (and a lot of good) in working from both ends (actually, many ends) at once, and what the two Pauls' respective projects (HEP and CIC) are doing is working on the centralized repository aspect, which will also be very helpful in getting the dominoes to fall.

As soon as a researcher establishes a personal ftp archive, it is on the global map. But what the two Pauls' projects will do is make the map all the more rationally structured and navigable. A veronica (or www) search on "lederberg" would already point to your personal ftp archive, but browsing a HEP or CIC catalogue, especially once hierarchical classification systems -- plus the all-important quality-control (peer review) tagging -- are implemented, will be extremely valuable too.

So let us encourage private archiving AND centralized archiving projects. Eventually, a rational method of automatic link-up and transfer will surely evolve too.

Stevan Harnad

Date: Tue, 28 Jun 94 10:43:31 -0600
From: Paul Ginsparg 505-667-7353 <ginsparg@qfwfq.lanl.gov>

> Date: Tue, 28 Jun 94 00:26:17 -0400
 > From: Joshua Lederberg <jsl@rockvax.rockefeller.edu>
 >
 > Institutions also compete with one another, so there is likely to
> be constructive emulation of the pioneers; and there is some tacit
> quality labelling just by the name of the institution.

sh> That is exactly right. The grass-roots initiative should be at the
sh> individual scholars' end: everyone should establish a personal ftp
sh> archive, starting now...

sh> But there's no harm (and a lot of good) in working from both ends
sh> (actually, many ends) at once, and what the two Pauls' respective
sh> projects (HEP and CIC) are doing is working on the centralized
sh> repository aspect, which will also be very helpful in getting the
sh> dominoes to fall.
sh> So let us encourage private archiving AND centralized archiving projects.
sh> Eventually, a rational method of automatic link-up and transfer will
sh> surely evolve too.

i have been through this argument many times. when i set up the first physics archives three years ago, it was clear that a distributed database, with only the indexing and pointers stored centrally, would be in principle much more desirable than a centralized one. the problem is that it would have been too restrictive back then to require even that every physicist have access to his/her own anon ftp site (much less gopher/www server). while the community may appear "homogeneous" from the exterior, it is nonetheless a global community with a wide variety of interests and wide variation in computer literacy and network access. (our indian, chinese, and russian colleagues have only recently established full internet access -- but still lagging in their local computational infrastructure, high quality workstations and printers rare i'm told). moreover a significant percentage of papers are written by transient grad students / postdocs / junior faculty. were they expected to establish and maintain control over their personal portable archives? if the anon ftp server was left to the institutional department or library to maintain, how could author maintain control after leaving? how many dept's have the competence/staffing to maintain such servers?

there were just too many unknowns had i not begun with a "lowest common denominator" e-mail interface and centralized archive, this never would have gotten off the ground. (and indeed earlier efforts e.g. in mathematics were stillborn for precisely the above reasons) now with platform for training the userbase, i can implement higher level functionality (e.g. the www interface) while continuing to democratically support the lowest common denominator. i estimate that it will still be years before a full distributed database will be logistically feasible (as opposed to technically feasible, which it already is), but a migration has begun where people insert pointers to additional resources (jpegs/mpegs/software/postscript) at their local ftp/gopher/www sites when available (and any http:... in title/abs is automatically converted to a link for www interface). people who do not have local archiving capability have recourse to the centralized database which automatically guarantees stable storage and high bandwidth network access through a variety of protocols at centralized site (and its mirrors).

Paul Ginsparg

Date: Tue, 28 Jun 1994 12:58:59 -0400 (EDT)
From: Paul Southworth <pauls@locust.cic.net>

On Tue, 28 Jun 1994, Paul Ginsparg 505-667-7353 wrote:

> Date: Tue, 28 Jun 94 11:53:03 EDT
> From: "Stevan Harnad" <harnad@Princeton.EDU>
>
> Eventually, a rational method of automatic link-up and transfer will
> surely evolve too.

>
> i have been through this argument many times. when i set up the first physics
> archives three years ago, it was clear that a distributed database,
> with only the indexing and pointers stored centrally,
> would be in principle much more desirable than a centralized one.

Obviously a centralized point of access for the end-user is desirable. The issue of local archives is really a matter of how to handle distributed maintenance by humans in different locations. We could possibly (a) give out accounts to maintainers on a central server and delegate areas to them completely, or (b) we could also evaluate wide-area distributed file systems (such as AFS) as a foundation for the server. Those are both alternatives (with their own problems) to relying on multiple servers. One other possibility, since I suspect we will be dealing with a number of specific highly-motivated experts in each area, would be to house subject-specific servers on location with their caretakers who would be responsible for coordinating with other archivists working on the same subject area (ie, physics) so as to have a handful of servers that we link to from the central access point, rather than thousands of them, one for each professor (in the worst case). Then we could approach organizations with a proposal for funding specific subject area servers, get them to agree to a standard for what type of server interfaces to support and how they should look, and then link them all up with a central access point at the server-application level (ie, http and gopher). Central access to distributed archives via ftp is not really possible unless we go the AFS route.

Date: Tue, 28 Jun 94 17:13:13 EDT
From: "Stevan Harnad" <harnad>

> From: Ann Okerson <ann@cni.org>
> Date: Mon, 27 Jun 1994 21:55:51 -0400 (EDT)
>
> Stevan,
>
> Thank you for forwarding me the two messages, though I don't really
> know what they are about (in context).

It was an abstract of a talk I'm to give in London in November, but it served a double purpose: I also branched it to other interested parties (as usual), including a UNESCO group headed by Joshua Lederberg that is interested in making the scientific literature available worldwide.

> However, you may be interested to know that one outcome of the AAU task

> force reports (Association of American Universities) is a recommendation
> from the Intellectual Property Task Force (the one I worked on) to
> involve universities more in publishing the works of their faculty
> electronically.

Bravo. But, as you know, "publishing" is an ambiguous term these days. There are two distinct questions here: Publishing of the refereed literature, and "publishing" of the preprint literature. My subversive proposal was intended to make the latter break down the doors for the former.

All help is welcome, but I find the present path to direct electronic refereed publication too slow, even with the good will and help of universities and libraries. My proposal would have all scholars AUTO-"publish" their preprints, in personal ftp archives at their institutions, and then the subversive step comes as they swap the refereed reprint for the preprint. (I may be wrong, and it may not do the trick, but there is a good chance it might; so please pause to note that this is NOT the same as having universities and libraries get directly into the publishing game. They are welcome to help now, but they will more probably be needed waiting in the wings when the dominoes fall, just in case the paper publishers are not ready to retool themselves to take up the slack. [How's that for a hopelessly miscegenated metaphor?])

> At this point a couple of the universities are interested in doing
> a prototype in which the works of their faculty go up on the Internet
> associated with that university. If the works are subsequently
> published in print or in a more formal way, the version can either
> be replaced or can point to the more formal one -- details to be
> worked out. It is not unlike the preprint model.

The devil is in the details. Before refereeing and publication, they are preprints, the author's property. After refereeing, acceptance and publication, they are (in virtue of copyright assignment), the publisher's property, and there immediately arises the critical question of whether a price-tag will be allowed to intercede between the work and its readers. Call it what you like, before, it's preprints, after, it's (usually copyrighted) reprints. And my subversive proposal is intended to shake off for ever the shackles of the pay-to-see model that reigns now. By the way, most ftp archives are ALREADY associated with the author's university, so we're on the same wave-length there. But I think the initiative will have to come from the author community, initially on an individual basis (though backed up by the electronic resources of the author's institution). When a critical mass is reached (as it has with the HEP community), then Universities and Libraries can be poised to jump in if publishers are not willing or able to do the right thing.

> I imagine we will have a meeting early in the fall (summer is too
> fragmented with vacations and stuff) of the interested parties to
> start to hammer out details. Or at least, I hope so. It seems to me
> that with key, well-endowed American institutions trying this and
> supporting it, we can prove that it can succeed. Or if we fail,
> we will have a better understanding of how/why. I'm very excited
> about this potential.

I agree that it will be helpful to have concerted efforts -- but concerted at what? If the Universities act preemptively (i.e., before a critical preprint inertial mass is formed) they will make publishers act preemptively, and authors will be intimidated ("If you publicize your preprint electronically, we will not consider it for publication; and if you make it available electronically after publication, you will be in violation of copyright.") That's why I think a natural subversive process rather than a premature formal confrontation might be the best.

IV.   What Does Electronic Publishing Cost?

Discourse by a leader from the American Chemical Society, one of today's largest and most electronically seasoned learned society publishers, takes the discussion to a new level and adds specific detail of costs and economics to the conversation. Whwrhwe electronic publishing will be cheaper or more expensive than print on paper, at least in the near term, is an important underlying question.

Date: Fri, 1 Jul 1994 08:41:11 EDT
From: Stevan Harnad <harnad@Princeton.EDU>

From: lrg96@acs.org (Lorrin Garson)
Date: Wed, 29 Jun 94 15:49:33 EDT

Stevan,

Re below, by all means post to a wide list of interested parties. I'd sincerely love to discover someone/somehow to reduce journal production costs so that a majority of our expenses were printing/paper-distribution.

Regards, Lorrin

Publications Division, American Chemical Society, Washington, D.C.
E-mail: lrg96@acs.org   Phone: (202) 872-4541   FAX (202) 872-4389

> From: lrg96@acs.org (Lorrin Garson)
> Date: Mon, 27 Jun 94 19:51:40 EDT
>
> Regarding the phrase "(which I estimate to be less than 25% of paper-page
> costs, contrary to the 75% figure that appears in most current publishers'
> estimates)" from your proposal below, do you mean that printing costs are
> 75% of the total publishing costs? If so, I can assure you this is certainly
> incorrect in scientific/technical publishing. Our experience at the American
> Chemical Society is that printing and paper costs are about 15% of total
> manufacturing costs and the "first copy", or prepress costs are about 85% of
> the total. Could you clarify what you mean? I'd be very interested on what
> basis you make your financial estimates.
>
> Lorrin R. Garson

Dear Lorrin,

Yes, in fact, the data you have often presented were among the ones I had in mind when I challenged the 75% figure (though many other publishers have come up with figures similar to yours 70-85%).

I challenge it on two bases, and they are these:

(1) The calculation according to which the "per-page" savings would be only 25%, leaving 75% still to be paid for is based on how much electronic processing will save in PAPER publication. The entire superstructure is set up to hurtle headlong toward print on paper, so if you recalculate that budget and leave out the print-run and a few other things, you find you're left with 75% of the original expenses. Solution? Exorcise everything having to do with going into paper, from the bottom up. Budget an electronic-ONLY journal, and the per-page cost will come out much, much lower (if anything, my 25% is an OVER-estimate).

To put it another way: Your way of doing the figures is rather like challenging the advantages of automobiles by calculating how much they would save on horse-feed.

(2) But, if that is not enough, I also speak from experience: I edit both a paper and an electronic journal. Although the two are not entirely comparable, and the paper one undeniably still has a much larger submission rate and annual page count, the true costs of the electronic one are an order of magnitude lower even making allowances for this. And this is not because anyone is working for free, or because the Net is giving the journal a free ride (it gives -- as I delight in showing audiences in (numerical) figures -- an incomparably bigger free ride to porno-graphics, flaming, and trivial pursuit, and THAT is much riper for being put onto a trade model than esoteric scholarly publication, the flea on the tail of the dog, which I believe we would all benefit from granting a free ride on the airwaves in perpetuum).

If we charged PSYCOLOQUY's readership (now estimated at 40,000) their share of the true costs, they would have to pay 25 cents per year (down from 50 cents a couple of years ago, as the readership grew and costs actually shrank; and thanks in part also to centralized subscriber-list handling at EARN, much of it automatized, as well as to developments such as gopher and world-wide-web, which are rapidly replacing the subscriber model by the browser model altogether in electronic publication).

PSYCOLOQUY is subsidized by the APA, which is also a large psychology paper publisher. I don't know what proportion of the APA's or ACS's publications are esoteric: I am NOT speaking about publications on which the author expects to make money from the sale of the text. But for that no-market portion of the literature, re-do your figures with the endpoint being a URL file in WWW for all those published articles. Reckon only the true costs of implementing peer review, processing manuscripts (electronically), editing, copy-editing, proof-reading, etc., and then finally electronic archiving and maintenance. I predict that you will be surprised by the outcome; but this cannot be reckoned by striking a few items from the ledger based on how you do things presently.

Best wishes, Stevan

> Date: Tue, 28 Jun 1994 16:28:49 +0100
> From: "Paul F. Burton" <paul@dis.strath.ac.uk>
> Subject: Re: Subversive Proposal
>
> A note to thank you for the notice of your "subversive proposal", but why
> be subversive about it? I've suggested at two conferences this year that
> universities should take back the electronic publication of work done by
> their staff (most of it research carried out with public funds), though I
> have not been as direct as your proposal :-). My personal view is that
> commercial publishers are running scared of electronic publishing, which is
> why they seem to be involved in so many projects.
>
> It seems to me that this is an idea whose time has just arrived. Do you
> think that the Follett Report proposals could include a feasibility study
> of this? I'd be interested in discussing the idea further with you, if you
> have time.
>
> BTW, I seem to have two addresses for you (Southampton and Princeton) so
> I'm sending this to both, as I'd value your comments.

Paul, It is indeed a subversive proposal, and here's why: Many of us already share the DESIRE for electronic publication in place of paper; the question is, How to get there from here? Life is short. The subversion is in not trying to do it directly, by taking on the all-powerful paper flotilla head-on. Forget about electronic publishing. Leave the "publishing" to them. Simply archive your PREprints (on which you have not ceded copyright to anyone) in a public ftp archive. Let EVERYONE (or a critical mass) do that. And then nature will take its course. (Everyone will, quite naturally, swap the reprint for the preprint at the moment of acceptance for publication, and before paper publishers can mobilize to do anything about it, the battle will be lost, and they will be faced with an ultimatum: either re-tool NOW, so that you recover your real costs and a fair return by some means other than interposing a price-tag between [esoteric, no-market] papers and their intended readership, or others will step in and do it instead of you.)

This IS subversive. Direct appeals (whether to authors or to publishers) to "publish electronically" are not subversive; they have simply proven hopelessly slow. And at this rate (esoteric) paper publishers will be able to successfully prolong the status quo for well into the foreseeable future -- to the eternal disadvantage of learned inquiry itself, which is the one that has been suffering most from this absurd Faustian bargain for the centuries that paper was the esoteric author's only existing expedient for PUBLICation at all.

Paper publishers, by the way, are, quite understandably, looking for much less radical solutions. These compromises are mostly in the category of "hybrid" publication (paper and electronic), and they share the fatal flaw of (esoteric -- remember, I am speaking only of esoteric, non-trade, no-market) paper publication: requiring a price for admission to a show that has virtually no audience, yet is essential to us all!

I have no animus against paper publishers. It's natural for them to do whatever they can to preserve the status quo, or something close to it. But necessity is the mother of invention, and my subversive proposal would awaken their creative survival skills. And if they wish to survive (in esoteric publication -- I cannot repeat this often enough: what I am proposing is NOT applicable to literature that actually has a market, one in which the author really has hopes of selling his words, and a market is interested in buying them, for there there is no Faustian pact; it is in the interests of BOTH parties, author and publisher, to charge admission at the door -- if publishers wish to survive in ESOTERIC publication, they will have to change from a trade to a subsidy model for recovering the substantially lower true costs of electronic-ONLY publication).

My claim that the true per-page cost of electronic publication will be 25% of current per-page paper costs rather than the 75% that has been quoted over and over, has been challenged (by Lorrin Garson of the American Chemical Society) and I have attempted to support my estimate above.

We can discuss this any time (we ARE doing so right now). I'm at Princeton till end of August, then at Southampton. Both email addresses will continue to reach me.

Stevan Harnad

Date: Fri, 1 Jul 94 11:36:59 -0600
From: Paul Ginsparg 505-667-7353 <ginsparg@qfwfq.lanl.gov>

stevan,
some quick comments re your lorrin garson and paul burton exchange.

sh> (1) The calculation according to which the "per-page" savings would be
sh> only 25%, leaving 75% still to be paid for is based on how much
sh> electronic processing will save in PAPER publication. The entire
...
sh> To put it another way: Your way of doing the figures is rather like
sh> challenging the advantages of automobiles by calculating how much
sh> they would save on horse-feed.

thank you for making this point so explicitly. the meeting with the amer
phys society is now set for mid oct, and i am more satisfied with the
agenda (it seems that it is not an entirely monolithic organization, and at
least some within are starting to respond to community pressure). if for
any reason you have had a long-standing urge to visit santa fe and would
be free that weekend, you would be more than welcome to participate at
our expense (especially when it comes to issues of quality control and
peer review).

sh> as the readership grew and costs actually shrank; and thanks in part
sh> also to centralized subscriber-list handling at EARN, much of it
sh> automatized, as well as to developments such as gopher and world-
sh> wide-web, which are rapidly replacing the subscriber model by
sh> the browser model altogether in electronic publication).

for the physics e-print archives, i have been observing the relative
"subscriber" and "browser" model activities. (for e-mail and ftp access, i
have data going back to '91; for gopher and www going back to '92 [the
www url btw is http://xxx.lanl.gov/, mentioned this last jan but wasn't
clear if you had client for that yet. useful as at least one model for how
to organize things, with no tendency to the feared chaos, at least in the
short term.] there seem to be two equally committed camps, the
"subscriber" camp by far the majority (in this case subscription means
receiving a daily list of new abstracts, typically 10 new abstracts per
weekday on the more active archives, about half that on the average
ones). i personally am in the minority browser camp, and don't really
understand the subscriber mentality (who needs all the intrusive daily e-
mail? in the old days we browsed journals or preprints when we felt the
urge, not when they invaded our privacy...), but "subscribers" here claim
that is a convenient *feature* of the electronic system that they get such
daily reminders, and that receiving things parcelled out in daily pieces
facilitates keeping up (and moreover being *forced* to go through them to

avoid a clogged mailbox). the minority "browsers", on the other hand, instantly cancelled their subscriptions when high quality gui browsing was enabled. bottom line is: evidently there will remain both kinds, and both should be accommodated.

pb>> My personal view is that commercial publishers
pb>> are running scared of electronic publishing, which is

bingo.

pb >> It seems to me that this is an idea whose time has just arrived. Do you
pb >> think that the Follett Report proposals could include a feasibility study
pb >> of this? I'd be interested in discussing the idea further with you, if you
pb >> have time.

again you are welcome to any of the data i've collected, if interested. the net result is certain to increase dramatically the pressure on publishers of esoteric material.

> From: harnad
sh> (Everyone will, quite naturally, swap the reprint for the preprint at
sh> the moment of acceptance for publication, and before paper publishers
sh> can mobilize to do anything about it, the battle will be lost, and they
sh> will be faced with an ultimatum: either re-tool NOW, so that you
sh> recover your real costs and a fair return by some means other than
sh> interposing a price-tag between [esoteric, no-market] papers and their
sh> intended readership, or others will step in and do it instead of you.)

yup, i forwarded these comments from you to the aps people so they can appreciate that the rest of the academic world shares many of our concerns, and may soon be catching up in preprint activity.

sh> I have no animus against paper publishers. It's natural for them to do
sh> whatever they can to preserve the status quo, or something close to it.

i didn't use to, one seems to be growing on me over past few years.

sh> if, as I say,
sh> publishers wish to survive in ESOTERIC publication, they will have to
sh> change from a trade to a subsidy model for recovering the substantially
sh> lower true costs of electronic-ONLY publication).

my current guess (hope?) is that the big publishing companies will ultimately drop out of the esoteric market, since the bottom line will not be so interesting to them (currently libraries spend over $10,000/year on subscriptions to single journals such as nuclear physics b -- those will be the first to go). professional societies, on the other hand, are likely to survive and still may be of use. my own professional society (aps) is coming to terms with a fait accompli, and is now ponsoring a major meeting on my home turf with what appears to be in principle a forward-looking agenda.

keep me informed on your initiative (though i too will be in europe for most of the summer, organizing a physics summer school in the french alps [les houches, near chamonix], will occasionally hunt and peck on minitel and transpose all my q's and z's)

Paul Ginsparg

V.   Suggestions and Strategies

Several scientists contribute.   One is a long-time editor of a substantive electronic newsletter for computer scientists and shares his economic perspectives. Another volunteers to promote the Harnad proposal.   Another, a creator of the World Wide Web, comments and offers encouragement for the future.   Yet another sees a role for the European Community.   Striking is the consensus of the proposal's proponents that practical actions can take precedence for the time being over broader considerations.

Date: Sat 2 Jul 94 00:18:20-PDT
From: Ken Laws <LAWS@ai.sri.com>

I'll second Stevan Harnad's economic estimate, and his general philosophy.   I publish a weekly 32KB newsletter.   The electronic circulation is irrelevant in terms of cost.   I also send out hardcopy, for which I charge postage and an extra $.25 per week for printing and handling. (I have *one* hardcopy subscriber, but would want to print out a copy for my own use in any case.   It takes me about half an hour to do the formatting, as I haven't purchased a good layout program yet.)

Total costs, including advertising and supplies, have been about $2,000 per year + network access costs (free, in my case) + an occasional purchase of computer hardware or software + whatever my time is worth.   I've included the cost of news sources (i.e., subscriptions and professional memberships) in that $2,000; obviously one could pay much more -- even millions, for a weekly such as Newsweek.   Harnad's proposal concerned esoteric publishing, which usually uses free material. The peer review -- which I omit -- is also free, except for the correspondence and "shepherding" expenses.

If you don't go after a large readership, there's no advertising expense.   If you don't edit authors' papers, there's very little editing expense.   If you use LISTSERV or MajorDomo, there's no clerical expense.   That's why most net services are free.

Unfortunately, the next level of quality requires at least one paid professional.   Money must be collected somehow; either sponsors must be courted or customers must be billed.   Net commerce isn't well developed yet, so billing and payment are major hassles. Clerical help with the billing can add to the cost, so sponsorship is usually the better option.
I've been advocating self-publication for several years now.   Stevan has

always insisted on the need for peer review, whereas I see it as optional. Peer review certainly adds an exciting dynamic to his e-journals, and may help in satisfying sponsors. Vanity publishing has entirely different benefits. I expect that both will do well. What will not survive is redundant publishing of slightly varying conference papers, journal articles, and collected works with delays of 1-3 years. Publish or perish has pushed academic publishing to the point of collapse, with library budgets no longer able to archive everything that any scientist wants to record for posterity. That function will now fall to FTP publishing as Stevan suggests, or possibly to CD ROM publishing of tech report archives. Hardcopy publication will become more reader-driven (reader pulled?) instead of author/sponsor-driven, and only the highest-quality collections will appear in print. For those, editing and publishing costs will remain high.

-- Ken Laws, Computists' Communique

Date: Mon, 4 Jul 1994 12:23:34 -0400 (EDT)
From: "Lloyd S. Etheredge" <letedge@access.digex.net>
Subject: Re: Possible Strategy re shift to electronic publishing
To: Stevan Harnad <harnad@Princeton.EDU>

> On Thu, 16 Jun 1994, Stevan Harnad wrote:
> Lloyd, can I have your permission to post the following to vpiej-l,
> the list of electronic journals editors and publishers (and perhaps
> a couple of other pertinent lists)?

Steve- Please feel free to post. Sorry for the delay - I was away from my desk for a bit. I'll have a more thoughtful response to you soon. Good points - I think we need a strategy. Lloyd

[Ed. Note: Below, Harnad extracts from original Etheredge message, sent to him personally from Etheredge. It had not appeared heretofore in the public discussion.]

le>> Date: Thu, 16 Jun 1994 00:53:24 -0400 (EDT)
le>> From: "Lloyd S. Etheredge" <letedge@access.digex.net>
le>>
le>> Re pushing over the house of cards we discussed (the 80% of scientific
le>> journals that might be more efficiently published in electronic form): It
le>> might be timely to talk with a range of people in American science, ask
le>> what they believe is needed, and whether a common strategy would help.
le>>
le>> I.e., perhaps UNESCO can help. But this is, first, an American problem -

le>> it's our journals, and our systems of payment, that are critical.
le>>
le>> I can devote shoe leather to this, esp. in the Washington area. Anyone
le>> you think might be useful to consult?

There is no single person or organization "in charge" of the current flotilla of paper journals. One can of course talk to individual authors, publishers, or societies, but the reason there is not much headway to be made there is that they wouldn't really know what to do. At the agency level, the best strategy is to encourage funders to encourage electronic "PREpublication," and to cover the expense in the research grant.

At the individual scholar level, as I said, by far the best strategy is public ftp/http archives for all preprints. This could be supplemented by encouraging learned societies to bundle and mirror their members' archives in a central repository (even just links and pointers to the home archives would do); the idea is to have high-profile global access TO all scientists' and scholars' work FOR all scientists/scholars. Scholars' societies, universities and other learned and scientific organizations can scale up the individual ftp/http archive visibility (already a huge step forward) by providing centralized subject-coded indices, etc. This should have low-end versions (ftp, archie, gopher) and high-end as well (www, mosaic, hytelnet), to include the full range of Internet users.

le>> A quick & practical solution might be to suggest a change in federal
le>> policy. The Clinton Administration could welcome the opportunity to
le>> take a leading role in developing the benefits of the Information Age in
le>> this area - and change the outmoded policies it inherited.
le>>
le>> E.g., What would you think about requiring that all publications based on
le>> research underwritten by public funds should, within one year of any
le>> initial publication in printed form, be made publicly available in (a
le>> standard) electronic form? (The copyright holders will still be entitled
le>> to a reasonable fee for use.)

Good idea, but "requiring" it may take some fight and time, whereas "encouraging" it might go more smoothly. Re-think the copyright issue, though, because it is a red herring: (Esoteric) scholars and scientists (i.e., most of us, most of the time) do not expect, and do not get, fees for their publications. None. Our publishers do (reasonably, because paper costs a lot of money to produce and disseminate). But in the electronic age, 75% or more of the real expense of paper is out of the loop!

So re-think copyright. It is no longer protecting an expensive technological investment in making the scholar's words "public" (that's what "publishing" does, after all). And since there is in reality virtually no "market" for those esoteric words, why not just scrap all thinking in terms of "fees" -- or, if anything, think of the fees as what the author's research grant PAYS in order to reach the limited number of esoteric peer-eyeballs there are in the world for a given scholarly work.

Also, there is a built in conflict of interest in this hybrid print/net idea, one that will either be (understandably) resisted by paper publishers outright, or used as a means of constraining the electronic version to the same pay-per-view economics as paper for a LONG time to come. That means the continuing irrational and counterproductive denial of the freedom of access to esoteric scholarly work that the economics of print have necessitated for centuries.

I prefer my noncoercive (but subversive) solution: Get all scholars to make ALL preprints of their work available publicly, by anonymous ftp/http NOW. The rest (replacing the preprint in due time by its refereed version, including in the archive "reprints" of previously published articles, etc. etc.) will take care of itself as the house of cards falls.

Your hybrid proposal is just extrapolating the Faustian alliance with paper, when what we should be trying to do is to shake free of it at last. The CORE of that freedom, is FREE GLOBAL ACCESS TO scholars' (esoteric) work FOR all scholars, in perpetuum, with the minimal true costs (less, probably much less, than 25% of what they are now) borne by those in whose interests the free access would exist: the scholars themselves (as authors, learned societies, learned institutions, and research-supporting arms of government).

In brief: Paper means substantial expense. Substantial expense means copyright protection. Copyright protection means fees. Fees mean "protection" of the scholars' work from nonpaying eyeballs. THAT is precisely what the scholar does NOT want. Hence the conflict of interest in the Faustian alliance. Solution: Break out of the paper mold entirely, not by brute force, but by the gentle force of the push of scholarly inquiry itself. With the preprint (and eventually the reprint) universally available for free electronically, the rest of the unnecessary edifice will peacefully vanish in the "perestroika" quietly occasioned by the ftp/http subversion...

le>> This might be a happy solution politically. It changes the incentives in a
le>> reasonable way, without imposing a ban. As a first step, it assures that
le>> print publication can continue (& with advertising revenue) & will be
l>> attractive (i.e., people will subscribe if they want the results quickly),
le>> but also assures that everything will be available electronically
le>> (worldwide) after the first year.

Advertising is a red herring too. First, most esoteric journals don't even carry any (or no significant amount). Second, it too is part of the old Faustian bargain: What do ads have to do with my research results? They are things I reluctantly swallow (along with paper access fees restricting my readership) in exchange for reaching my audience AT ALL. Why resurrect these gratuitous barriers in a new medium where they are not needed or wanted?

le>> This first step also breaks open the current mindset & *de facto*
le>> might get everything available in electronic form almost immediately -
le>> i.e., if a journal or authors are expected to overcome the inertia and
le>> prepare the electronic form anyway, why not just mount the tape now?
le>> They can create a pricing structure for the first year that costs more than a
le>> membership & paper subscription & slowly reduce prices, under pressure
le>> from their members & with the benefit of experience, to see how far they
le>> can go without losing total income. And they may be pleasantly surprised
le>> to find that the elasticities are in their favor - i.e., a much larger, and
le>> growing, global N of new readers whose fees for early on-line accessing of
le>> individual articles sums to more than the revenue they lose.]

I doubt it, because the hybrid solution you are hoping will generate a benign transition has all the incentives for self-perpetuation built into it. FREE UNIVERSAL ACCESS (to esoteric scholarly and scientific work) is the goal. Paper costs money, and is the only justification for charging money. What we need is a solution that gets paper out of the loop entirely. A hybrid structure, with fees blocking both paper and electronic access, can only DELAY the day, rather than hasten it. In fact, it is no doubt paper publishers' dream that such a hybrid solution will hold back the day forever! How are you envisioning the shrinking prices, given the low "hit" rate for the average esoteric article?

The goal is indeed to switch to a system where the remaining true expenses of publication are covered, but that's going to have to be up-front payment (subsidy through author page charges or learned society or institutional consortium support). There is just no continuous line that will get you from THERE (a subscription-based trade model) to HERE (a subsidy-based free model). All the internal forces of the hybrid structure are conspiring against it. Hence the need for a noncoercive, parallel solution (that will subvert the whole house of cards).

I do think that publishers can play a role in this, but then they must explicitly rejoin on the subsidized-model end, rather than hoping to continue on the trade model.

le>> If the new rule goes through, I suspect lots of folks (in addition to
le>> AT&T) will step-forward to offer the global services. To judge from

le>> yesterday's *Times*, Sprint & its new global (European) partners might be
le>> interested; and the MCI/British Telecom alliance.
le>> Any alternative ways to get this going with changes in federal
le>> policy? (I'll also ask for advice about a wider range of strategies,
le>> including appeals to statesmanship, etc.)

Let's talk and think some more before making policy recommendations...

Stevan

Date: Tue, 5 Jul 94 12:37:45 EDT
From: "Stevan Harnad" <harnad>

Here is a reply from Paul Ginsparg, with whom I completely concur, deferring to his greater technical expertise and experience on every point where he corrects my own errors and inaccuracies.

-- Stevan Harnad

P.S. Paul: whenever I give talks about this, I ALWAYS describe your project as the model for it all.

Date: Tue, 5 Jul 94 00:04:46 -0600
From: Paul Ginsparg 505-667-7353 <ginsparg@qfwfq.lanl.gov>
To: letedge@access.digex.net
Subject: Re: Possible Strategy re shift to electronic publishing
Cc: harnad@Princeton.EDU, serialst@uvmvm.BITNET, vpiej-l@vtvm1.BITNET

lloyd (le),
stevan h (sh) forwarded to me your message. few quick comments:

le>> Re pushing over the house of cards we discussed (the 80% of scientific
le>> journals that might be more efficiently published in electronic form): It
le>> might be timely to talk with a range of people in American science, ask
le>> what they believe is needed, and whether a common strategy would help.
le>>
le>> I.e., perhaps UNESCO can help. But this is, first, an American problem -
le>> it's our journals, and our systems of payment, that are critical.

sometimes stevan forgets to mention that some such archives have already been on-line for as much as three years, and can serve as a useful model (especially as an existence-proof that they need not necessarily lead to chaos in the short term, as many would predict -- the longer term remains an open question). the physics and related e-print archives, for example, have over 20,000 dedicated users and already over 30,000 accumulated submissions, typically processing over 35,000 transactions per day.

(the submissions are processed, archived, and indexed automatically -- and are made available by e-mail, anonymous ftp, and www from the main site and various mirrored sites [full text, including equations and in-line figures]. subscribers are automatically notified of new submissions via e-mail'ed abstracts. for www access, use: http://xxx.lanl.gov/; for e-mail help, send a message e.g. To: hep-th@xxx.lanl.gov Subject: help; for more info see the "blurb" link on the xxx frontpage, or send a message to the above e-mail address with Subject: get blurb. the system is unstaffed and unsupported -- to date i have had little success with certain funding agencies but a decision on an nsf proposal is due sometime before the fall).

these systems have entirely supplanted recognized journals as the primary disseminators of research information in certain fields (with their sole current virtue being instant retransmission -- the next generation of hypertexted submissions and discussion threads, currently undergoing implementation, will further reconfigure the landscape). my own professional society (and sometimes publisher), the American Physical Society, has at last been jolted from complacency and has scheduled a meeting to take place this fall in Santa Fe to start plotting their future role in the electronic realm. their role remains uncertain, but the overwhelming commitment of the community to electronic distribution is a fait accompli.

sh> At the individual scholar level, as I said, by far the best strategy is
sh> public ftp/http archives for all preprints. This could be supplemented by
sh> encouraging learned societies to bundle and mirror their members'
sh> archives in a central repository (even just links and pointers to the
sh> home archives would do); the idea is to have high-profile global access
sh> TO all scientists' and scholars' work FOR all scientists/scholars.
sh> Scholars' societies, universities and other learned and scientific
sh> organizations can scale up the individual ftp/http archive visibility
sh> (already a huge step forward) by providing centralized subject-coded
sh> indices, etc. This should have low-end versions (ftp, archie, gopher)
sh> and high-end as well (www, mosaic, hytelnet), to include the full range
sh> of Internet users.

actually since mosaic is just one of many co-equal www clients, it doesn't make sense to say (www,mosaic,...) [would be like saying (gopher, xgopher, ...)] - also the gopher people might object to being characterized in the low-end (it is after all a stateless protocol like the http used by www, unlike the stateful protocol of ftp, and nothing to do with archie indexing), but no matter they are not long for the world.

as i have commented to stevan, even in my own highly computer literate community (2nd only *perhaps* to the computer science community) it would still be unrealistic to expect everyone to be in a position to maintain his/her own public server (due to transient nature of students, postdocs, junior faculty active in research; and also given global nature of community -- this is not just an american problem -- where not everyone is entirely caught up). that is why the short-term must include a combination of centralized archives and centralized indices with pointers to distributed local archives (and why i maintain a fully functional lowest common denominator e-mail interface for submission/retrieval so that no one is left behind, while the more fortunate can preferentially use the higher level interfaces).

le>> E.g., What would you think about requiring that all publications based on
le>> research underwritten by public funds should, within one year of any
le>> initial publication in printed form, be made publicly available in (a
le>> standard) electronic form? (The copyright holders will still be entitled
le>> to a reasonable fee for use.)

a fine idea, except i don't believe that authors should sign over their copyrights at all. i intend to retain 100% possession of my ideas in the form i produce them, publishers are welcome to keep their alleged "value-added" (i.e. the superficial appearance they produce, typically with added typos and other errors). starting 10 years ago, we no longer needed publishers to turn our drafts into something that had a polished superficial appearance. starting more recently, we no longer need them for their distribution network -- we have something much better. what we really need now is to extract just their certification and filtering roles to organize the information for more efficient retrieval of quality material. this can be implemented in a large number of creative ways (some discussed by stevan in his earlier "scholarly skywriting" articles, some others will be hammered out with the amer phys society this fall, and perhaps even implemented shortly thereafter [with or without them]).

let me know if i can provide any further info, Paul Ginsparg

Date: Tue, 5 Jul 94 11:55:53 +0200
From: Tim Berners-Lee <timbl@www3.cern.ch>
Subject: Re: Possible Strategy re shift to electronic publishing

sh: "Stevan Harnad" <harnad@Princeton.EDU>
le: "Lloyd S. Etheredge" <letedge@access.digex.net>

sh> There is no single person or organization "in charge" of the current
sh> flotilla of paper journals. One can of course talk to individual
sh> authors, publishers, or societies, but the reason there is not much
sh> headway to be made there is that they wouldn't really know what to do.
sh> At the agency level, the best strategy is to encourage funders to
sh> encourage electronic "PREpublication," and to cover the expense in the
sh> research grant.

In my experience of trying to promote a change, those "in charge" are liable to be the least susceptible to persuasion. Change spreads from the grass roots -- to get from one state of society to another you have to make a path each step of which is taken by a different person somewhere, and each step of which is downhill. In the case of high energy physics, for example, scientists resorted to the net because they needed the speed of publication. There was no mandate from above. A way that you could expedite such a move in other disciplines would be for example to set up a free preprint repository which would accept papers in whatever form it is easiest for the author to provide, for example in postscript by email, and make them easily findable by providing good indexing. Put a cheerful front page to the archive: put some graphics in at the top to encourage readers. Let the thing run with a few gigabytes of disk space, and see whether society responds. You will have to jump start it probably with an injection of existing archives of papers, or pointers to them: otherwise, you will never get a critical product of readership and information base.

sh> At the individual scholar level, as I said, by far the best strategy is
sh> public ftp/http archives for all preprints. This could be supplemented by
sh> encouraging learned societies to bundle and mirror their members'
sh> archives in a central repository (even just links and pointers to the
sh> home archives would do);

Yes -- though the societies may see this as being in competition with their own journals. The interests of their members should be pointed out.

sh> the idea is to have high-profile global access TO all scientists' and
sh> scholars' work FOR all scientists/scholars. Scholars' societies,
sh> universities and other learned and scientific organizations can scale up
sh> the individual ftp/http archive visibility (already a huge step forward)
sh> by providing centralized subject-coded indices, etc.

I see this as one excellent role for the academies of science -- to provide indexes of the works of their members, and of their members.

sh> This should have low-end versions (ftp, archie, gopher)
sh> and high-end as well (www, mosaic, hytelnet), to include the full range
sh> of Internet users.

Given lynx, the www client for the vt100, one hardly has to be a "high-end" user to use www. WWW was designed to cover the range. (Terms: archie is an index of ftp sites, and so is not appropriate to this set of retrieval systems. "www" is a line-mode interface to the WWW, and mosaic is one of the graphic user interfaces to WWW. Hytelnet is a database of telnet sites, and so is not appropriate to this set.)

le>> A quick & practical solution might be to suggest a change in federal
le>> policy. The Clinton Administration could welcome the opportunity to
le>> take a leading role in developing the benefits of the Information Age
le>> in this area - and change the outmoded policies it inherited.
le>>
le>> E.g., What would you think about requiring that all publications based
le>> on research underwritten by public funds should, within one year of any
le>> initial publication in printed form, be made publicly available in (a
le>> standard) electronic form?

Possible -- though federal policy change is not always the quickest and easiest solution.

sh> In brief: Paper means substantial expense. Substantial expense means
sh> copyright protection. Copyright protection means fees. Fees mean
sh> "protection" of the scholar's work from nonpaying eyeballs. THAT is
sh> precisely what the scholar does NOT want. Hence the conflict of interest
sh> in the Faustian alliance. Solution: Break out of the paper mold
sh> entirely, not by brute force, but by the gentle force of the push of
sh> scholarly inquiry itself. With the preprint (and eventually the reprint)
sh> universally available for free electronically, the rest of the
sh> unnecessary edifice will peacefully vanish in the "perestroika"
sh > quietly occasioned by the ftp/http subversion...

You might find it is already happening anyway...(But when it has happened, you may want to pay for the filtering done by a good review system, I suspect!)

Tim Berners-Lee
CERN
Geneva, Switzerland

Date: Tue, 5 Jul 94 13:08:03 EDT
From: "Stevan Harnad" <harnad@princeton.edu>

Note: I have to point out that behind the desideratum shared by many of us -- that the esoteric scientific and scholarly literature can and should be made available electronically to all for free, and that public ftp/http archives may well hasten the day when they are -- there are some NONdivisive differences of opinion regarding the need for quality control (peer review, editing/copy-editing). Nothing hinges on them for the matter at hand. I just happen to be relatively conservative on that subtopic, and Andrew Odlyzko relatively laissez-faire.

Stevan Harnad

From: david@arch.ping.dk (David Stodolsky)
Date: Tue, 5 Jul 94 11:13:21 +0200 (MET DST)

sh> I do think that publishers can play a role in this, but then they must
sh> explicitly rejoin on the subsidized-model end, rather than hoping to
sh> continue on the trade model.

If we can locate a European Publisher that will cooperate, then there is a good chance of getting at least of few years of subsidy under the EU's Fourth Framework for R & D. In the Telematics area, there is supposedly going to be an emphasis on applications, as opposed to infrastructure development, which has been the main line so far. Directorate General XIII/E has already funded exploratory actions in multimedia publishing, using Third Framework money for feasibility projects preparing for the Information Engineering program under the new Fourth Framework. Two of the examples of areas suitable for pilot applications listed:

> o the development of new forms of Sci. & Tech. publishing
> using networks and exchangeable media

> o sector specific demo projects from electronic products and
> services such as electronic newspaper or magazine development

My feeling, however, is that the publishers are a lost cause due to the conflict of interest. I think a better option is a company that benefits from the move to on-line access. If scientists are going to develop their reputations on-line, then security is essential. Maybe one of the smart card producers would cooperate. I am investigating these companies in connection with another project and can bring this up as an option. Network operators also are a possibility. RARE is coordinating some activity, but I have yet to see anything definite.

For further info fax to:

European Commission
DG XIII, Directorate E
JMO C4/024
L-2920 Luxembourg
Fax: (352) 430132847
Contact: R. F. de Bruine

David S. Stodolsky, PhD   Internet: stodolsk@andromeda.rutgers.edu
Peder Lykkes Vej 8, 4. tv.   Internet: david@arch.ping.dk
DK-2300 Copenhagen S, Denmark
Voice + Fax: + 45 32 97 66 74

VI.   Reprise

Ginsparg and Harnad return to speculation about the practical elements of the proposal. The first of a series of responses from the library community follows.

Date: Tue, 5 Jul 94 16:45:23 EDT
From: "Stevan Harnad" <harnad>

> Date: Tue, 5 Jul 94 13:02:05 -0600
> From: Paul Ginsparg 505-667-7353 <ginsparg@qfwfq.lanl.gov>
>
> tks for forwarding latest group of messages. sounds exciting, almost
> regret i'm about to go incommunicado for two months
> (but will try to check in with berners-lee later this month at cern on my
> way to the french alps [les houches, near chamonix] for the summer school
> i'm organizing). Paul Ginsparg

Paul, if possible, please tune in one more time to reply to Lorrin Garson's reply to me. I'll be posting that next. He makes two points, one correct (that my journal is mostly text, and that text costs less than Tex and graphics) and one incorrect (that Tex and graphics will cost more rather than less than paper). I continue to stand by my <25% figure but for technical text and graphics I am on weaker ground because I don't have data of my own. Please chime in if you feel it is appropriate. I know that David Stodolsky has said he will; and there are already several technical e-journal editors who can give figures too. But your project is the biggest, and it's certainly not primarily text.

A reply to your earlier message follows. Sorry for the delay. I was swamped. In it I discuss our slight differences on the need for quality control (I want to make sure they are not conflated with the cost issue).

Stevan Harnad

> Date: Fri, 1 Jul 94 11:36:59 -0600
> From: Paul Ginsparg 505-667-7353 <ginsparg@qfwfq.lanl.gov
>
>From: "Stevan Harnad" <harnad@Princeton.EDU
>To: lrg96@acs.org
>Subject: Re: Subversive Proposal
>Date: Fri, 1 Jul 94 05:51:45 EDT
>
sh> (1) The calculation according to which the "per-page" savings would be
sh> only 25%, leaving 75% still to be paid for is based on how much
sh> electronic processing will save in PAPER publication. The entire
sh>
sh> To put it another way: Your way of doing the figures is rather like
sh> challenging the advantages of automobiles by calculating how much
sh> they would save on horse-feed.
sh>
pg> thank you for making this point so explicitly. the meeting with the
pg> amer phys society is now set for mid oct, and i am more satisfied with
pg> the agenda (it seems that it is not an entirely monolithic
pg> organization, and at least some within are starting to respond to
pg> community pressure). if for any reason you have had a long-standing
pg> urge to visit santa fe and would be free that weekend, you would be
pg> more than welcome to participate at our expense (especially when it
pg> comes to issues of quality control and peer review).

Hi Paul,

I'll be in Southampton by then, but if you can get my trip and lodging covered, I'd be happy to come (though I'll need to know the exact dates very quickly, so I can get it on my schedule at Southampton).

I'm aware that you and I don't see quite eye-to-eye on the quality-control/peer-review question, but I think it will be a central one in a lot of people's minds, so I think it's important to be very explicit (and aware) about the options. I'm in the middle here, between those who argue that it's the cost of quality control that necessitates sticking to the trade model (I completely disagree) and those who argue that quality control itself is unnecessary and the Net can control its own quality (I completely disagree). In some ways (in my view), these two opposing positions (status-quo versus anarchy), especially if they are seen as the two main options, are among the main obstacles to reaching a sensible solution soon. The reactionaries will cling to the paper/pay-per-view model, even on the Net, in the name of maintaining the quality of the literature, and the anarchists will reject refereeing and editing in the name of "democracy."

It's for this reason that it would be good to see the quality-control issue pulled out of this fray. I oppose the pay-per-view model completely, yet I advocate a very conventional form of quality control. The critical point is that the two are dissociable, so going purely electronic does NOT leave only two options: paying for quality control on the trade model or else giving it up for anarchic self-regulation. You can have a rigorously refereed and carefully edited electronic literature and still make it available for free to all. THAT's the point of view I'd like to represent. And if you yourself happen to favor a model with looser quality-control constraints, it is still to your advantage (and mine) to have allies on the free-access issue (which is the really radical one) who happen to have different views on quality control. Then no one can link the two factors, dividing and conquering by pitting the radicals against one another (free-access/controlled-product vs. free-access/uncontrolled-product), as if the issue were quality information vs. free information.

sh> as the readership grew and costs
sh> actually shrank; and thanks in part also to centralized subscriber-list
sh> handling at EARN, much of it automatized, as well as to developments
sh> such as gopher and world-wide-web, which are rapidly replacing the
sh> subscriber model by the browser model altogether in electronic publication)

pg> for the physics e-print archives, i have been observing the relative
pg> "subscriber" and "browser" model activities.
pg > but "subscribers"
pg> here claim that is a convenient *feature* of the electronic system
pg> that they get such daily reminders, and that receiving things
pg> parcelled out in daily pieces facilitates keeping up (and moreover
pg> being *forced* to go through them
pg> to avoid a clogged mailbox). the minority "browsers", on
pg> the other hand, instantly cancelled their subscriptions when high
pg> quality gui browsing was enabled. bottom line is: evidently there
pg> will remain both kinds, and both should be accommodated.

I've had the same experience: I've encouraged PSYCOLOQUY subscribers to unsubscribe and browse the archives instead, but about 3000 continue to prefer having everything emailed to them. The whole issue could eventually be finessed with "virtual" email, in which "hot links" are simply activated whenever you look at your "mail": You wouldn't really be clogging the Net by actually mailing everything to everyone; the mailer would simply do an active browse for you, dressed as email. Eventually these will simply be parameters you set: Autobrowse X, Y and Z.

> Date: Tue, 28 Jun 1994 16:28:49 +0100
> From: "Paul F. Burton" <paul@dis.strath.ac.uk
> Subject: Re: Subversive Proposal

pb> It seems to me that this is an idea whose time has just arrived. Do you
pb> think that the Follett Report proposals could include a feasibility study
pb> of this? I'd be interested in discussing the idea further with you, if you
pb> have time.

pg> again you are welcome to any of the data i've collected, if
pg> interested. the net result is certain to increase dramatically the
pg> pressure on publishers of esoteric material.

I will forward this to Paul, suggesting he get directly in touch with you.

sh> (Everyone will, quite naturally, swap the reprint for the preprint at
sh> the moment of acceptance for publication, and before paper publishers
sh> can mobilize to do anything about it, the battle will be lost, and they
sh> will be faced with an ultimatum: either re-tool NOW, so that you
sh> recover your real costs and a fair return by some means other than
sh> interposing a price-tag between [esoteric, no-market] papers and their
sh> intended readership, or others will step in and do it instead of you.)

pg> yup, i forwarded these comments from you to the aps people so they
pg> can appreciate that the rest of the academic world shares many of our,
pg> concerns and may soon be catching up in preprint activity.

But notice the crucial "invisible hand" factor: Swapping the reprint for the
preprint assumes that at some point there is a quality-control stage, with
what is before it being "pre" and what is after it being "post." The
invisible hand is being provided by the PAPER literature right now. THIS
is the (seeming) weak point at which the divide-and-conquer strategy will
be aimed, squarely. You have to make sure you are fore-armed against it,
so the whole project doesn't get locked into the anarchy issue.

sh> I have no animus against paper publishers. It's natural for them to do
sh> whatever they can to preserve the status quo, or something close to it.

pg> i didn't use to, one seems to be growing on me over past few years.

sh> But necessity is the mother of invention, and my subversive
sh> proposal would awaken their creative survival skills.

pg> you may be giving them too much credit. there seem very few
pg> visionaries in that industry, and their investment in the
pg> status quo leaves the rest blinded.

They're not facing necessity yet (though your preprint archive is what is bringing them the closest to the brink so far -- and wide following of my subversive proposal would simply generalize your effect across disciplines; my electronic journal is no threat till it has hundreds of counterparts, across disciplines). So far 99.99% of the cards are still paper, and they are in their hands. Necessity (and the creativity it gives birth to) will only intervene when those cards really begin to fall; until then, vision will be limited, and delaying the inevitable will be the best strategy for paper publishers.

sh> if, as I say,
sh> publishers wish to survive in ESOTERIC publication, they will have to
sh> change from a trade to a subsidy model for recovering the substantially
sh> lower true costs of electronic-ONLY publication).

pg> my current guess (hope?) is that the big publishing companies will
pg> ultimately drop out of the esoteric market, since the bottom line will not
pg> be so interesting to them (currently libraries spend over $10,000 / year on
pg> subscriptions to single journals such as nuclear physics b -- those will be the
pg> the first to go). professional societies, on the other hand, are likely
pg> to survive and still may be of use. my own professional society (aps) is
pg> coming to terms with a fait accompli, and is now sponsoring a major
pg> meeting on my home turf with what appears to be in principle
pg> a forward-looking agenda.

But since virtually all of our intellectual goods are currently being carried by the paper flotilla it is in ALL of our best interests (not just publishers') to make sure that the transition period does not turn into anarchy. Worst scenario: Paper publishers decide to cut their losses instead of restructuring, and simply pull out of esoteric publication. Do you think the editorial offices of all those esoteric journals could simply go electronic overnight? In fact, paper journal editorial offices (and paper journal editors) for the most part wear the same paleolithic blinkers as paper publishers.

No, the transition process should be a (preferably speedy but) graded one, a peaceful one, and preferably one in which paper publishers, those with the expertise in the quality control, re-tool themselves for electronic-only publication with advance subsidy (from author page charges, learned society dues and subsidies, university and library subsidies, and research publication grants), rather than a sudden pull-out leaving others (with no quality-control expertise) scrambling to pick up the pieces.

This is where necessity born of subversion comes in: With preprints/reprints becoming accessible for free to all it will be clear that costs will HAVE to be covered some other way. Going to electronic-only publishing will first cut costs down to size; and going for advanced subsidy will put them into phase with the non-trade model.

pg> keep me informed on your initiative (though i too will be in europe
pg> for most of the summer, organizing a physics summer school in the
pg> french alps [les houches, near chamonix], will occasionally hunt and
pg> peck on minitel and transpose all my q's and z's), Paul Ginsparg

I hope you will be invited to join the gs/UNESCO group directly, and then you will be a part of the initiative de jure (as you already are de facto).

Stevan Harnad

Date: Tue, 5 Jul 94 14:42:44 EDT
From: Peter Graham <psgraham@gandalf.rutgers.edu>

One of the points Paul Ginsparg makes that bears thinking about is the proposal that various archives be established, e.g. by scholarly societies but also presumably by other agencies.

Let me condense an argument very much by suggesting that this function is what libraries are for, perhaps uniquely for: the long-term preservation function. Some of us in the library community have been discussing what it is that libraries bring distinctively to the electronic environment. One of the functions is the continuing one of assuring that information that is here today is also here tomorrow (as I sometimes like to put it, If I love this information in May will it still be here in December?).

Libraries, unlike publishers, individual scholars, and scholarly societies, are explicitly in this for the long term. I think it is our responsibility in the library community to determine what is necessary for long-term provision of information. This will include matters such as

- backup
- technology (hardware) refreshing (e.g. from vax to unix to ?, from 5.25" floppy to 3.5" floppy to ?, from magnetic disk to optical disk to crystal, etc.)
- technology (software) refreshing (e.g. from Wordperfect 1.1 to v6.0, from DisplayWrite to Word, from LaTeX to ?, from CorelDraw to ?, etc.).
- accessibly search engines
- authenticity and completeness
- long-term commitments of people, money and systems (this

being the hardest thing of all) in an environment where budgets are typically only annual.

There's more to say but this thread tends to bunch up in indigestible chunks anyway, so I shove this out to get this ball rolling. (metaphor?)

Peter Graham (psgraham@gandalf.rutgers.edu)
Rutgers University Libraries
169 College Ave
New Brunswick, NJ 08903
phone: (908)445-5908

VII. E-Journal Publishing; Infrastructure Investments

The American Chemical Society's Lorrin Garson returns to the discussion with detailed comments about the significant planning and investment course the Society has already taken in moving into non-print publication. He makes the case that scaling up and sustaining production require considerable thought and infrastructura support. More numbers are introduced; Harnad differentiates esoteric publication from other sectors of the information market.

From: lrg96@acs.org (Lorrin Garson)
Subject: Publication costs (cont.)
Date: Sun, 3 Jul 94 15:57:07 EDT

Stevan,

As of yesterday I am on vacation for three weeks, and about to leave for British Columbia and Alaska. However, before going, I wanted to respond to your latest message in our exchange of thought and comments on publishing costs.

Perhaps the disparity of our cost figures is a consequence of the type of material we publish. My impression is that journals in the humanities are much simpler and would therefore be less expensive to create in the front-end process. In fact, chemistry may be the most challenging of the sciences with much information in complex tables, display math, graphics -- including chemical structures and other line art, half-tones and color. Tables, math, and artwork are labor intensive (expensive) to handle whether for print or electronic products. Also, in the sciences, there are many special characters and multi-level positioning which must be handled; we have over 500 special characters for our journals and seven levels of super- and subscripts (on line, 3 levels above and 3 levels below). These special characters must also be handled whether on paper or electronically. I must confess I don't read humanities journals and my experience in this domain is limited to undergraduate textbooks. But even with undergraduate text books, there is a marked difference in manufacturing costs because of the difference in complexity of material.

We are indeed both addressing the issue of what you call "esoteric publications," that is, scholarly journals for which authors submit manuscripts without receiving payment or royalty.

Your statement "The entire superstructure is set up to hurtle headlong toward print on paper ..." is incorrect. Since 1974 the ACS has been publishing its journals on a database structure aimed toward the day when electronic products would be created. We started preserving our journal data in an SGML-like structure long before SGML became an ISO standard. Our print products are spun-off from the database, not the other way around. I am afraid your perception of how we produce journals is quite erroneous. Approximately 80-85% of our costs are for creating this database and 15-20% for printing. The majority is for peer review, processing manuscripts (50% are now done electronically; this will probably reach 60-80% by the end of 1995), editing, copy-editing, proof-reading, etc.

Also your statement "It's natural for them [paper publishers] to do whatever they can to preserve the status quo, or something close to it." is also very inaccurate---certainly incorrect for the the ACS. Let me give you a few highlights of the ACS' electronic publishing activities:

(a) 1980: One thousand articles from the Journal of Medicinal Chemistry were loaded on BRS as the first fulltext file in chemistry, probably the first fulltext file in the sciences. This was an experimental prototype file which was tested by a few dozen volunteers.

(b) 1981: An experimental file of 16 ACS journals was loaded at BRS. The coverage was 1976 to current for the Journal of Medicinal Chemistry and 1980 to current for the other journals. The file was evaluated by about 300 individuals.

(c) 1982: The fulltext of ACS journals file at BRS became a commercial product in November.

(d) 1984: Our colleagues at Chemical Abstracts Service (CAS) established STN International in cooperation with node operators in Karlsruhe, Germany and Tokyo, Japan. This is a true network with files located at any one node accessed from Europe, North America and the Pacific Rim. Users are not aware in day-to-day searching/retrieving on which continent the files are located.

(e) 1985: We developed a prototype CD-ROM in cooperation with OCLC using the chemistry journal Inorganic Chemistry. This prototype was fulltext searchable and provided on-the-fly composition with display of our full character set, including super- and subscripts.

(f) 1986: On September 28th, the ACS made the fulltext of all its chemistry journals available on STN (the CJACS file). This file allows fulltext searching and display, but does not contain mathematics, tables or math. The file is available today and contains our journal data from

1982 to the present. The file is updated every two weeks.

(g) 1987-90: Files from John Wiley (CJWILEY file), the Royal Society of Chemistry (CJRSC file), VCH Publishers (CJVCH), and Elsevier Science Publishers (CJELSEVIER file) were loaded on STN International. These files are still available and regularly updated. [My group processes the data for these publishers for file loading.]

(h) 1990 to date: The ACS has been involved with colleagues at Bellcore, OCLC, CAS, and Cornell University to create a prototype electronic library at Cornell University. This is called the CORE project; a non-commercial, experimental endeavor.

(i) 1993: The ACS made supplementary material for the Journal of the American Chemical Society available on an Internet server (acsinfo@acs.org). These are TIFF-Group-4-FAX compressed files available for downloading by anonymous ftp or through a Gopher interface. There are approximately 20,000 pages per year loaded on the server. The file is still available and is updated weekly.

(j) 1994-1996: The ACS is a participant in the Red Sage project at the University of California at San Francisco. Approximately 20 publishers are involved (with Springer-Verlag being the dominant publisher) along with UCSF and Bell Laboratories, to create a prototype electronic library in the fields of radiology and molecular biology.

(k) 1994: On June 19th, the ACS/CAS made electronic pages of all its chemistry journals available via STN International, thus tables, mathematics, line art and half-tones are now available by downloading via the Internet, direct dial modem or by FAX.

(l) 1994: Later this month we will ship the first CD-ROMs of two of our titles: Journal of the American Chemical Society and Biochemistry. The CD-ROMs contain fielded, full-text searching capabilities, capability to display and print journal page images, with special processing of half-tone images to accommodate non-grey scale printers, display and printing of color images, etc.

(m) By the end of this year we will have all of the graphics for our journals as separately callable objects, linked to the text, along with SGML encoded data, including tables and mathematics.

Stevan, I assure you the ACS as well as most main-line traditional, commercial publishers of scientific information are not trying to preserve the status quo but rather are very active in developing electronic information products. Other not-for-profit organizations in the sciences, notably physics, astronomy, medicine/biology and engineering, are also very active in this domain.

By the way, the ACS is a not-for-profit organization, but it is also a not-for-loss institution. The Publications and Chemical Abstracts Service Divisions are not subsidized from external sources, nor from ACS members' dues. These two divisions are charged by the ACS Board of Directors to annually return a small net to the ACS' reserves.

I would like to suggest that publishing electronic journals is in fact going to be more expensive than printing. For example, I believe most of the data we currently publish in journals today will in the future be acquired as coherent, digital data. This is starting now in the field of x-ray crystallography and will likely spread to other areas of structure such as spectroscopy (IR, UV, MS, NMR, etc.), biological data, in vitro testing, etc. The journal Protein Science (published by Cambridge University Press for the Protein Society) now publishes with each issue a floppy disk which contains protein/enzyme structure data which can be visualized with a program called Kinemage, which is also provided with the journal. The Protein Society plans to make these data also available on CD-ROM and via the Internet. The collection, maintenance (including indexing and cataloging), and dissemination of these data will, I believe, be more costly than printing, but the information will be much more valuable to the scientific community. Of course, when we get to this point we won't be publishing journals; the output will be called something else.

I am afraid you haven't convinced me to your view point and our cost figures are so diametric we can't possibly both be correct. As I mentioned in my opening, perhaps the great disparity lies in the nature of the information we publish. Have I through my verbiage above changed your perceptions of publishing and associated costs? Probably not . . .

It seems we are unlikely to resolve the issue by merely exchanging messages. Sometime when you are in Washington area, or when I am in Princeton, why don't we sit down and try to thrash this out. If on some occasion you should be in Columbus, Ohio, I would be very happy to walk you through our production facilities (data entry, database building, composition but not printing, which is done in Easton, Pennsylvania). In any case, please count on being my guest for lunch or dinner when and where we might meet.

I won't be responding to e-mail until after July 25th.

Finally, I would like to ask that you forward this message to those to whom you sent your last message. Thank you.

Best regards,

Lorrin

************************ From: Lorrin R. Garson **************************
Publications Division, American Chemical Society, Washington, D.C.
E-mail: lrg96@acs.org   Phone: (202) 872-4541   FAX (202) 872-4389
****

Date: Tue, 5 Jul 94 17:56:39 EDT
From: "Stevan Harnad" <harnad@princeton.edu>
Subject: Lorrin Garson (Amer. Chem. Soc.) Reply to Subversive Proposal

Dear Lorrin,

Thanks for your detailed reply about publication costs and electronic innovations at the American Chemical Society. I am very impressed by the scale of electronic innovativeness you describe taking place at the ACS.

The status quo I should have said that paper publishers would be endeavoring to preserve was the trade model itself: pay-to-see, whether on screen or on paper. You raise a valid point about technical and graphical capabilities and expenses, and you are right that my own data, from a mostly-text discipline, are insufficient to establish the generality of my < 25% per-page claim. I will accordingly allow colleagues in the more technical disciplines to bring forward their own figures in response to what you write below. My own reaction to the impressive panorama of innovations you describe (apart from admiration for what you have accomplished) would be the following:

(1) Many the graphical capabilities you describe are likely to be available on the author/researcher's end these days, as are the technical-text generating capabilities. So what authors submit for publication may be very close to the final product (and they could incorporate editing and design feedback into it in their revision). It is not at all clear that having these functions instead performed by the publisher will be either optimal technically or a justification for sticking to the pay-to-see model instead of the free-access-to-all model for esoteric publication.

(2) The coding will soon be standardized, or near standardized, so that

will be provided from the author's end too (guided, of course, by feedback from editors, copy editors and production editors, to which I will return below), and hence no justification for sticking to the pay-to-see status quo.

(3) Powerful public-domain search/storage/retrieval tools are already being developed and made available to all (e.g., wais, www, etc.). So this too need no longer be something the publisher does for the author, and is again not a justification for preserving the status quo.

So what seems to remain in the calculations you describe -- assuming author's end graphics and text-processing plus archive management tools are in place for all -- is (as I suggested) the true cost of quality control: refereeing and editing (include copy-editing and design). I regret that I have to say that I continue to believe that the true cost of this essential service is well under 25% per page in all fields of science and scholarship. I will allow those who are more technically expert than I to follow up on (1) to (3).

One last point: ACS is noncommercial, but is it not worrisome that, as you describe below, it so readily makes common cause with so many others who most decidedly are not? Esoteric publishing simply does not belong in this paradigm.

Stevan Harnad

Date: Tue, 5 Jul 94 23:19:57 -0600
From: Paul Ginsparg 505-667-7353 <ginsparg@qfwfq.lanl.gov>
To: harnad@Princeton.EDU
Subject: Re: Lorrin Garson (Amer. Chem. Soc.) Reply to Subversive Proposal

> I will allow those who are more technically
> expert than I to follow up on (1) to (3).

stevan,

essentially your responses are correct, but tentative due to unfamiliarity with publishing technical material including in-line equations, graphics, etc. in physics, we've been transmitting such material without compromise over the networks for close to a decade now so i can make slightly more definitive comments below.

i've lost track of all the different lists (please forward to whichever may be relevant -- feel free to edit if necessary, have been through this many times in many forums and answers grow increasingly abrupt).

Paul Ginsparg

lg> From: lrg96@acs.org (Lorrin Garson)
lg> Subject: Publication costs (cont.)
lg> To: harnad@Princeton.EDU (Stevan Harnad at Princeton University)
lg> Date: Sun, 3 Jul 94 15:57:07 EDT

lg> Perhaps the disparity of our cost figures is a consequence of the type of
lg> material we publish. My impression is that journals in the humanities are
lg> much simpler and would therefore be less expensive to create in the
lg> front-end process. In fact, chemistry may be the most challenging of the
lg> sciences with much information in complex tables, display math, graphics-
lg> including chemical structures and other line art, half-tones and color.

i suspect physics is roughly as challenging as chemistry. who is providing all of the above material? in physics, we the authors produce the tables and graphics ourselves, and can typically integrate them into in electronic end product better than can the publishing companies on paper.

lg> Tables, math, and artwork are labor intensive (expensive) to handle
lg> whether for print or electronic products. Also, in the sciences, there are
lg> many special characters and multilevel positioning which must be
lg> handled; we have over 500 special characters for our journals and seven
lg> levels of super-and subscripts (on line, 3 levels above and 3 levels below).

why would a publisher re-typeset all submissions? in physics, the journal publications are frequently lower quality precisely because of the errors introduced in the typesetting process (it is very difficult to proofread yet again something that has already been proofread hundreds of times for our own versions; especially when many of the conventional pub co's weren't even running spellcheckers to catch their trivial errors.)

lg> These special characters must also be handled whether on paper or
lg> electronically. I must confess I don't read humanities journals and my
lg> experience in this domain is limited to undergraduate textbooks. But even
lg> with undergraduate text books, there is a marked difference in
lg> manufacturing costs because of the difference in complexity of material.

if handled properly, scientific research can be propagated electronically as easily as can non-scientific. this is not conjecture -- the e-print archives on xxx.lanl.gov have from their inception been full text with all in-line figures and equations (and the astrophysicists have begun to submit .mpeg files with on-line animation), all author-prepared, and in no case are any compromises necessary for professional research communication. as i say, the author produced material is frequently superior in quality to the ultimate print form from the publisher.

lg> Your statement "The entire superstructure is set up to hurtle headlong
lg> toward print on paper . . ." is incorrect.
lg>
lg> Also your statement "It's natural for them [paper publishers] to do
lg> whatever they can to preserve the status quo, or something close to it." is
lg> also very inaccurate---certainly incorrect for the the ACS. Let me give you
lg> a few highlights of the ACS' electronic publishing activities:

i am afraid that the litany of "achievements" below tends to support rather than refute stevan's statement. instead they are strawpeople that convey the impression of forward-looking, but remain too firmly rooted in the status quo. essentially this view of the electronic format is literally to repeat the entire process, and then *after* the final stage, essentially as an afterthought, take an electronic photo (i.e. bitmap) of the finished version, post it somewhere, and suggest that that constitutes vision for the future. from this myopic viewpoint, of course the electronic version appears to add to the overall expense. this just means you'll be hard-pressed to compete when someone else comes along with a better optimized and more streamlined operation.

lg> (a) 1980: ...

prior to 1984 the relevant word processing and graphics simply was not available. any info on usage patterns, cost, etc., is irrelevant. totally different medium. continuing...

lg> (f) 1986: On September 28th, the ACS made the fulltext of all its chemistry
lg> journals available on STN (the CJACS file). This file allows fulltext
lg> searching and display, but does not contain mathematics, tables or math.
lg> The file is available today and contains our journal data from 1982 to the
lg> present. The file is updated every two weeks.
lg> (g) 1987-90: Files from John Wiley (CJWILEY file), the Royal Society of
lg> Chemistry (CJRSC file), VCH Publishers (CJVCH), and Elsevier Science
lg> Publishers (CJELSEVIER file) were loaded on STN International.

no mathematics, tables, or math. in physics, this would have been less than useless and would convince people of the superiority of paper.

lg> (h) 1990 to date: The ACS has been involved with colleagues at Bellcore,
lg> OCLC,CAS, and Cornell University to create a prototype electronic library
lg> at Cornell University. This is called the CORE project; a non-commercial,
lg> experimental endeavor

isn't this just another scan and shred project to post bitmaps of existing journals? for some reason, many journals seem unable to distinguish superficial appearance from information content and insist that they are *defined* by their superficial appearance. (the american physical society, for example, proposed an electronic version of its journals which retained every artifact of the paper version -- including a two column format with equations that occasionally cross between columns. [a format that many physicists have grown to despise. aps would likely be subject to a full-scale network attack if they ever ventured to post new material in such an electronic format.]

it is important to rethink the compromises embodied in the current paper format and not robotically propagate them to the electronic format. indeed when i demo-ed a bitmap server to some physics postdocs, the uniform response was incredulity ["my god, it's a picture of each page."] then laughter -- they were just not interested in the static formats promoted in general by OCLC and e.g. Bell's "rightpages". and, again, of course your costs are unaffected or increased -- everything proceeds as before with an extra step added at the end. very soon we will demand functionality (hypertext, in-line links to other resources and applications, public annotation threads, etc.) that can *only* be embodied in the electronic format from the start.

lg> (i) 1993:The ACS made supplementary material for the Journal of the
lg> American Chemical Society available on an Internet server
lg> (acsinfo@acs.org). These are TIFF-Group-4-FAX compressed files
lg> available for downloading by anonymous ftp or through a Gopher interface.
lg> There are approximately 20,000 pages per year loaded on the server. The
lg> file is still available and is updated weekly.

more after-the-fact bitmaps. not as useful, unfortunately, as text.

anyway, rather than continue point by point, i am just trying to emphasize how all of this substantiates the point that publishers base their cost estimates of the electronic format on an outmoded mentality, viewing it as an "add-on" to existing activities rather than as a means to alter, improve, optimize, and streamline communication of research in a fundamental manner. there is nothing fundamentally different about highly technical scientific material as compared with the humanities -- researchers across the board, once empowered to produce a final format that suits their standards, and given the means of distribution, will take full advantage. the likely outcome is to force established publishers to rethink what they're doing and concede that their cost estimates were based on the wrong analysis.

lg> Stevan, I assure you the ACS as well as most main-line traditional,

lg> commercial publishers of scientific information are not trying to preserve
lg> the status quo but rather are very active in developing electronic
lg> information products. Other not-for-profit organizations in the sciences,
lg> notably physics, astronomy, medicine/biology and engineering, are also
lg> veryactive in this domain.

i have met with a continuous stream of representatives from "main-line, traditional, commercial publishers of scientific information" over the past three years and yes, they are trying to do *something*, mainly stay in the ballgame somehow, but that *something* is not necessarily optimized for the interests of researchers, either in cost, functionality, or means of access. no idea to which "not-for-profit organizations" you refer in physics -- there, at least, i believe i know what is going on (perhaps the confusion is over what constitutes "very active" as opposed to "very productive").

lg> I would like to suggest that publishing electronic journals is in fact going
lg> to be more expensive than printing.

i would like to suggest that those institutions and organizations for whom publishing electronic journals will in fact prove more expensive than printing do not have a very bright future in store.

Paul Ginsparg

Date: Tue, 5 Jul 1994 18:54:41 -0400
From: lesk@bellcore.com (Michael E. Lesk)

Steve, Lorrin

I wonder if you both know about an article "Reader rip-off: why are books so expensive" by Tony Rothman in the New Republic for Feb. 3, 1992. He is mostly talking about trade books, and finds most of the cost in distribution. He says that a $20 book costs about $3 to produce. (The author gets $2, the publisher gets $4 for overhead, the distributor gets $3 and the bookstore gets $8). For a 20,000 copy run typesetting is not important -- it is 10% of the production cost. Paper is only slightly more, about 15% of production cost.

Unfortunately, scientific journals have already achieved his most obvious recommendation: eliminate the bookstore retail markup and go to mailorder.

But his overall point is still true- most of the money in the current system is NOT going to run presses. It's distribution and organization that is taking the money, not the production side. I think that's true for scientific journals as well.

Michael

Hi Mike,

I'm sure Rothman's right about those figures, but I think that's probably more general even than book economics and probably gets to the heart of capitalism (and middlemen. etc.).

Rather than take all of THAT on, I think the simple pertinent fact in the case of ESOTERIC (no-market) publication (which makes it different from sell-your-words trade publication) is that it is NOT a "product" from which the author does, can or expects to make money through selling it! That is something peculiar to esoteric publication, independently either of the mark-ups of trade book/magazine publishing or commerce in general: THE AUTHOR WANTS YOU TO READ THE WORK, THAT'S ALL. That motive should never have had to make common cause with an economic model in which there is a MARKET for the work, people ready to pay for it, and the author writing it in hopes of getting part of that revenue -- a model in which it is in the interests of the author as well as the publisher to interpose a price-tag between the author and the readership.

This anomaly in the special case of esoteric publishing is now in a position to be remedied in short order WITHOUT taking on either the inefficiencies of trade publishing in general, or of trade in general.

Stevan Harnad

VIII. A Researcher's Perspective

Andrew Odlyzko of AT&T Bell Labs, himself a proponent of similar enterprises, joins the discussion as a third strong voice after Harnad and Ginsparg and presents an essay about staging the transition to electronic scholarly journals..

From: amo@research.att.com
Date: Tue, 5 Jul 94 08:02 EDT
To: harnad@Princeton.EDU

Thank you very much for sending your proposal. It's been my contention for a long time (for example, in the original draft of the "Tragic Loss ..." essay that follows) that widespread distribution of preprints through electronic media, either via preprint servers such as Ginsparg's, or through ftp directories, would subvert paper journals. One thing that is worth emphasizing, though, is just how easy it is for a scholar to do this with modern tools. Enclosed below is a revision of my essay (which will hopefully be finished in a couple of days) that dwells on this point.

Concerning Lorrin Garson's message, I agree completely with your [Harnad's] estimates, and will have some quantitative arguments in my essay to support them.

The novel methods of scholarly information dissemination that have been made possible by modern technology can be seen in the system that I have started to use recently. All my recent preprints can be accessed through Mosaic at URL

  ftp://netlib.att.com/netlib/att/math/odlyzko/index.html.Z

(Preprints of some older, already published papers are also available there, but may have to be removed if publishers complain.)

For those without access to Mosaic, ftp access is available on machine netlib.att.com. After logging in as "anonymous" and giving the full email address as password, all the user has to do is give the commands

    cd netlib/att/math/odlyzko
    binary
    get index.Z

to obtain a copy of the (compressed) index file, which describes what preprints are available. Finally, those without ftp access can send the message

      send index from att/math/odlyzko

to netlib@research.att.com, and the index file will arrive via return mail, with instructions for retrieving individual papers. (This system contains the work of other colleagues. For papers of my colleague Neil Sloane, use the same commands as above, but with "odlyzko" replaced by "sloane," for example.)

The system described above gives all the 20 million users of the Net access to my colleagues; and my own preprints. Moreover, this access is almost always free (although that might change), and available around the clock (except when networks or computers malfunction, of course). Further, this access is very easy. What is most remarkable about it, though, is that it is also easy to add papers to it. All I need to do (once a paper has been typeset in TeX or LaTeX, say) is to give the commands

latex analytic dvips analytic.dvi >/usr/math/odlyzko/analytic.comp.ps

and edit the file /usr/math/odlyzko/index by adding to it the lines

      file att/math/odlyzko/analytic.comp.ps
      title Analytic Computations in Number Theory
      by Andrew M. Odlyzko
      (to appear in "Mathematics of Computation 1943-1993," W. Gautschi, ed., Amer. Math. Soc., Proc. Symp. Appl. Math., 1994.)

Everything else is done automatically by the system, which was written by Eric Grosse, and which is available for free. (In practice there is a bit more work, since I also make the source files available in the src directory, to make text searches easier, but it is not much.)

The only time-consuming part in using Grosse's system is the typesetting of the paper, but that is something that would be done in any case. The extra effort needed to make the preprint available is a matter of a minute or two. This is a dramatic change compared to the situation of even a few years ago, and certainly to that of a few decades ago, when the only way for a scholar to communicate with a wide audience was to go through the slow and expensive process of publishing in a conventional journal. Now it is possible to reach a much broader audience with just a few keystrokes.

From: amo@research.att.com (Andrew Odlyzko)
Date: Wed, 6 Jul 94 07:57 EDT
To: harnad@Princeton.EDU
Subject: more subversion

Stevan,

Concerning a bunch of your postings from yesterday, I agree wholeheartedly that the issue of costs of electronic publications can and should be separated from that of peer review. I felt you had confused the two in your comment on my message to you. The section from the forthcoming revision of my essay that I had sent you was meant just to demonstrate how easy it is to disseminate information with modern technology. It did not deal with quality of the information at all. The next paragraph in the essay (which I did not send to you) talks of how the same mechanism can be used by the editor of a journal to disseminate refereed papers.

Concerning Mike Lesk's message, I agree with you that the figures he cites are not directly relevant to esoteric scholarly publishing. However, it is interesting to note that even in the trade press, electronics is likely to cause substantial changes, and will squeeze out some of the distribution costs that Mike cites. Publishers are talking of producing customized textbooks, for example. For one of your future courses in cognitive psychology, for example, you might choose from a publisher's catalog what sections you want to go into your students' textbook. The students will then go to your school's bookstore and have a copy printed for them on the new machines that companies like Xerox are developing. (As I recall, Xerox is already marketing one such machine.) This will eliminate the need for publishers and bookstores to overstock and ship back and forth tons of paper that is not used. (The driving force for this development is not so much the college textbook market, but all the myriad corporate documents, computer manuals, etc., which are frequently changed and are typically needed only in small quantities. However, the same technology will be used in the college textbook market.)

Best regards, Andrew Odlyzko

[Ed. Note: Because the Odlyzko article is frequently referenced in the discussion, we have reprinted the abridged version next, with permission.]

Tragic loss or good riddance?
The impending demise of traditional scholarly journals

September 26, 1994

Condensed version
Published in the Notices of the American
Mathematical Society, Jan. 1995.

Andrew M. Odlyzko
AT&T Bell Laboratories
amo@research.att.com

Author's Note: The full version, with more data and detailed arguments, appeared in the Intern. J. Human-Computer Studies (formerly Intern. J. Man-Machine Studies). A preprint can be obtained via email by sending the message

    send tragic.loss.txt from att/math/odlyzko

(for the ascii version) or

    send tragic.loss.long.ps from att/math/odlyzko

(for the PostScript version) to:

      netlib@research.att.com.

If your mailer cannot handle large files, include in your message the line "mailsize 40k", if you wish the revision to be sent in chunks of at most 40 KB, say.

[Ed. Note: Bracketed citations in the paper are references to end notes that appear at the end of this abridged version of "Tragic Loss ... "]

I. Introduction

Traditional printed journals are a familiar and comfortable aspect of scholarly work. They have been the primary means of communicating research results, and as such have performed an invaluable service. However, they are an awkward artifact, although a highly developed one, of the print technology that was the only means available over the last few centuries for large-scale communication. The growth of the scholarly literature, together with the rapidly increasing power and availability of electronic technology, are creating tremendous pressures on journals. The purpose of this article is to give a broad picture of these pressures and their likely outcome, and to argue that the coming changes may be abrupt.

It is often thought that changes will be incremental, with perhaps a few electronic journals appearing and further use of email, ftp, etc. My guess is that change will be far more drastic. Traditional scholarly journals will likely disappear within 10 to 20 years. The electronic alternatives will be different from current periodicals, even though they may carry the same titles. There are obvious dangers in discontinuous change away from a system that has served the scholarly community well [Quinn]. However, I am convinced that future systems of communication will be much better than the traditional journals. Although the transition may be painful, there is the promise of a substantial increase in the effectiveness of scholarly work. Publications delays will disappear, and reliability of the literature will increase with opportunities to add comments to papers and attach references to later works that cite them. This promise of improved communication is especially likely to be realized if we are aware of the issues, and plan the evolution away from the present system as early as possible. In any event, we do not have much choice since drastic change is inevitable no matter what our preferences are.

Predictions and comments in this article apply to most scholarly disciplines. However, I will write primarily about mathematics, since I am most familiar with that field and the data that I have is clearest for it. Different areas have different needs and cultures and are likely to follow somewhat different paths in the evolution of their communications.

II. Growth of literature

The impending changes in scholarly publications are caused by the confluence of two trends. One is the growth in the size of the scholarly literature; the other is the growth of electronic technology. The number of scientific papers published annually has been doubling every 10-15 years for the last two centuries [Price]. Similar growth has been occurring in mathematics alone. In 1870 there were only about 840 papers published in mathematics. Today, about 50,000 papers are published annually. The growth has not been even, and a more careful look at the statistics shows that from the end of World War 2 until 1990, the number of papers published has been doubling about every 10 years [MR]. Growth has stopped recently, but this is likely to be a temporary pause of the kind that have occurred before.

The exponential growth in mathematical publishing has interesting implications. Adding up the numbers in [MR] or simply extrapolating from the current figure of about 50,000 papers per year and a doubling every 10 years, we come to the conclusion that about 1,000,000 mathematical papers have ever been published. What is much more surprising to most people (but is a simple consequence of the geometric growth rate) is that almost half of them have been published in the last 10 years. Even if the rate of publication were to stay at 50,000 papers per year, the size of the mathematical literature would double in another 20 years. While this rapid growth is a sign of vitality of our field, it creates problems.

Scholarly publishing has some features that sharply differentiate it from the popular fiction or biography markets, and make rapid growth difficult to cope with. Research papers are written by specialists for specialists. Furthermore, scholars do not receive any direct financial remuneration for their papers, and give them to publishers only in order to disseminate the information to other scholars. This means that radical changes are more likely to occur in scholarly journals than in mass market publishing, since the interests of scholars and publishers are different.

Scholarly publishing would be facing a minor inconvenience and not a crisis if the scale of this enterprise were small enough. If a university department were paying $ 5,000 per year for journals, it could deal with several decades of doubling in size and cost of the subscriptions before anything drastic had to be done. However, good mathematics libraries spend well over $ 100,000 per year just for journal subscriptions, and the cost of staff and space is usually at least twice that. Budgets that large are bound to be scrutinized for possible reductions.

III. Technological advances

A doubling of papers published each decade corresponds to an exponential growth rate of about 7% per year. This is fast, but nowhere near as fast as the rate of growth in information processing and transmission. Microprocessors are currently doubling in speed every 18 months, corresponding to a growth rate of 60% per year. Similarly dramatic growth figures are valid for information storage and transmission. For example, the costs of the NSF-supported backbone of the Internet increased by 68% during the period 1988-91, but the traffic went up by a factor of 128 [MacKieV]. The point of citing these figures and those below is that advances in technology have made it possible to transform scholarly publishing in ways that were impossible even a couple of years ago. Recall that about 50,000 mathematical papers are published each year. If they were all typeset in TeX, then at a rough average of 50,000 bytes per paper, they would require 2.5 GB of storage.

We can now buy a 9 GB magnetic disk for about $ 3,000. For archival storage of papers, though, we can use other technologies, such as optical disks. A disk with a 7 GB capacity that can be written once costs $ 200-300. Digital tapes with 250 GB capacities are expected to become available soon. Thus the electronic storage capacity needed for dissemination of research results in mathematics is trivial with today's technology.

We conclude that is it already possible to store all the current mathematical publications at an annual cost much less than that of the subscription to a single journal. What about the papers published over the preceding centuries? Since there are 1,000,000 of them, it would require about 50 GB to store them if they were all in TeX. Conversion of old papers to TeX seems unlikely. However, storage of bitmaps of these papers, compressed with current fax standards, requires less than 1,000 GB. This is large, but it is still less than 150 of the current large optical disks. For comparison, Wal-Mart has a database of over 1,000 GB that is stored on magnetic disks, and is processed intensively all the time.

Within a decade we may have systems for personal computers that can store 1,000 GB. Even before that, university departments will be able to afford storage systems able to store all the mathematical literature. This ability will mean a dramatic change in the way we operate. For example, if you can call up any paper on your screen, and after deciding that it looks interesting, print it out on the laser printer on your desktop, will you need your university's library?

Communication networks are improving rapidly. Most departments have their machines on Ethernet networks, which operate at almost 10 Mbs (millions of bits per second). Further, almost all universities now have access to the Internet, which was not the case even a couple of years ago. The Internet backbone operates at 45 Mbs, and prototypes of much faster systems are already in operations. Movies-on-demand will mean wide availability of networks with speed in the hundreds of megabits per second. If your local suppliers can get you the movie of your choice at the time of your choice for under $ 10 (as they will have to, in order for the system to succeed financially), then sending over the 50 MB of research papers in your specialty for the last year will cost pennies. Scientists might not like to depend on systems that owe their existence to the demand for X-rated movies, but they will use such systems when they become available.

Not only have information storage and transmission capacities grown, but the software has become much easier to use. Computerized typesetting systems have become so common that it is rare to encounter a manuscript typed on an ordinary typewriter. Moreover, scholars are increasingly doing their own typesetting. This trend is partially due to cutbacks in secretarial support, but is caused primarily by scholars preferring the greater control and faster execution that they obtain by doing their own typesetting. With modern technology, doing something is often easier than explaining to another person what to do.

Two centuries ago there was a huge gap between what a scholar could do and what the publishers provided. A printed paper was far superior in legibility to hand-written copies of the preprint, and it was cheaper to produce than hiring scribes to make hundreds of copies. Today the cost advantage of publishers is gone, as it is far cheaper to send out electronic versions of a paper than to have it printed in a journal. The quality advantage of journals still exists, but it is rapidly eroding.

IV. Preprints and electronic journals

Advances in technology allow for much more convenient dissemination of information. Preprints have already become the main method in mathematics and many other fields for experts to communicate their latest results among each other. Electronics is making this process much easier. Two approaches are becoming common. One is for departments to set up publicly accessible directories from which anyone can copy the latest preprints via anonymous ftp. The other is to use preprint servers, with scholars sending their preprints to a central database. Wide use of these methods is a great boon to scholars, but it is extremely subversive of journal publications. (Cf. [Harnad3]) If I can get a preprint of a published paper for free, why should I (or my library) pay for the journal?

The subversive effect of wide preprint distribution is bound to force changes on the traditional scholarly journals. Moreover, the changes could be sudden. For example, within one year the preprint server that Paul Ginsparg had set up for high energy theoretical physics became the standard information dissemination method in that area [Ginsparg]. It has since been adopted by other fields as well. Such sudden changes are common in high technology areas (as in the dramatic rise in popularity of fax machines, or the catastrophic decline of the mainframe) and could occur in journal publishing. During a future financial squeeze at a university, a dean might come to a mathematics department and offer a deal: "Either you give up paper journal subscriptions, or you give up one position." Today such an offer would not be considered seriously, since journals are still indispensable. However, in 10 years or so once preprints are freely available, giving up the journals is likely to be the preferred response.

Preprints have a deservedly different status than refereed journal publications. However, the new technologies are making possible easy publication of electronic journals by scholars alone. It is just a easy for editors to place manuscripts of refereed papers in a publicly accessible directory or a preprint server as it is to do so for their own preprints. The number of electronic journals is small, but it is rising rapidly.

I expect that scholarly publishing will move to almost exclusively electronic means of information dissemination. This will be caused by the economic push of having to cope with increasing costs of the present system and the attractive pull of the new features that electronic publishing offers.

V. The interactive potential of electronic publications

Because conventional print journals have been an integral part of scholarly life for so long, their inflexibility is often not appreciated. Most mathematical journals are available at only about 1,000 research libraries around the world. Even for the scholars at those institutions, access to journals requires a physical trip, often to another building, and is restricted to certain hours. Electronic journals will make access available around the clock from the convenience of the scholar's study. It will also make literature searches much easier. For journals without subscription fees, access will be available from anywhere in the world.

Frank Quinn [Quinn] argues that the reliability of mathematical literature justifies extreme caution in moving away from paper journals, lest we be tempted into "blackboard-style" publishing practices that are common in some fields. He advocates keeping a strong distinction between informal preprint distribution and the formal refereed publications, even in an electronic format. I agree that mathematicians should strive to preserve and enhance the reliability of mathematical literature. However, I feel that Quinn's concerns are largely misplaced, and might serve to keep mathematicians and other scholars from developing better methods for communicating their results. I feel a better solution is to have an integrated system that combines the informal netnews-type postings with preprints and electronic journal publication. Stevan Harnad has been advocating just such a solution [Harnad1], and has coined the terms scholarly skywriting and prepublication continuum to denote the process in which scholars merge their informal communications with formal publications. Where I differ from Harnad is in the form of peer review that is likely to take place. Whereas Harnad advocates a conventional form, I feel that a reviewing continuum that matches the publication continuum is more appropriate.

I will describe the system I envisage as if it were operating on a single centralized database machine. However, this is for convenience only, and any working system would almost certainly involve duplicated or different but coordinated systems. I will not deal with the software aspects of this system. There will surely be hypertext links, so that a click on a reference or comment would instantly bring up a window with that paper or comment in it, but the precise features are not important for this article.

At the bottom level of future systems, anyone could submit a preprint to the system. There would have to be some control on submissions, but it could probably be minor. Standards similar to those at the Abstracts of the AMS might be appropriate, so that "proofs" that the Earth is flat, or that special relativity is a Zionist conspiracy, would be kept out. Discussions of whether Bacon wrote Shakespeare's plays might be accepted (since there are interesting statistical approaches to this question). There would also be digital signatures and digital timestamping, to provide authentication. The precise rules for how the system would function would have to be decided by experimentation. For example, one feature of the system might be that nothing that is ever submitted could be withdrawn. This would help enforce quality, since posters submitting poorly prepared papers risk having their errors exposed and publicized for ever.

Once a preprint was accepted, it would be available to anyone. Depending on subject classification or keywords, notification of its arrival would be sent to those subscribing to alerting services in the appropriate areas. Comments would be solicited from anyone (subject again to some minor limitations), and would be appended to the original paper. There could be provisions for anonymous comments as well as signed ones. The author would have the opportunity to submit revised versions of the paper in response to the comments (or the author's further work). All the versions of the papers, as well as all the comments, would remain part of the record. This process could continue indefinitely, even a hundred years after the initial submission. Author X, writing a paper that improves an earlier result Y(123) of author Y, would be encouraged to submit a comment to Y(123) to that effect. Even authors who just reference Y(123) would be encouraged to note that in comments on Y(123). (Software would do much of this automatically.) This way a research paper would be a living document, evolving as new comments and revisions were added. This process by itself would go a long way towards providing trustworthy results. Most important, it would provide immediate feedback to scholars. While the unsolicited comments would require evaluation to be truly useful, and in general would not compare in trustworthiness with formal referee reports, they would be better than no information at all. Scholars would be free to choose their own filters for this corpus of preprints and commentary. For example, some could decide not to trust any unrefereed preprint that had not attracted positive comments from at least three scholars from the Big Ten schools.

Grafted on top of this almost totally uncoordinated and uncontrolled system there would be an editorial and refereeing structure. This would be absolutely necessary to deal with many submissions. While unsolicited comments are likely to be helpful in deciding on the novelty and correctness of many papers, they are unlikely to be sufficient in most cases. There is need to assure that all the literature that scholars rely on is subject to a uniform standard of refereeing (at least as far as correctness is concerned), and at the same time control the load on reviewers by minimizing duplicate work. Both tasks are hard to achieve with an uncoordinated randomized system of commentary. A formal review process will be indispensable. There would have to be editors who would arrange for proper peer review. The editors could be appointed by learned societies, or even be self-appointed. (The self-correcting nature of science would take care of the poor ones, I expect. We do have vanity presses even now, and they have not done appreciable damage.) These editors could then use the comments that have accumulated to help them assess the correctness and importance of the results in a submission and to select official referees. (After all, who is better qualified to referee a paper than somebody who had enough interest to look at it and comment knowledgeably on it? It is usually easy to judge someone's knowledge of a subject and thoroughness of reading a manuscript from their comments.) The referee reports and evaluations could be added as comments to the paper, but would be marked as such. That way someone looking for information in homological algebra, say, and who is not familiar with the subject, could set his or her programs to search the database only for papers that have been reviewed by an acknowledged expert or a trusted editorial board. Just as today, there would be survey and expository papers, which could be treated just like all the other ones. As new information accumulated with time, additional reviews of old papers might be solicited as needed, to settle disputes.

The proposal above is designed to work within the confines of what we can expect both technology and ordinary fallible people to accomplish. It would integrate the roles of authors, casual readers, and official referees. The main advantage of this proposal is that it would provide a continuum of peer review that more closely matches the publication continuum that is likely to evolve.

VI. The future of publishers, journals, and libraries

It is impossible to predict the date or speed of transition to a system like the one outlined in the previous section, but only because they will be determined primarily by sociological factors. The technology that is necessary for future systems is either already available or will be in a few years. The speed with which this technology will be adopted by scholars will depend on how quickly we are prepared to break with traditional methods in favor of a superior but novel system. For example, how quickly will tenure and promotion committees start accepting electronic publications as comparable to those in traditional journals?

What would be the role of publishers in the projected system? Scholars can run electronic journals themselves, with no financial subsidies or subscription fees, using only the spare capacity of the computers and networks that are provided to them as part of their job. This is the model under which most of the current electronic journals in mathematics operate. There is more work for authors and editors in such a system than with traditional print journals, but advances in technology are decreasing the effort that is required. A major advantage of such a system is that the journal can be available for free anytime everyplace that data networks reach. However, the lack of copy editing that is likely to prevail in such a system may not be acceptable. I expect that what editing assistance might be required will not cost anywhere near what print journals cost, and so might be provided by the authors' institutions. If that happens, electronic journals can also be distributed freely. If such assistance is not provided, then subscription fees will have to be imposed, together with access restrictions to the information. However, to compete successfully with free preprint distribution and free journals, any subscription journals will have to keep their fees low. In any event, I expect that publishers will have to shrink.

Paper journals will have to convert to electronic publication or disappear. The role of paper is likely to be limited to temporary uses, and archival storage will be electronic.

Review papers are likely to play an increasingly important role, but they are written by scholars and can be published in regular electronic journals. On the other hand, short bibliographic reviews, such as are common in Math. Rev. and Zentralblatt, might be replaced by computerized searches, since the entire literature will be available on each scholar's workstation. This might mean the demise of Math. Rev. and Zentralblatt. However, I suspect that they will do well, although they will have to change. They are inexpensive enough that they do not need to offer much extra service to justify their price. There will always be need for classifying papers, ensuring that all significant ones are reviewed, and keeping track of all the changes in the databases. Review journals are positioned to provide these services. Still, they will have to change. They will need to be accessible electronically, and will most likely be paid for by a site license fee, giving unlimited access to the database to all scholars affiliated with the customer institution. They will provide much more current information than is true today, since there will be no publications delays. The formats of reviews might vary from those used today. The main distinction from today is likely to be the presence of hypertext links from reviews to the papers and the commentaries associated to those papers. Combined with easy electronic access to the primary materials, review journals will then provide all the functions of a specialized library.

What about libraries? They will also have to shrink and change their role. The transition to the new system is likely to be less painful for them than for publishers. There is much more inertia in the library system, with old collections of printed material that will need to be preserved and converted to digital formats. Eventually, though, we are even likely to need many fewer reference librarians. If the review journals evolve the way I project, they will provide directly to scholars all the services that libraries used to. With immediate electronic access to all the information in a field, with navigating tools, reviews, and other aids, a few dozen librarians and scholars at review journals might be able to substitute for a thousand reference librarians.

Acknowledgements

This article provides my own personal view of the future of mathematical journals. Few of the observations and predictions are original, and I have freely drawn on the ideas in the papers listed below. I have benefited greatly from extensive email correspondence with Paul Ginsparg and Frank Quinn, and especially with Stevan Harnad. Helpful comments and useful information were also provided by a large number of colleagues and correspondents, who are acknowledged in the full version of this paper. The full version contains more data, detailed arguments, and additional references.

References

[APS] Report of the APS task force on electronic information systems, Bull. Amer. Phys. Soc. 36, no. 4 (April 1991), 1119-1151.

[Franks] J. Franks, The impact of electronic publication on scholarly journals, Notices Amer. Math. Soc. 40 (1993), 1200-1202.

[Franks2] J. Franks, What is an electronic journal?, unpublished report, available at gopher://gopher.cic.net/11/e-serials/related.

[Ginsparg] P. Ginsparg, First steps towards electronic research communication, Computers in Physics, 8, no. 4, July/August, (1994), 390-396. Also available at URL http://xxx.lanl.gov F/blurb/.

[Harnad1] S. Harnad, Scholarly skywriting and the prepublication continuum of scientific inquiry, Psychological Science 1 (1990), 342-343. Reprinted in Current Contents 45 (November 11, 1991), 9-13.

[Harnad2] S. Harnad, Implementing peer review on the Net: Scientific quality control in scholarly electronic journals, Proc. Intern. Conf. on Refereed Electronic Journals: Towards a Consortium for Networked Publications, to appear. (Available via anonymous ftp, along with [Harnad1] and other related papers, from princeton.edu, in directory pub/harnad/Harnad.)

[Harnad3] S. Harnad, Publicly Retrievable FTP Archives for Esoteric Science and Scholarship: A Subversive Proposal. To be presented at: Network Services Conference, London, England, 28-30 November 1994. (Available via anonymous ftp from princeton.edu, in directory pub/harnad/Psycoloquy/ Subversive.Proposal.)

[Lederberg] J. Lederberg, Digital communications and the conduct of science: The new literacy, Proc. IEEE 66 (1978), 1314-1319.

[Licklider] J. C. R. Licklider, "Libraries of the Future," MIT Press, 1965.

[Loeb] D. Loeb, An Electronic Journal of Mathematics: Feasibility Report 5, electronically circulated manuscript, 1991.

[MacKieV] J. K. MacKie-Mason and H. R. Varian, Some economics of the Internet, in "Networks, Infrastructure and the New Task for Regulation}, W. Sichel, ed., to appear. (Available via gopher or ftp together with other related papers from gopher.econ.lsa.umich.edu in /pub/Papers.)

[MR50] Mathematical Reviews, 50th Anniversary Celebration, special issue, Jan. 1990.

[Okerson] A. Okerson, The electronic journal: What, whence, and when?, The Public-Access Computer Systems Review 2, no. 1 (1991), 5-24.

[Price] D. J. Price, The exponential curve of science, Discovery 17 (1956), 240-243.

[Quinn] F. Quinn, Roadkill on the electronic highway? The threat to the mathematical literature, Notices Amer. Math. Soc., Jan. 1995, to appear.

[Schaf1] A. C. Schaffner, Electronic journals in the sciences, Brandeis internal report, available from the author, schaffner@logos.cc.brandeis.edu.

[Schaf2] A. C. Schaffner, The future of scientific journals: Lessons from the past, Information Technology and Libraries, vol. 13, Dec. 1994, to be published. Preprint available from the author, schaffner@logos.cc.brandeis.edu.

IX. A Librarian Speaks

One of the proposal's proponents' regular strategies is to insist that moving to electronic journals is a much simpler process than other participants believe to be the case. Richard Entlich, a librarian at Cornell, with substantial hands-on experience in implementing online journals for university researchers, shares his experience and points to the complexity of the publishing landscape and the interrelated nature of the various parts.

Date: Thu, 7 Jul 94 14:58:46 EDT
From: "Stevan Harnad" <harnad@princeton.edu>

From: Richard Entlich <rentlich@oldal.mannlib.cornell.edu>
Subject: Re: Ginsparg's Reply to Garson
To: harnad@Princeton.EDU
Date: Thu, 7 Jul 94 13:53:12 EDT

Stevan,

You forwarded Paul Ginsparg's comments on Lorrin Garson's response to your "subversive" proposal to VPIEJ-L and perhaps elsewhere. Please forward my comments to whatever lists you sent his comments.

Dr. Ginsparg['s]... comments on the CORE (Chemistry Online Retrieval Experiment) project are ill-informed. First of all, CORE was not conceived, nor has it ever been portrayed as a model for de novo electronic publishing. CORE is a retrospective conversion project, designed to test the efficacy of a variety of approaches to capturing previously published material, using whatever combination of machine-readable formats may be available or obtainable through conversion. Perhaps high energy physicists have no interest in anything published more than a few picoseconds ago, but in most disciplines, the existing print corpus has ongoing value.

Yes, CORE is using bitmapped page images, but it is hardly "another scan and shred project to post bitmaps of existing journals." Full-page bitmaps are used 1) because they are a reasonable alternative for conversion of existing print archives to machine-readable form, and 2) to capture portions of pages which were not available in machine-readable form, mainly illustrations of various types. However, the heart of the CORE project is over ten years of marked-up machine-readable text files from twenty ACS journals. These files are converted from ACS proprietary markup to SGML.

The resulting files can be searched, displayed and navigated via a sophisticated X Window based interface developed by OCLC called Scepter. Full-text searching is provided (including about two dozen fields, from author and title to CAS registry number and figure captions) and supports Boolean and adjacency operators, truncation, and direct searching on Greek letters and diacritics. Text is displayed using standard and custom-designed X Window fonts. The interface also supports direct access to article subsections, hypertext searching and citation linking, and full article printing.

Article text, equations and tables are all displayed based on the existing machine-readable files. Only figures are displayed as bitmaps. CORE makes the best possible use of these bitmaps by extracting them from the full-page image file and making them accessible from icons embedded in the text. In Scepter, they are also displayed thumbnail size along with the article front matter so they can be browsed as a kind of "visual abstract."

Another important element of CORE is that it is based on a large corpus of highly regarded publications, spanning many subdisciplines within chemistry. In addition to working out technical problems, CORE was designed to test user acceptance of network journal delivery in a variety of formats. A large enough body of material to create more than a "toy" system was seen as essential to the user testing process. Perhaps physicists are content with downloading TeK source or PostScript, but Ginsparg's system will not necessarily translate smoothly to other disciplines, at least not right away.

Not every group of scholars has the same degree of computing sophistication, or access to state-of-the-art computing equipment. Not everyone has ready access and familiarity with Unix workstations or can afford to replace equipment in order to keep pace with the latest network fad. For instance, there are still plenty of Macintoshes and PCs around which cannot run NCSA Mosaic.

I recognize that Ginsparg wants to make every physicist a self-publisher and believes that his colleagues all share that desire and are equipped to do so. Perhaps the pervasive use of computers in physics and established standard of TeK for manuscript preparation makes this reasonable--for physics. But even physicians, who are, as a group, wealthy and fairly technically literate, have expressed doubts about electronic journals. (See, for example, JAMA, May 6, 1992, vol. 267, no. 17, p. 2374 and The New England Journal of Medicine, Jan. 16, 1992, vol. 326, no. 3, pp. 195-97). Some of their concerns focus on the peer review process, but others focus on the expense of computing equipment, and lack of format standardization for manuscript generation.

And speaking of medicine, Ginsparg takes a shot at "...dead formats promoted in general by OCLC." OCLC happens to co-publish (with AAAS) an electronic journal in medicine, the Online Journal of Current Clinical Trials. Though I am in no way a spokesperson for OCLC, I am puzzled at Ginsparg's comments. OCLC has done pioneering work in the creation of de novo networked electronic journals, most of which is based on TeK and SGML. These hardly qualify as "dead formats."

Lest I come off sounding like an apologist for the publishing community, let me make my position clear. As a librarian, I am acutely aware of the down side of print publishing in terms of cost, distribution, access, time lag, functionality, space requirements, preservation, etc. Libraries have been too reluctant to embrace new technologies which offer potential solutions to some of these problems. But it is also hardly the case that Ginsparg's system resolves all the myriad issues involved in the transition from print to electronic publishing and distribution of scholarly articles. Some of the reticence on the part of libraries reflects the tremendous flux and lack of standardization in information technology. One does not throw out a proven, centuries old system, whatever its flaws and limitations, without solid assurance that its replacement is a reliable, stable substitute for the long-term.

I am as excited as anyone working in the electronic journal area about the promise of new technologies; I also recognize that progress towards network publishing will probably cause upheaval within libraries and very likely the disappearance of some. Libraries will attempt to find continuing relevance. Nevertheless, we will not support print publishing when it ceases to meet the needs of our patrons. In the meantime, despite the success of Ginsparg's preprint system, more research is needed in the areas of interface design, organization and classification of machine-readable files, the creation of machine-readable archives which will remain accessible for centuries, etc. Even though it is based on previously published material, CORE is helping to address these thorny issues.

Richard Entlich   Technical Project Manager
Albert R. Mann Library   Information Technology Section
Cornell University   entlich@cornell.edu

(Note: some of the above comments are based on a talk I gave at the 9th annual NASIG (North American Serials Interest Group) conference in Vancouver, BC last month and will subsequently appear in the conference proceedings.)

Date: Thu, 7 Jul 94 20:17:21 -0600
From: Paul Ginsparg 505-667-7353 <ginsparg@qfwfq.lanl.gov>
Subject: Re: Entlich Reply to Ginsparg

richard entlich's remarks miss the point. the point i was trying to make was that garson's examples of electronic involvement were all irrelevant to the argument at hand, that of cost estimates for true electronic research distribution, and were just confusing the issues.

i'm eager to see other kinds of publishing efforts that look promising. i offer the physics and related servers as an example to others who might want to do something similar; various features clearly will not be applicable for all communities. others can learn from our mistakes. (o'donnell's Chicago Journal of Theoretical Computer Science (MIT Press) will be a most interesting experiment -- to see if they can provide sufficient "value-added" for which people will voluntarily pay.)

> [Ginsparg's] comments on the CORE (Chemistry Online Retrieval
> Experiment project are ill-informed. First of all, CORE was not conceived, nor
> has it ever been portrayed as a model for de novo electronic publishing. CORE
> is a retrospective conversion project,

correct, that's precisely why i identified it as irrelevant to the question of costs of an enterprise that starts electronic from inception.

> Perhaps high energy physicists have no interest in anything
> published more than a few picoseconds ago, but in most
> disciplines, the existing print corpus has ongoing value.

my community accesses the archival database (journals in libraries) as well as the growing electronic one, never argued otherwise -- not sure why we're being reviled here. how best to port the archival database to electronic format is an important question, it is just not relevant to the issue at hand, as mentioned above. (and this is neither the proper forum to give an exhaustive technical critique of the "sophisticated X Window based interface developed by OCLC called Scepter.")

> In addition to working out technical problems, CORE was
> designed to test user acceptance of network journal delivery in a
> variety of formats.

the report i heard from the head librarian at cornell (harvard "gateways to knowledge" meeting last fall) was that user acceptance was remarkably low for reasons they did not yet understand.

> Perhaps physicists are content with downloading TeK source or

> PostScript, but Ginsparg's system will not necessarily translate
> smoothly to other disciplines, at least not right away.

that's TeX (the X according to Knuth is a chi, hence the pronunciation). undoubtedly it won't transfer smoothly, i have no doubt there are many features peculiar to my community. but we are looking towards the future and can envision a gradual transition. different communities will have different standards. perhaps no matter what word-processor is used, they may be able to choose the final output format (as we currently choose postscript for some applications): acrobat pdf, sgml, or some other -- all readily interconvertible. five years from now, the options for author-prepared documents are guaranteed to be dramatically improved over now; and each generation of more sophisticated software grows *easier* to use. the point is to start thinking ahead now.

> For instance, there are still plenty of Macintoshes and PCs
> around which cannot run NCSA Mosaic.

not sure i understand this comment. we've got macmosaic running here on the lowest end mac classic -- probably just means there are some macs and pc's not connected to the internet because no one installed mactcp or equivalent. it is true that the windows version of mosaic will not run on a pc that cannot run windows, but there will always be a mix of technology at any given time and servers can always provide a lowest common denominator interface (the systems i set up still allow for equal low-end e-mail access via dumb terminal and printer). the important point is that many communities will find self-sufficiency in their interests, and they will proceed accordingly.

> OCLC happens to co-publish (with AAAS) an electronic journal in medicine,
> the Online Journal of Current Clinical Trials.

yes, this was announced with great fanfare in mid '92. it required proprietary software that ran on low-end pc's ("for instance there are still plenty" of high end machines that do not run low-end pc emulation. in a few years will there be more of these or more "macs and pcs around which cannot run ncsa mosaic"?) and was far from state-of-the-art even at the time (i remember discussing this with representatives of other publishing companies.) after more than half a year it had published a grand total of only seven submissions (as reported in Science, another AAAS publication), and was used as the standard example of how not to proceed. i do not have statistics for how it is currently faring, but perhaps they have since made improvements to correct the deficiencies -- might even provide some solid basis for the 25% vs 75% cost question, but not if they're still too remote from critical mass.

> OCLC has done pioneering work in the creation of de novo
> networked electronic journals, most of which is based on TeX and
> SGML. These hardly qualify as "dead formats."

as i mentioned in my message to andrew o., as a member of an aps advisory board i've seen their more recent proposals and while it is inappropriate to comment in detail here, i can readily affirm that there's nothing that impacts the issue of costs of publishing scientific vs. non-scientific material.

> Lest I come off sounding like an apologist for the publishing community,
> let me make my position clear. As a librarian, I am acutely aware of the
> down side of print publishing in terms of cost, distribution, access,
> time lag, functionality, space requirements, preservation, etc.
> Libraries have been too reluctant to embrace new technologies which
> offer potential solutions to some of these problems.

and i am entirely sympathetic to the plight of librarians for whom committing prematurely to the wrong technology would be a disaster. and i am sympathetic because i've always been a fan of libraries and librarians (aren't all academics?) and they're as much victims of the practices of pub co's as we are.

> But it is also hardly the case that Ginsparg's system resolves all the
> myriad issues involved in the transition from print to electronic
> publishing and distribution of scholarly articles.

no argument.

> Some of the reticence on the part of libraries reflects the tremendous flux
> and lack of standardization in information technology. One does not throw
> out a proven, centuries old system, whatever its flaws and limitations,
> without solid assurance that its replacement is a reliable, stable
> substitute for the long-term.

no argument. this is why it's so much easier for us to test the envelope -- the consequences of failure are less pronounced.

> I am as excited as anyone working in the electronic journal area about
> the promise of new technologies. I also recognize that progress towards
> network publishing will probably cause upheaval within libraries and
> very likely the disappearance of some. Libraries will attempt to find
> continuing relevance.

important issues. and by no means clear at present what will be the evolving role of libraries (and in particular of university research libraries which satisfy a wide variety of different needs). perhaps they will be out of the loop entirely for many aspects of scholarly research communication, or perhaps they will become the natural local repositories to organize and serve this information to the rest of the world. cornell's mann library is clearly ahead of the game in technical sophistication (i have no problem with that, i got my doctorate from cornell) so may not be the best short-term model for involvement from the library community.

> the creation of machine-readable archives which will
> remain accessible for centuries, etc. Even though it is based
> on previously published material, CORE is helping to address
> some of these thorny issues.

very few libraries currently have dedicated resources to address these issues. but in the most optimistic scenario, perhaps this will become commonplace in a few years and libraries and research communities can become partners in subversion to their mutual benefit. time will tell.

none of these issues impact the cost distinction between scientific and non-scientific publication, however, and that was the original issue.

Paul Ginsparg

PS it is still not clear exactly how things will proceed from community to community -- harnad's original "subversion" proposal passed to an economist got back:

>> ... but Harnad is a bit off (at least for econ types). Most of
>> them care less about whether others read their stuff, what is important is
>> publishing because that is what determines salary and promotion.
>> My guess is that around 2011 his vision will happen and journals
>> will be a thing of the past, and I will be retired.

(c.f. harnad on compos mentis; but also comment a bit off of course for usual reason that the on-line versions will ultimately receive similar certification in your scheme and be used [or abused] for allocation of jobs, promotions, and grant money.)

[Ed. Note: Entlich's reply to Ginsparg, copied to Harnad, follows. At the time, this remained a private communication between the three, but is now used with permission to clarify the sequence of messages and ideas. This is followed by a final, private exchange between the three correspondents.]

From To:ginsparg@qfwfq.lanl.gov Fri Jul 8 14:52:38 1994
Date: Fri, 8 Jul 94 14:52:38 EDT
To: ginsparg@qfwfq.lanl.gov
From: Richard Entlich <rentlich@oldal.mannlib.cornell.edu>
Subject: Ginsparg reply to Entlich
Cc: harnad@princeton.edu

Paul,

re>> His comments on the CORE (Chemistry Online Retrieval Experiment)
re>> project are ill-informed. First of all, CORE was not conceived, nor has it
re>> ever been portrayed as a model for de novo electronic publishing. CORE is
re>> a retrospective conversion project,

pg> correct, that's precisely why i identified it as irrelevant to the question
pg> of costs of an enterprise that starts electronic from inception.

I understand that the economics are the same whether we're using
bitmaps or recycled phototypesetting tapes, since both involve
reprocessing material that has already been through the print publishing
process. But your comments did not focus on the retrospective aspect of
CORE, but on the use of bitmaps of pages. I have no problem with your
making the point that ACS' participation in CORE fails to address the
cost issues your raised. I was disturbed by the incorrect characterization
of CORE as primarily a bitmap scanning effort and the subsequent
ridicule of such efforts.

re>> Perhaps high energy physicists have no interest in anything
re>> published more than a few picoseconds ago, but in most
re>> disciplines, the existing print corpus has ongoing value.

pg> my community accesses the archival database (journals in libraries) as
pg> well as the growing electronic one, never argued otherwise -- not sure why
pg> we're being reviled here. how best to port the archival database to
pg> electronic format is an important question, it is
pg> just not relevant to the issue at hand, as mentioned above.

Well, from what I've read of your preprint system, it did sound like
archiving the submissions was something of an afterthought. However,
the main point is that you seemed to be condemning all use of bitmaps,
despite the fact that they may be the only practical way to "port the
archival database to electronic format."

pg> (and this is neither the proper forum to give an exhaustive technical
pg> critique of the "sophisticated X Window based interface developed by
pg> OCLCcalled Scepter.")

Again, being unsure of how far your comments were promulgated, I was trying to set the record straight about CORE. You criticized all "scan and shred" projects, in which category you placed CORE, for being "unable to distinguish superficial appearance from information content" and for not "rethink[ing] the compromises embodied in the current paper format and robotically propagat[ing] them to the electronic format." The description of Scepter was included to clear the air and to indicate that we _are_ working on the very functionality "that can *only* be embodied in the electronic format from the start," even if we are not producing new electronic journals.

The fact is, CORE has not done a very good job of publicizing what it's been doing (which may explain your own misperceptions), and I would hate for people to write us off because of your comments.

re>> In addition to working out technical problems, CORE was
re>> designed to test user acceptance of network journal delivery in a
re>> variety of formats.

pg> undoubtedly it won't transfer smoothly, i have no doubt there are many
pg> features peculiar to my community. but we are looking towards the
pg> future and can envision a gradual transition. different communities
pg> will have different standards. perhaps no matter what word-processor
pg> is used, they may be able to choose the final output format (as we
pg> currently choose postscript for some applications): acrobat pdf, sgml, or
pg> some other -- all readily interconvertible. five years from now, the options
pg> for author-prepared documents are guaranted to be dramatically
pg> improved over now; and each generation of more sophisticated
pg> software grows *easier* to use. the point is to start thinking ahead now,
pg> though it is still not clear exactly how things will proceed from community
pg> to community -- your original "subversion" proposal passed to an economist
pg> got back:

I basically agree, though I still think the pace of change alone will leave users in certain disciplines out.

re>> For instance, there are still plenty of Macintoshes and PCs
re>> around which cannot run NCSA Mosaic.

pg> not sure i understand this comment. we've got macmosaic running here
pg> on the lowest end mac classic -- probably just means there are some macs
pg> and pc's not connected to the internet because no one installed mactcp
pg> or equivalent.

No, I wasn't talking about network connectivity here. It's true that you can get MacMosaic to run on a "porthole" Mac. But, with 4 Meg of RAM available, System 7 needs 2, Mosaic itself wants another 1, and if you want to run several helper programs and load, say a 2 Mb QuickTime Movie, well, you're really out of luck. My main point is that the CPU speed, RAM, hard drive space, etc. ante gets upped regularly with each new network software innovation. Equipment replacement schedules in poorer disciplines are way behind the curve of such changes.

pg> it is true that the windows version of mosaic will not run on a pc that
pg> cannot run windows, but there will always be a mix of technology at
pg> any given time and servers can always provide a lowest common
pg> denominator interface (the systems i set up still allow for equal low-end
pg> e-mail access via dumb terminal and printer).

Yes, and we are very aware of the need to do this at the library, where equitable access is always a concern. On the other hand, you did describe full-text access to technical journals which lacked "mathematics, tables, or math" as "less than useless" and I agree with that evaluation. We may feel good about providing vt100 emulation as an alternative, but we should at least admit that such users, as a result of their technological poverty, are not being well served.

pg> the important point is that many communities will find self-sufficiency
pg> in their interests, and they will proceed accordingly.

Agreed.

re>> OCLC happens to co-publish (with AAAS) an electronic journal in
re>> medicine, the Online Journal of Current Clinical Trials.

pg> yes, this was announced with great fanfare in mid '92.
pg> it required proprietary software that ran on low-end pc's
pg> ("for instance there are still plenty" of high end machines that do not run
pg> low-end pc emulation. in a few years will there be more of these or more
pg> "macs and pcs around which cannot run ncsa mosaic"?)
pg> and was far from state-of-the-art even at the time (i remember discussing
pg> this with representatives of other publishing companies.)
pg> after more than half a year it had published a grand total of only seven
pg> submissions (as reported in Science, another AAAS publication),
pg> and was used as the standard example of how not to proceed.
pg> i do not have statistics for how it is currently faring, but perhaps
pg> they have since made improvements to correct the deficiencies -- might
pg> even provide some solid basis for the 25% vs 75% cost question, but not
pg> if they're still too remote from critical mass.

I intentionally avoided addressing the success or failure of OJCCT. I only wanted to say that, to my knowledge, OCLC was not emphasizing

bitmaps in its electronic journal projects.
re>> OCLC has done pioneering work in the creation of de novo
re>> networked electronic journals, most of which is based on TeX and
re>> SGML. These hardly qualify as "dead formats."

pg> as i mentioned in my message to andrew o., as a member of an aps advisory
pg> board i've seen their more recent proposals and while it is inappropriate
pg> to comment in detail here, i can readily affirm that there's nothing
pg> that impacts the issue of costs of publishing scientific vs.
pg> non-scientific material.

You may well have heard something that I'm not privy to.

re>> Lest I come off sounding like an apologist for the publishing community,
re>> let me make my position clear. As a librarian, I am acutely aware of the
re>> down side of print publishing in terms of cost, distribution, access,
re>> time lag, functionality, space requirements, preservation, etc.
re>> Libraries have been too reluctant to embrace new technologies which
re>> offer potential solutions to some of these problems.

pg> and i am entirely sympathetic to the plight of librarians for whom
pg> committing prematurely to the wrong technology would be a disaster.
pr> and i am sympathetic because i've always been a fan of libraries
pg> and librarians (aren't all academics?) and they're as much victims of
pg> the practices of pub co's as we are.

Libraries have been in a difficult position with respect to serials publishers for years. Some of the responses to the ongoing "serials crisis" have not been very productive. We need to work with our faculty and other constituents to determine how we can best continue to provide service in an environment where the library is no longer _the_ center of the information universe.

Thanks for all your comments.

Date: Mon, 11 Jul 94 02:34:13 -0600
From: Paul Ginsparg 505-667-7353 <ginsparg@qfwfq.lanl.gov>
To: rentlich@oldal.mannlib.cornell.edu
Subject: Re: Ginsparg reply to Entlich

Richard, some minor dangling issues.

pg>> (the systems i set up still allow for equal low-end
pg >> e-mail access via dumb terminal and printer).

re> ..full-text access to technical journals which lacked "mathematics, tables,
re> or math" as "less than useless" and I agree with that evaluation. We may
re> feel good about providing vt100 emulation as an alternative, but we should
re> at least admit that such users, as a result of their technological poverty,
re> are not being well served.

i was not clear enough. the low-end access is nonetheless full eqns/figs,
just printed on laserprinter (so users are no worse off than they were with
print -- and still somewhat better for the faster distribution -- they just
miss out on all the higher end capabilities, e.g., hypertext access, window
interface for searches, embedded hypertext in target text, links to
.mpeg/.qt movies and other external software apps, etc.) this is again the
advantage of starting from electronic material and not having to worry
about transporting large bitmaps or reliability of ocr.

pg

[Ed. Note: The following is a message sent by Entlich to VPIEJ-L only
reiterating a few of the points he made above. Though not, strictly speaking, a
part of the subversive discussion, it tidies up some important points.]

Date: Mon, 11 Jul 1994 13:57:57 EDT
From: Richard Entlich <rentlich@oldal.mannlib.cornell.edu>
Subject: Re: Ginsparg's Reply to Entlich
To: Multiple recipients of list VPIEJ-L <VPIEJ-L@VTVM1.CC.VT.EDU>
In-Reply-To: from "Stevan Harnad" at Jul 11, 94 8:43 am

pg> richard entlich's remarks miss the point. the point i was trying to
pg> make was that garson's examples of electronic involvement were all
pg> irrelevant to the argument at hand, that of cost estimates for true
pg> electronic research distribution, and were just confusing the issues.

Paul Ginsparg's intention may have been as stated above, but part of the
effect was to promulgate a highly misleading description and unjustified
criticism of a project in which I (and many others) have invested several
years. (This accounts for the angry tone of my original response). The
CORE Project is obviously fair game for criticism, but even if that
criticism was a sidebar to Ginsparg's thesis, it should have been based on
fact, not speculation.

pg> (and this is neither the proper forum to give an exhaustive technical
pg> critique of the "sophisticated X Window based interface developed by
pg> OCLC called Scepter.")

Since the technical aspects of the CORE Project were inaccurately portrayed in this forum, what forum but this should be used to provide technical details which set the record straight?

Anyone interested in a brief summary and bibliography about the CORE Project may request one from me at the address given below.

Richard Entlich
Mann Library, Cornell University
entlich@cornell.edu

X.   Reprise -- *Prima Facie* Worries

For several years, Harnad has spoken out about objections to electronic publishing that he sees as ill-founded.   Here he takes the opportunity of a contribution to this discussion to review those worrisome issues.

From: harnad Fri Jul 8 21:04:39 1994
To: vpiej-l@vtvm1.bitnet (Pub-EJournals)
Subject: Familiar prima facie worries...

The following questions from Bill Turner at Cornell Library fall in the category of "prima facie" worries that get voiced over and over. One replies to the them, only to hear them resurface somewhere else as vociferously as ever.   There ARE some profound questions about electronic publishing, but, alas, these are not they! These are questions based entirely on old papyrocentric thinking and habits. Nothing personal about Bill! Many, many others have asked the exact same questions. I had planned to write an article for Serials Review, laying them to rest once and for all (and still hope to do so, if I ever find the time to for it); and I carry them around (along with 30 or so further prima facie questions) on transparencies, ready to fix their wagon every time I give a talk.

> Date: Wed, 06 Jul 94 10:55:33 EDT
> From: Bill Turner - Cornell University Library <WRT@CORNELLC>
> Status: RO
>
> Steven, I am in agreement with much of what you are saying about
> electronic publishing etc., but I think you (and MANY others) are
> totally ignoring the hard questions about electronic publishing.
>
> Is there a real archive? Is it guaranteed to always be there?

Bill,

Is there a real paper archive, and is it guaranteed to be always there? If so, why? and who/what underwrites the guarantee? Whatever your reply in the case of paper, the SAME reply (mutatis mutandis) applies to electronic archiving. Paper is an object; tapes are objects; disks are objects. The safest way to protect a flotilla of objects is to make them redundant, distribute them the world over, and have professionals (scholars and librarians for the most part, in the case of scholarly texts) devoted to preserving them for posterity. In the case of electronic archives, this includes making sure that texts get transferred with every technology upgrade.

There is absolutely no problem in principle here. Nothing unique to electronic archiving. And in fact the electronic archive is potentially much more powerful, efficient, accessible, and inexpensive.

> How do I know that what I have retrieved from the network is what you
> wrote?

How do you know in the case of a paper text? Chicanery is possible there too. Why don't we worry about it? Well, in the case of esoteric paper publication (which is the kind I'm interested in) it's rarely of any interest to anyone to tamper with it, but if it is, it COULD be protected, at least to the level of the encryption of military secrets: Is that secure enough?

> If you decide your work contained an error, how do you correct the
> multitude of copies out there?

How do you do it in paper? Publish an erratum or a second edition. The Net has the virtue of being able to make prominent pointers and links to other items along a "thread" of scholarship, including errata and new editions.

Again, no problem WHATSOEVER that is peculiar to electronics over paper; the instinct that there somehow is is simply a paper-bred illusion.

> If you notice that someone ELSE's work contains errors, how do you do
> anything about it?

Need I go on? What do you do in paper? Do the same (much more powerfully and efficiently) in the Virtual Library.

> What do you do about malicious mischief?

There ARE some real security problems on the Net. But esoteric publication is far from being at the greatest risk; encrypted, distributed, off-loaded archives, faithfully maintained, are probably more than good enough for scholarship and science except in rare special cases where even more stringent measures are possible.

> We have a real "caveat emptor" situation being actively pursued by
> people who in some cases have a particular axe to grind (they think
> publishers are getting filthy rich and want to stop it), and they are

> willing to accept great losses so long as the publishers are hurt
> worse.

I know there are some such people, but I am certainly not one of them. I am quite aware that esoteric scholarly publication is not a gold mine, like movies and the tabloids. I'm grateful publishers do it; I would just like to see them adjust to the new, non-trade model that electronic publishing now makes possible.

> Would you REALLY entrust any critical information to the Internet right
> now?   Bill Turner

Please address this to the 20,000 physicists world-wide who are doing just that, in Paul Ginsparg's Archive, to the tune of 35,000 "hits" per day! In the past I had had occasion to call much of Usenet a "global graffiti board for trivial pursuit," but thanks to Paul Ginsparg, plus the editors of some brave new electronic journals, a portion of cyberspace is now being carved out where scholars and scientists really CAN feel secure in entrusting their intellectual wares.

Stevan Harnad
Editor, Behavioral & Brain Sciences, PSYCOLOQUY

Cognitive Science Laboratory
Princeton University
221 Nassau Street
Princeton NJ 08544-2093
harnad@princeton.edu
609-921-7771

P. S. My abstract of paper presented at ASIS 1992 SESSION follows:

FULL-TEXT ELECTRONIC ACCESS TO PERIODICALS
Sponsored by the ASIS Special Interest Group on Library Automation and Networking (SIG/LAN) and the Association of Research Libraries (ARL)

55th ASIS Annual Meeting, Pittsburgh Hilton, Pittsburgh, Pennsylvania October 26-29, 1992

Session II. Full-Text Electronic Access to Periodicals: Strategies for Implementation

WHAT SCHOLARS WANT AND NEED FROM ELECTRONIC JOURNALS

Stevan Harnad

It is useful to remind ourselves now and again why scholars and scientists do what they do, rather than going straight into the junk bond market: They presumably want to contribute to mankind's cumulative knowledge. They have to make a living too, of course, but if doing that as comfortably and prosperously as possible were their primary motive they could surely find better ways. Prestige no doubt matters too, but here again there are less rigorous roads one might have taken than that of learned inquiry. So scholars publish not primarily to pad their CVs or to earn royalties on their words, but to inform their peers of their findings, and to be informed by them in turn, in that collaborative, interactive spiral whereby mankind's knowledge increases. My own estimate is that the electronic medium has the potential to extend individual scholars' intellectual life-lines (i.e., the size of their lifelong contribution) by an order of magnitude.

For scholars and scientists, paper is not an end but a means. It has served us well for several millennia, but it would have been surprising indeed if this manmade medium had turned out to be optimal for all time. In reality, paper has always had one notable drawback: its turnaround time. Although it allowed us to encode, preserve and share ideas and findings incomparably more effectively than we could ever have done orally, its tempo was always significantly slower than the oral interactions to which the speed of thought seems to be organically adapted. Electronic journals have now made it possible for scholarly publication to escape this rate-limiting constraint of the paper medium, allowing scholarly communication to become much more rapid, global and interactive than ever before. It is important that we not allow the realization of the new medium's revolutionary potential to be retarded by clinging superstitiously to familiar but incidental features of the paper medium.

What scholars accordingly need is electronic journals that provide: (1) rapid, expert peer-review, (2) rapid copy-editing, proofing and publication of accepted articles, (3) rapid, interactive, peer commentary, and (4) a permanent, universally accessible, searchable and retrievable electronic archive. Ideally, the true costs of providing these services should be subsidized by Universities, Learned Societies, Libraries and the Government, but if they must be passed on to the "scholar-consumer," let us make sure that they are only the real costs, and not further unnecessary ones arising from emulating inessential features of the old medium.

For scholars and scientists the greatest disadvantage of paper publication has always been its turnaround time, which is hopelessly out of phase with the human thought process. Electronic networked publication now makes it possible for the first time in the history of learned inquiry to explore the full interactive potential of the human brain in a medium that provides the discipline, permanence, and quality control of the peer-reviewed written medium along with the speed, scope and interactiveness of a "live" global symposium. PSYCOLOQUY is a refereed electronic journal sponsored by the American Psychological Association and dedicated to "Scholarly Skywriting": "target articles" reporting important new ideas and findings followed closely by multiple peer commentary and authors' responses. It is in its unique capacity for interactive publication that the revolutionary potential of the new medium lies rather than in its capacity to duplicate the features of paper publication in a faster and cheaper form.

XI.   A Librarian's View from Europe

Bernard Naylor is the University Librarian at the University of Southhampton. He initially joined the discussion through a paper coincidentally written at about the moment the "subversive" discussion was beginning. This section begins his various contributions to the subversive proposal.

[Ed. Note: Because a great deal of the discussion from here on includes comments on Bernard Naylor's essay written for a meeting of Euorpean librarians, we reproduce it here. It was published in the LIBER Quarterly, 4 [1994], pp. 283-289. We thank Dr. Heiner Schnelling, of the Universitaetsbibliothek of Giessen, for permission to reprint.]

From: "Bernard Naylor" <B.Naylor@soton.ac.uk>
Date: Fri, 15 Jul 94 17:30:01 BST

THE FUTURE OF THE SCHOLARLY JOURNAL

Paper delivered to the general meeting of LIBER on Thursday 7 July 1994

Bernard Naylor, University Librarian
University of Southhampton

CLEARING THE GROUND

Before entering onto the main substance of this paper, it will be useful to clear the ground on a number of points.

The first thing to remember is that publishing journals is a large international industry. Much of the content of journals is brought to fruition in universities, and universities are prominent buyers of the ultimate product. What goes on in between is an industry. The shares of journal publishing companies and subscription agents are quoted on the Stock Exchange. Journal publishing companies draw up accounts which reveal profits and losses. They raise capital for new ventures. In the final analysis, they know that unless they trade profitably, they will end up in liquidation.

Some academic publishers take a longer term and less commercial view of their operations, but their constraints are getting tighter, too. Some societies have hived off their journals to commercial companies, either to be rid of the administrative burden, or with the object of generating increased income. Sponsoring institutions also take a much less indulgent view about the spending of the institution's money on a journal, for example by the provision of administrative support in the office of a teaching department. Where they might once have done this just for the prestige, now they are more likely to demand financial compensation.

If we are speculating about the future of the journal, we are also anticipating change in the industry. Large international industries do not make radical change tidily, and fortunes can be made and lost in the process. I cannot think of any industry which has successfully restructured itself solely as a result of customers (which is what we librarians are) sitting round tables and talking about their problems. So, while I think that exchanges of views among players in the journals industry are very much needed at the present time, I do not expect miracles of readjustment to flow from them.

The second introductory point concerns the number of players in the journals industry, librarians, publishers, serials agents, document delivery services, writers, editors, users of journals. Some players do more than one thing. Writers of articles are usually readers of journals. Blackwells is an agent and a publisher. CARL is a document delivery service based on libraries. The result of this is some confusion of roles. Obviously, the players do not all have identical interests. A particularly interesting question is: who are journals published for? Is it for librarians who buy them but rarely read them? Is it for library users, who curse if they are cancelled, but have little financial stake in the purchasing process? Is it for writers (usually themselves library users also) who want to see their work in print because of the academic prestige attached -- and even though they may suspect that very few people will ever read it? Journal publishing clearly is an industry but in some respects it is a very strange industry.

My third introductory point concerns the complexity of the journals problem. There are some features, copyright for example, which are worth a whole series of lectures in themselves. Every debate on the future of journals risks foundering on interventions like: "yes, but you have forgotten to mention such a thing." I propose to concentrate mainly on two factors, the economics of the situation and the impact of technology. This is for two reasons. First, because I think they are, in the final analysis, the most important, and secondly, because the other problems are often produced or intensified by these two. For example, the problems of copyright often arise because of activities libraries get up to in respect of journals to which they cannot afford to subscribe or because of the remarkable opportunities opened up by information technology -- opportunities which many journal publishers regard as threats to their ownership of copyright.

ECONOMIC ASPECTS OF THE JOURNALS PROBLEM

There are many ways of looking at the economic aspects of the journal problem. Let me get one of them out of the way to begin with. In all the conflicts about the cost of journals, I have little time for the demonising of any of the parties to the conflict. Some publishers are no doubt wicked profiteers, just as a few (but very few) librarians are cavalier about the rights of copyright owners. On the whole, I think publishers want to make a decent living like most people in an industry, and some of the economic problems of dwindling circulation lists and price increases which continually exceed the rise in the retail price index are problems they would prefer to do without if only they thought they could.

I therefore need to restate the economic problem, and I present it, first, as follows:

"The scholarly community in general and academic libraries in particular cannot at present afford as much scholarly communication of a print-on-paper kind as they would like."

Economists would probably say there is an excess of supply over demand, and it was one of those economists who identified the journals problem in those terms, and asked me in a rather exasperated way: "Then why are prices going up instead of down?"

One answer undoubtedly is that demand for journals is quite a funny concept in economic terms. Normally, we associate demand for a product with the economic power to purchase it. Most managers of academic libraries do not themselves demand journals; the demand comes more from their users who do not have to pick up the bills. This is a potent factor in the way that supply and demand in the journals industry operates. I could therefore try a further restatement of the economic problem in the following terms:

"The scholarly community in general would like more scholarly communication of a print-on-paper kind but academic libraries consider that they cannot afford it from their present resources and have often been unable to achieve the increase in resources necessary to afford it."

If there is an excess of supply over demand in the journals industry, and there seems no prospect of an increase in demand, the obvious alternative is that supply ought to fall. However, whichever way you look at it, supply is tending to increase. We are getting more articles in our existing journals. We are getting more new journals -- though old ones are dying too. All this should be evidence of burgeoning demand; and so it is, but demand from the users of journals rather than their purchasers, the libraries. The normal self-readjusting tension between supply and demand fails to operate.

In effect, we have looked at two possible responses to the mismatch between supply and demand. One is to increase demand -- but libraries cannot seem to get more money. The other is to reduce supply - but it is increasing. A third would be to reduce costs -- but costs too are increasing. So cancelling subscriptions is very understandable, and many economists would see it as tending to remedy the mismatch between supply and demand. Unfortunately, the whole situation is so atypical that the librarians' response has so far shown few signs of putting things right.

JUST IN TIME AND JUST IN CASE

Another noteworthy thing about journals as a product is that you can consume journals in one of two ways. The normal way we consume journals is by subscribing to them. We can also consume them by ordering individual journal articles from document delivery services. This is not unique to journals. Some people do not own cars but can nevertheless avail themselves of motorised transport. They can hire a self-drive car or take a taxi. The car owner has made a "just in case" purchase; he spends because he has a general expectation of his needs. The hired car or taxi user is a "just in time" consumer who spends because of a precise and immediate need.

It is now becoming clear to me that the future of the journal involves a battle over "just in case" and "just in time" in the journals industry. Like the consumer who does not want to afford to own a car and falls back on "just in time" car hire, the librarian who cannot afford to subscribe to a journal "just in case", falls back on "just in time" provision, that is from a document delivery service. We may care to note, in passing that, in a user service environment, "just in time" is usually more accurately described as "just too late." The user normally would like something at the time of asking and the delay while the document is delivered may be acceptable but is usually second best.

The more important thing is this. The "just in time" car user makes a fairly realistic contribution towards the cost of the product, paying the car hire firm or the taxi driver. By contrast, the "just in time" journal user makes a very poor contribution - but the contribution is increasing as document delivery services increasingly collect royalties on behalf of the owners of the journals from which they supply copies. Royalties are not liked by librarians but they do make for a more realistic choice for the consumer between "just in time" and "just in case." They also help to ensure that the "just in time" approach does not irretrievably damage the financial viability of the product on which it is dependent.

As we all know, document delivery services are improving dramatically at the present time, and it looks as though information technology will allow further improvements. I have already referred to document supply as an example of "just too late" provision. With improvements in networking and in the terminals available to end users, and with the advances in such technologies as CD-ROM, it is becoming increasingly possible to take journals in electronic form, either by subscription, or by the purchase of individual articles as required. There is an increasing number of experiments taking place. Some publishers are offering electronic versions of their journals, alongside the traditional product. Some are pursuing new service concepts, in such experiments as ADONIS, TULIP and RED SAGE. Some are launching entirely new journals in the electronic medium only, such as PSYCOLOQUY. The number of those is growing steadily but from a very small base. Some document supply services -- and CARL is the obvious example -- are making increasing use of fax. The overall effect is that the tardiness of document supply looks like a diminishing factor. Libraries and end users feel increasingly confident that document supply services will soon be able to meet their needs quickly enough - at a price.

CONTINGENT FACTORS

This welcome trend contains lots of problematical factors and I ought to enumerate some of them.

There are technical problems. Can the networks cope with the bandwidth? The answer seems to be "yes" as long as we are talking of a few experiments, but "possibly not" if we are thinking of this as a heavily-used technique. Can the end user terminals cope with the bandwidth? The answer is "by no means all of them", and for the time being a terminal adequate to present high resolution illustrations is more expensive than a standard terminal for word-processing and spread sheets. Are the formats for articles satisfactorily standardised? No. Are there outstanding questions about user interfaces? Most certainly. The trouble-free transmission of journal articles of all kinds and in large numbers is still technically some way in the future.

Then there are the financial problems. In principle, one copy of a journal in Boston Spa or Hanover can feed photocopies of articles to every library there is, and the price the user would pay at present is mainly one of delay. With technical advance, one electronic copy of a journal could satisfy the world, and delay would be minimal or nil. So far, the way of paying for such a development has not emerged. Indeed, plenty of people are not sure it needs to be paid for. They believe "the age of the free lunch" has really arrived. I think a way will be found to enable people to pay in advance "just in case" for electronic journals as they do for printed ones. There are examples such as CD-ROM and the BIDS services, launched in recent years in the UK, which can help us to sort this out. I also believe that some system of licensing users will impose the necessary controls to protect revenue.

Questions of copyright are tightly bound up with the financial problems. I can remember the days when photocopies were spewed slowly and wetly from a foul smelling chemical sink -- and nobody attached any importance to copyright, because it was very difficult to contravene to any significant extent. Copyright became a serious issue with the growing ease of photocopying. With the lightning ease of electronic transfer, the serious issue has become a potential nightmare for a publisher interested in protecting copyright, and by implication the revenue stream. So far, we are barely at the stage of defining the issues sufficiently clearly to suggest a blueprint for a possible solution.

An increase in dependence on photocopied articles has made some people question whether the journal or the journal part will survive as a unit of publication. It is suggested that the individual article, identified through an indexing or abstracting service and obtained through a document delivery service, is now the focal point. However, the demand for journals of a traditional kind continues among library users, and I hear a great deal from ordinary library users in defence of browsing, or rather in enthusiastic advocacy of browsing, enough to satisfy me that it has to be taken seriously and allowed for, if possible. To my mind, the forecast that the individual article as publishing unit would rise in triumph, like a phoenix, from the ashes of the dead journal, was more fashionable a year or two ago than it is now.

The last point I want to make in this section of my paper concerns the question of how the great abundance of conventional printed journals will decline and disappear. Our own behaviour and the behaviour our users expect of us suggest that the least popular journals will be replaced first, because those are the ones we cancel and for which we first come to depend on modern methods of document supply. This makes the exciting new technology a crutch for our weakness rather than a banner for our ambitions for the future, a strange role indeed. What does look certain is that secondary source periodicals, such as indexing and abstracting tools, in printed form, are in terminal decline. Otherwise, the broad image of the future shape of events is still surprisingly unclear.

REBIRTH OF THE JOURNAL

In addressing the economic aspects of the journal problem, I have slipped imperceptibly into talking about technology. I now embark on a more formal discussion of technology from one significant aspect. Let us imagine, if we can, that the potential of the network had emerged in a setting where the exchange of knowledge was not already underpinned by a host of printed journals. What do we observe on the network? We can see people informally exchanging information in the most natural way. We can see this process being organised into discussion groups so that people with common interests can have readier access to one another's views.

We can see a controversy starting to emerge as to whether the flow of knowledge should be entirely unmoderated or whether there should be some discipline and some prior assessment of the value of each contribution. We can sense increasing concern about the sheer exuberant volume of communication. How can we be sure we are not missing something significant? How can we avoid being swamped by masses of trivia and irrelevant detail?

We can already notice anxieties about the economic future of this massive information flow. For now, it is all happening for nothing, but persistent rumours about charging for the Internet at the point of use refuse to lie down. We can hear some people saying that a policy of charging for access to information over the Internet would simply be a sensible mechanism for securing the future of this medium of communication. We can hear other voices saying that freedom of information means that access to information should be free and that the chance to implement such a radical proposal is with us now. We can also identify the demand that the system should have a means of clearly fixing each intellectual contribution to the exchange, so that there is no argument about who said something, what they actually said and whether they can establish a claim to be the first to say it.

The interesting thing to me in all this is that I can see history repeating itself. In the early growth of scientific communication, and in the appearance of the first scientific journals, we can see some of these same important considerations asserting themselves, especially the individual's desire to establish the primacy of his or her discovery, and the role of the peer group in establishing the authority of a medium of communication and in assessing the intellectual value of a particular finding or report, before it is promulgated. As the history of the journal has developed, we can see the same considerations about the importance of scientific communication as a social process coming to the surface. There is a kind of special irony in the fact that, as the printed journal is today trying to face up to the difficult challenges of its uncertain financial future, the electronic equivalent is already posing the question: how can we ensure that, as a medium of communication, it can serve its purposes, and, at the same time, pay for itself?

CONCLUSION

I therefore see two convergent developments taking place as a result of the availability of electronic networks. In the first, I can see the possibility that electronic networks will remove most of the delay involved in the "just in time" provision of journal articles. This process has already raised questions about the nature of the journal, why articles are bundled together in the way they are, and whether a new communication technology will provoke radical change. In the second, I can see a new parallel process of knowledge communication growing up; and the present signs are that it is tentatively moving towards operating conventions which strongly echo the conventions of the traditional print-on-paper product.

As for how quickly these changes will take place, I would first say that it is likely to vary from subject to subject. Having said that, I am very mindful of the so-called millennial religious sects. From time to time the end of the world, like the end of the printed journal, is prophesied. So far, it has never come about and so we tend to laugh at further such predictions. Some people say that the world will never end, just as they say the printed journal will always be with us. They could be right but on the whole I don't believe them. Whether I will be around to see them being proved wrong, I wouldn't like to predict.

Bernard Naylor
Southampton
July 1994

Date: Mon, 18 Jul 94 11:01:36 EDT
From: "Stevan Harnad" <harnad@princeton.edu>
To: gs@reagan.ai.mit.edu (UNESCO List EJ LIB),
serialst@uvmvm.bitnet (Lib Serials list),
vpiej-l@vtvm1.bitnet (Pub-EJournals)
Subject: Paying for the Pipe vs. the Piper in Esoteric Publishing

Below are my annotations to the draft of a paper by Bernard Naylor, Director of the University of Southampton Library and much involved in the future of journal publication in the UK. Further discussion is invited.

[Ed. Note: The full text of the paper appears above.]

Stevan Harnad

> From: "Bernard Naylor" <B.Naylor@soton.ac.uk>
> Date: Fri, 15 Jul 94 17:30:01 BST
>
> The first thing to remember is that publishing journals is a large
> international industry. Much of the content of journals is brought to
> fruition in universities, and universities are prominent buyers of the
> ultimate product. What goes on in between is an industry. The shares of
> journal publishing companies and subscription agents are quoted on the
> Stock Exchange. Journal publishing companies draw up accounts which
> reveal profits and losses. They raise capital for new ventures. In the
> final analysis, they know that unless they trade profitably, they will
> end up in liquidation.

The possibilities opened up by electronic scholarly publishing allow us to make finer distinctions: There's (1) trade publishing; then there's (2) trade scholarly publishing; then there's (3) "esoteric" (no market) scholarly publishing, which until now has also had to be treated on the trade model, but now this is no longer true. The trade model is the selling of the author's words; both publisher and author expect to make some money from this. In esoteric publishing, where there is virtually no market for the author's words, the trade model has continued to be applied because paper (and its attendant sizeable expenses) offered no alternative. Electronic-only publication (at less than 25% of the cost of paper publication) offers a radical alternative. The author, his learned societies, institutions and grants pay these much lower per-page expenses and the words are then available to all for free. This is also in agreement with the motivational structure of esoteric publication, where the scholar/scientist's main interest is in reaching the eyes and minds of his peers in cumulative, collaborative research, not in making revenue from the sale of his words.

> I cannot think of any industry which has successfully
> restructured itself solely as a result of customers (which is what we
> librarians are) sitting round tables and talking about their problems.
> So, while I think that exchanges of views among players in the journals
> industry are very much needed at the present time, I do not expect
> miracles of readjustment to flow from them.

Libraries may be the paying customers, but the real consumers (and also the producers) of esoteric publications are the scholars themselves. Libraries have been hostages in the Faustian bargain scholars have had to make with paper publishers in order to reach the eyes and minds of their fellow-scholars. Libraries are now much better advised to ally themselves with those scholars, forming consortia to help pay in advance the much reduced per-page costs of electronic publication, with the product then available for free to all, rather than inadvertently prolonging the status quo by merely readjusting the trade model to which publishers will no doubt cling until forced to adopt the advance-subsidy model out of necessity.

> A particularly interesting question is: who are journals
> published for? Is it for librarians who buy them but rarely read them?
> Is it for library users, who curse if they are cancelled, but have
> little financial stake in the purchasing process? Is it for writers
> (usually themselves library users also) who want to see their work in
> print because of the academic prestige attached - and even though they
> may suspect that very few people will ever read it? Journal publishing
> clearly is an industry but in some respects it is a very strange
> industry.

Your last alternative is closest to the truth for esoteric publication. This has been irrelevant in paper-only days, because the true costs simply made it impossible to adapt to the true motivational structure of esoteric publication. Now this is at last possible, and science and scholarship will be much better served once the need for the requisite restructuring is recognized and met.

But, again, issues are confused if one mixes apples and oranges. What is appropriate for ESOTERIC scientific and scholarly writing (and that's a huge chunk of the literature) is not appropriate for trade scientific and scholarly writing, where there really is and always has been money to be made for both author and publisher from the sale of the text, because there really is a large market of readers willing to pay for it.

> For example, the problems of copyright often arise because of activities
> libraries get up to in respect of journals to which they cannot afford
> to subscribe or because of the remarkable opportunities opened up by
> information technology - opportunities which many journal publishers
> regard as threats to their ownership of copyright.

It is a foregone conclusion that copyright is a very different matter in the trade model -- where it is assigned to the publisher to protect him and the author from "theft of intellectual property" -- as compared to the esoteric model, where subsidies are paid so the property can reach as many interested peers as possible, with no arbitrary and counterproductive price-tag acting as a barrier to access.

Needless to say, if they contributed to up-front subsidy of electronic page charges (for free-for-all acquisitions), libraries would save vastly over anything they could hope for on the trade model -- in paper, because of its true [but now unnecessary] expenses, and in a pay-per-view or similar electronic system where the price-barrier would be artificially re-introduced, needlessly raising prices for all, while at the same time blocking rather than promoting access to the esoteric work, which is what, after all, is the purpose of esoteric publication.

I agree that it's absurd to treat scholarly publishers as villains: They could obviously do much better in tabloids, best-sellers or movies. But they ARE linked to the status quo, just as tobacco producers are, and only necessity will be the mother of invention on their part. I am grateful that they are willing to publish learned work rather than more money-making stuff, but my gratitude tapers off as their interests come into conflict with those of (esoteric) scholars. In libraries they have the kind of "inelastic" demand that produces price spirals and even the kind of situation in which a virus is so "effective" that it causes the extinction of both itself and its host. Electronic-only publication now offers a path out of this cycle; publishers will only adapt to that new path if they are forced to take it. If I were them, I too would probably want to preserve the trade model and the status quo for as long as possible.

> Economists would probably say there is an excess of supply over demand,
> and it was one of those economists who identified the journals problem
> in those terms, and asked me in a rather exasperated way: "Then why are
> prices going up instead of down?"

Simple answer: The wrong people are being taken to be the "consumers," by analogy with trade publication: The consumers are authors, their institutions, societies and research grants. What they are consuming is a (quality-controlled) "public address" (PA) system that allows them to influence the minds and work of their intended readership, present and future. When paper was the only option, we had to pretend this was not so, as if the intended readers were the consumers. (They never were the real consumers, of course; libraries and universities, their proxies, subsidized their consumership by paying for paper journals.)

Remedy this topsy-turvy situation, now that the vastly reduced expenses and vastly enhanced reach of electronic publication make this possible, by paying for esoteric publication where it makes sense: Up front. Then prices will indeed go down instead of up, as more and more information is produced.

> One answer undoubtedly is that demand for journals is quite a funny
> concept in economic terms. Normally, we associate demand for a product
> with the economic power to purchase it. Most managers of academic
> libraries do not themselves demand journals; the demand comes more from
> their users who do not have to pick up the bills. This is a potent
> factor in the way that supply and demand in the journals industry
> operates. I could therefore try a further restatement of the economic
> problem in the following terms:

In other words, scholarly publication is ALREADY subsidized: Electronic publication now makes it possible to recoup the greatly reduced true costs at the logical point -- the (near negligible) price of using the PA system -- instead of the absurd one of a subsidized (and largely nonexistent) esoteric readership.

> "The scholarly community in general would like more scholarly
> communication of a print-on-paper kind but academic libraries consider
> that they cannot afford it from their present resources and have often
> been unable to achieve the increase in resources necessary to afford
> it."

Like publishers, the scholarly community will only become more imaginative and inventive under the pressure of necessity. Their reading is now subsidized; all they do is lobby libraries for their favorite esoteric lore. If they could have their fill from an electronic source, they would no longer press for the paper and its attendant limits.

> We are getting more articles in our existing journals. We are getting more
> new journals - though old ones are dying too. All this should be evidence
> of burgeoning demand; and so it is, but demand from the users of journals
> rather than their purchasers, the libraries. The normal self-readjusting
> tension between supply and demand fails to operate.

And, per-(esoteric)-article, those users are precious few! If many (unrelated, uninteresting) articles were not artificially drawn together into issues and volumes, the constituency for any given (esoteric) article would have no clout at all (the average article in SCI is cited by no one and read by not many more). The solution is not to keep thinking of it all the old, trade-based way but to do the requisite perestroika: The real consumers are the "suppliers" -- the authors and their institutions, etc. The real costs of electronic publication are much lower. So the literature could afford to keep growing if these true minimal costs were simply shifted to those in whose interests it is that they should be paid. It is in universities' interests that their scholars should publish. If page-charges were part of their research grants or even their salaries, we could afford to let an unlimited number of flowers bloom, with their individual cultivators paying the minimal expenses of displaying them to all, and all scholars being the beneficiaries (when they swap their esoteric-authors' hats for their esoteric-readers' hats).

> In effect, we have looked at two possible responses to the mismatch
> between supply and demand. One is to increase demand -- but libraries
> cannot seem to get more money. The other is to reduce supply -- but it
> is increasing. A third would be to reduce costs -- but costs too are increasing.

Costs may be increasing in paper, but certainly not in electronic-only publication: They are shrinking, and will continue to do so as the software and hardware for the global virtual library continues to be developed.

> JUST IN TIME AND JUST IN CASE
>
> Another noteworthy thing about journals as a product is that you can
> consume journals in one of two ways. The normal way we consume journals
> is by subscribing to them. We can also consume them by ordering
> individual journal articles from document delivery services. This is
> not unique to journals.

Both models are inappropriate -- whether journal-subscription or pay-per-view, the price-tag interposed between author and reader is completely at odds with the true motivational structure of (esoteric) scholarship and science.

> It is now becoming clear to me that the future of the journal involves
> a battle over "just in case" and "just in time" in the journals industry.

Catchy as they have become, neither option is optimal, and they do not cover the true options: subsidized, free-for-all electronic publication is a third way (and should perhaps be seen as "just in case" for us all: writers and readers).

> By contrast, the "just in time" journal user makes a very poor contribution --
> but the contribution is increasing as document delivery services increasingly
> collect royalties on behalf of the owners of the journals from which they
> supply copies. Royalties are not liked by librarians but they do make for a
> more realistic choice for the consumer between "just in time" and "just in
> case." They also help to ensure that the "just in time" approach does
> not irretrievably damage the financial viability of the product on
> which it is dependent.

All old, papyrocentric ways of looking at things, unfortunately.

> There is an increasing number of experiments taking place. Some publishers
> are offering electronic versions of their journals, alongside the
> traditional product. Some are pursuing new service concepts, in such
> experiments as ADONIS, TULIP and RED SAGE. Some are launching entirely
> new journals in the electronic medium only, such as PSYCOLOQUY. The
> number of those is growing steadily but from a very small base. Some
> document supply services -- and CARL is the obvious example -- are making
> increasing use of fax.

Something very basic is being lost in mixing apples and oranges like this. Some of these "delivery" systems are hybrid and trade-based, just like paper, and charge admission to the reader; others are not, and apply their much lower expenses for quality control, distribution and archiving in the form of an up-front subsidy, with resulting free delivery to all! The implications are radically different -- one a minor improvement on the status quo, the other a radical restructuring of the means of production and access to (esoteric) knowledge.

> There are technical problems. Can the networks cope with the bandwidth?

No insoluble problems here, and again necessity will be the mother of invention. Once an irreversible commitment to electronic-only delivery of esoteric scholarship is made, the hardware, user-friendliness, familiarity, channel capacity and standardization will all follow suit. There are no problems of principle here.

> Then there are the financial problems. In principle, one copy of a
> journal in Boston Spa or Hanover can feed photocopies of articles to
> every library there is, and the price the user would pay at present is
> mainly one of delay. With technical advance, one electronic copy of a
> journal could satisfy the world, and delay would be minimal or nil. So
> far, the way of paying for such a development has not emerged. Indeed,
> plenty of people are not sure it needs to be paid for. They believe
> "the age of the free lunch" has really arrived. I think a way will be
> found to enable people to pay in advance "just in case" for electronic
> journals as they do for printed ones.

I hope I have provided some support for my view that this may not be the right way to conceptualize the true cost or demand structure, or how to accommodate it optimally.

> Copyright became a serious issue with the
> growing ease of photocopying. With the lightning ease of electronic
> transfer, the serious issue has become a potential nightmare for a
> publisher interested in protecting copyright, and by implication the
> revenue stream.

But what about the AUTHOR? Is the author worried about all the people photo-copying or electronically retrieving the work, or is the author happy about it? Remember, this is an esoteric author who is not making and never has made or expected REVENUE from all those little-read papers. In the old, Faustian days, the reluctant choice was to accept the Faustian pact (of allowing access to a work only to paid ticket-holders) because that was the only way to reach an audience AT ALL. But now that there is another option, it's time to rethink all of this (as I've argued, for example, in Harnad 1994).

The usual red herring that is introduced in copyright laws plays on the author's fear of plagiarism; but this has NOTHING to do with copyright as used to deter unpaid readers. There are other, better ways to protect one's work from plagiarism (especially in the Virtual Library, with its all powerful search/retrieve/compare tools) than by assigning copyright to a publisher who blocks non-ticket-holders at the door....

> I hear a great deal from ordinary library users in defence
> of browsing, or rather in enthusiastic advocacy of browsing, enough to
> satisfy me that it has to be taken seriously and allowed for, if
> possible. To my mind, the forecast that the individual article as
> publishing unit would rise in triumph, like a phoenix, from the ashes

> of the dead journal, was more fashionable a year or two ago than it is
> now.

I'm afraid I completely disagree. Journals will continue to exist (because they are a sensible way of taxonomizing and filtering the literature by subject matter and by the level of quality control [peer review] that their contents have undergone), but the pertinent "item" will of course be the individual article -- and there will of course be no need for date-locked issues in which an arbitrary set of apples and oranges co-appear: The year-number and journal-name will be a sufficient first cut. The rest will be done by sophisticated search/retrieval tools and archiving links and pointers.

> The last point I want to make in this section of my paper concerns the
> question of how the great abundance of conventional printed journals
> will decline and disappear. Our own behaviour and the behaviour our
> users expect of us suggest that the least popular journals will be
> replaced first, because those are the ones we cancel and for which we
> first come to depend on modern methods of document supply. This makes
> the exciting new technology a crutch for our weakness rather than a
> banner for our ambitions for the future, a strange role indeed. What
> does look certain is that secondary source periodicals, such as
> indexing and abstracting tools, in printed form, are in terminal
> decline. Otherwise, the broad image of the future shape of events is
> still surprisingly unclear.

This unfortunately takes the status quo for granted. Electronic-only publication is for ALL of the (esoteric) scholarly/scientific literature, and within that medium the rest can be taken care of by the quality control mechanisms (peer review) and reader preferences.

> What do we observe on the network? We
> can see people informally exchanging information in the most natural
> way. We can see this process being organised into discussion groups so
> that people with common interests can have readier access to one
> another's views.

So far, the amount of quality control on the Net is negligible. The Net began as a Global Graffiti Board for Trivial Pursuit (as I've had occasion to call it) because it was put together mostly by hackers and students, rather than by scientists and scholars; it is a mistake, though, to assume that this initial anarchy is something intrinsic to the medium. There is plenty of room in the skyways for unconstrained discussion as well as for a rigorously peer-reviewed literature -- plus everything in between. In particular, everything that was possible in paper can be duplicated on the Net (including, if anyone really wants it, lie-in-bed, leafable, virtual magazines and books).

> We can see a controversy starting to emerge as to whether the flow of
> knowledge should be entirely unmoderated or whether there should be
> some discipline and some prior assessment of the value of each
> contribution. We can sense increasing concern about the sheer exuberant
> volume of communication. How can we be sure we are not missing
> something significant? How can we avoid being swamped by masses of
> trivia and irrelevant detail?

The medium that generated the information glut is also the best means of managing it. Tools are being developed for navigating the anarchy: dynamic filters, set to search for and include/exclude whatever the user specifies, based on header tags as well as content analysis. You could receive everything on everything, or only the top 3 refereed journals of ornithology.

> We can already notice anxieties about the
> economic future of this massive information flow. For now, it is all
> happening for nothing, but persistent rumours about charging for the
> Internet at the point of use refuse to lie down.

We have to distinguish "public access radio" uses of the Internet (the Global Graffiti Board) from its use for esoteric scholarship. Commercial and Dilettante-Chat-Group uses will eventually have to pay their way (one of the biggest current bandwidth-gobblers is porno-graphics), and that will be no great loss to anyone; but esoteric science and scholarship will be but a flea on the tail of that dog, and EVERYONE would be better served if it continued to get a free ride in perpetuum.

> CONCLUSION
>
> I therefore see two convergent developments taking place as a result of
> the availability of electronic networks. In the first, I can see the
> possibility that electronic networks will remove most of the delay
> involved in the "just in time" provision of journal articles. This
> process has already raised questions about the nature of the journal,
> why articles are bundled together in the way they are, and whether a
> new communication technology will provoke radical change. In the
> second, I can see a new parallel process of knowledge communication
> growing up; and the present signs are that it is tentatively moving
> towards operating conventions which strongly echo the conventions of
> the traditional print-on-paper product.

I think it's simpler than this: The Net has opened up some remarkable possibilities -- for example, interactive ones -- that are not feasible in any other medium, and they will develop and flourish. But in addition to these, it has made it possible to take over completely the scholarly and scientific literature that has so far appeared only in refereed paper journals, and in doing so to emulate all of the paper literature's pertinent properties, whilst prominently improving on only one of them: It will no longer be necessary to apply the entirely inappropriate trade model (with the price tag it interposes between text and reader) to esoteric scholarly and scientific work. Accessibility will be free for all scholars and will be augmented by powerful and sophisticated search and retrieval tools as well as the resource that is entirely unique to the Net: Interactive publication (peer commentary and response on both the refereed and unrefereed literature; Harnad 1992).

> Some people say that the world will never
> end, just as they say the printed journal will always be with us. They
> could be right but on the whole I don't believe them. Whether I will
> be around to see them being proved wrong, I wouldn't like to predict.
>
> Bernard Naylor
> Southampton, July 1994

I make no specific predictions either. But I hope that if the growing number of free peer-reviewed electronic journals is not sufficient to make the paper cards fall, then perhaps something like my subversive proposal -- that all scholars in all disciplines should make their preprints (and then their refereed reprints) available in public ftp/http archives starting NOW -- will help bring them down.

Best wishes, Stevan

From: amo@research.att.com (Andrew Odlyzko)
Date: Mon, 18 Jul 94 16:48 EDT
Subject: comments on Naylor's article

Stevan,

As usual, I largely agree with your comments on the Naylor paper. However, I would like to make a couple of points.

1. You say:

> I agree that it's absurd to treat scholarly publishers as villains: They
> could obviously do much better in tabloids, best-sellers or movies. But
> they ARE linked to the status quo, just as tobacco producers are, and

> only necessity will be the mother of invention on their part. I am
> grateful that they are willing to publish learned work rather than more
> money-making stuff, but my gratitude tapers off as their interests come
> into conflict with those of (esoteric) scholars. ...

There is no evidence that publishers would be much better off publishing "tabloids, best-sellers or movies." Scholarly publishing is carried out by the commercial publishers and many nonprofit ones because it is profitable. (The profits of the nonprofit publishers are not called that, but they do exist, and are substantial in many cases.) In fact, I would not be surprised if the profits in scholarly journals were higher than in tabloids, since there is less competition and much greater barriers to entry. (One of the reasons that ethical drug companies are so much more profitable than the typical industrial companies is that government safety regulation requires huge investments and long lead times before a new drug can be marketed. In publishing investments are not huge, but it takes a while for a journal to reach a reasonable level of subscribers.)

2. The arguments in favor of "just in time," often known as "pay-per-view," do have validity. However, as I argue in the long version of my essay, this method cannot possibly succeed in esoteric scholarly publishing (at least not with today's high costs) because of the prohibitively high prices that would be involved. A typical copyright fee that publishers print in some journals seems to be in the range of $ 5-10, and scholars are upset by this. However, if an article costs $ 4,000 to produce, as I estimate, then you would need to find 400 to 800 scholars willing to pay for it just to recover the costs. I don't see that as realistic for the overwhelming majority of esoteric scholarly publications.

Best regards,
Andrew

XII.   Graffiti, Esoterica or Scholarship?

A return to a question of distinguishing "publishing" from other forms of network-public discourse. What seemed fairly simple in the world of print (for example, knowing the difference between a publication and a private letter) begins to be more complicated in a medium where formal discourse and chit-chat flow in the same pipeline. Does "esoteric" do justice to the significance of scholarly publishing?

> From harnad Tue Jul 19 12:12:54 1994
> serialst@uvmvm.bitnet (Lib Serials list)
> vpiej-l@vtvm1.bitnet (Pub-EJournals)
> Subject: Re: Paying for the Pipe vs. the Piper in Esoteric Publishing

Date: Mon, 18 Jul 94 19:56:04 -0600
From: Paul Ginsparg 505-667-7353 <ginsparg@qfwfq.lanl.gov>

stevan,

little to add to what you say (reminds me how helpful your participation would have been in october for us were you not already slated to be abroad).

i do have one minor nit to pick regarding the occasional:

sh> So far, the amount of quality control on the Net is negligible. The Net
sh> began as a Global Graffiti Board for Trivial Pursuit (as I've had
sh> occasion to call it) because it was put together mostly by hackers and
sh> students, rather than by scientists and scholars;

while a delightful metaphor, i believe the "GGBfTP" tends to promote some confusion. there is a very important distinction between UseNet (a collection of distributed access newsgroups) and the Internet (a linked group of networks that includes UseNet as a small subset) -- indeed this distinction is frequently blurred in the popular press (for example during recent mass advertising postings to usenet newsgroups, so-called "spamming" incidents, the n.y. times et al. write this as a dreaded challenge to The Internet [read prototype infobahn], not understanding that usenet is irrelevant to the vast majority of internet usage. indeed these news reports are universally "flamed" on comp.admin.misc with USENET != INTERNET [!= shorthand for "not equal"]).
surely you do not mean the internet when you say "put together mostly by

hackers and students" though later on you do specify:

sh> ... uses of the Internet (the Global Graffiti Board) from

in fact my little corner of the internet *was* assembled by "scientists and scholars," starting from the high energy physics decnet in the early 80s (one of a number of autonomous networks that in the mid 80's joined together to form "the internet"). as i mentioned in some earlier correspondence, we never formed the negative association of "electronic communication = low quality" since the electronic communication within my community by electronic mail, etc., was always of arbitrarily high quality and has been an invaluable research resource for the past decade (part of the reason the "e-print archives" were such a natural development for us). the nature of the internet is such that any background static never affected us since it never came unsolicited.

moreover it is not even true that the majority of material available via the Internet is unmoderated. currently, anyone who sets up a www server gives some thought to the construction of the pages, and as well some thought to the links to other resources collected. we may not agree with much of the judgment exhibited at some sites, but then we simply avoid them. (just as in research where i can learn whom to trust, when i browse web sites i can get a feeling for who has assembled the higher than average quality information). similar remarks apply to long standing automated anonymous ftp sites -- typically someone puts some thought into organization and what is archived (it is much rarer for anon ftp sites to allow arbitrary uploads; usually things go into incoming/ and are archived or removed). i am not of course arguing that the standards are at the levels of conventional peer review, but it is important to note that they are far from nonexistent.

sure there are many silly bulletin boards that spring up, and we've seen the usenet statistics from news.admin, but have a look at

http://www.gatech.edu/gvu/stats/NSF/merit.html

for the overall nsfnet backbone traffic to see just how negligible a fraction of the overall internet traffic usenet constitutes.

so i think you may be doing a minor disservice by coming down *too hard* on the current quality of electronic communication with an all-too-colorful metaphor that applies only to a small segment of the current total bandwidth. and my impression is that many new entries are continuously increasing in quality (you recently mentioned unsworth et al's iath site which includes pmc -- for numerous other such examples see http://wings.buffalo.edu/contest/).

it will be far easier to build what we want metaphorically on the much larger sector of the internet that possesses incipient quality, rather than overemphasizing the much smaller anarchic sector at this point.

hope these comments are helpful.

regards, pg

From: Stevan Harnad
Tue Jul 19 12:12:54 1994

Paul,

You may be right that there is and has all along been more quality in some regions of cyberspace than I have given it credit for. Historians will have to sort this out.

But my concerns are specifically with scholarly/scientific PUBLICATION, and, as far as I know, the uucp-style Usenet Groups and the BITNET listserv groups were the first mass circulation electronic forums. Personal email, file retrieval, collaborative computation, data exchange, etc. among scholars and scientists certainly constitute traffic on the Internet, but they are not the kind of mass-circulation communication that is directly comparable with the paper scholarly literature -- at least not until your HEP preprint archive came into existence.

In any case, for present purposes this much can be said with high confidence, and without the aid of careful historic research (and I don't think you'll disagree): With the prominent exception of your preprint archive (which is a special case, because, for the time being at least, it is parasitic on the refereed paper literature for which most of its PREprints are ultimately destined -- the "Invisible Hand" effect I have spoken of before), if one were to make a direct comparison between (say) the latest 20-, 10-, 5- or 1-year paper scholarly/scientific literature, within or across disciplines, and the electronic literature, there would be ABSOLUTELY NO CONTEST. The current electronic literature's quantity and quality is still infinitesimal in comparison to the corresponding paper literature. The point of my metaphor was to emphasize that this is just an artifact of demographic initial conditions (which is certainly is), and not intrinsic to the two respective media, as many Luddites are eager to infer. (And the point of my "Subversive Proposal" was that this very disparity could be turned to the dramatic and speedy advantage of electronic publication through immediate universal public ftp archiving by all authors of the esoteric scholarly preprint/reprint literature).

I don't really think you disagree with this; you number among the converted, where it is safe to insist that the Net HAS generated a good deal of quality to date after all. But that's an absolute judgment, whereas I was making a relative judgment. I admire the nuggets that the anarchy has generated so far, but the fact is still, I think, that the lion's share of it is junk, just as the paper scholarly literature would be mostly junk if it were unconstrained by economics and anarchically generated (with mostly students and hackers at the helm, instead of the peers of the realm, who are so far still the UNconverted to whom I am preaching).

Out of this anarchy are now at last emerging the traditional structures of scholarly/scientific quality-control; once these achieve a critical mass, what I said about the Global Graffiti Board will be past history. But for now, to hasten that day, those who sample or hear about the Net's CURRENT state (qua publication medium) -- in comparison, I stress, with the paper scholarly literature -- must be reassured that these are just initial conditions and not at all representative of the potential steady state.

I do know the distinctions among Net, Internet, Usenet, etc., and use them loosely because, as I said, my preaching is intended for the UNconverted, who are not impressed by computational nuggets from DARPA days but can see clearly (if they even go so far as to look) that most of what passes for scholarly/scientific publication and communication on the Net to date looks a lot more like Trivial Pursuit among dilettantes than the quality-controlled literature they associate exclusively with paper.

Best wishes,

Stevan

————————————

Date: Tue, 19 Jul 94 11:54:31 -0600
From: Paul Ginsparg 505-667-7353 <ginsparg@qfwfq.lanl.gov>

stevan,

tks for clarifications. my comments (doubt these need public posting...):

> that most of what passes for scholarly/scientific publication and
> communication on the Net to date looks a lot more like Trivial Pursuit
> among dilettantes than the quality-controlled literature they associate
> exclusively with paper.

yes, i had forgotten your concerns to be focused entirely on scholarly/scientific PUBLICATION (and of course this will never be more than an infinitesimal fraction of overall network bandwidth, but we hope a larger percentage than at present of the scholarly communication that's to be network available).

regards, pg

p.s. to some extent, this recalls to me the "n.y.er's map of the u.s." which shows manhattan and n.y. city reaching somewhere out past the mississippi, and the rest of the country squeezed onto the western coast (states like kansas, maybe even texas, appear as small towns in california). in a medium which sees few geographic and physical constraints (excepting of course speed of light limits on propagation), it is easy (and probably beneficial) to conceptualize the "majority" of the network as the part with which we're regularly in contact, and to ignore the rest. i can usually get what i want with relative ease from the network, so that's my overall picture (and i'm anxious to see it remain that way despite the upcoming commercial onslaught), hence my current reaction to "global graffiti" (which a half-year ago seemed perfectly accurate, so perhaps i've since changed more than the network...)

Date: Tue, 19 Jul 94 14:32:49 EDT
From: "Stevan Harnad" <harnad>
Subject: Esoterica

> From: Ann Okerson <ann@cni.org>
> Date: Tue, 19 Jul 1994 09:18:03 -0400 (EDT)
>
> Stevan, for what it's worth, your use of this word makes me and a number
> of others quite edgy and uncomfortable. I know the dictionary meaning
> of "esoteric" and you kindly provided it recently as well. However, the
> commonly understood meaning of the word (among the general educated
> population) is something related to the inner circle, the anointed, and
> often the somewhat mysterious, occult, etc. It is not a word that
> creates a positive impression throughout the land.
>
> As in Joe Citizen: why should I fund universities if what they are doing
> is esoteric? I thought they were doing research and scholarship that
> promoted, whether directly or indirectly, the well-being and progress of
> society...if what they are doing is so esoteric, let them find ways to
> pay for it themselves.
>
> Please, for the sake of the continuance of the research and information

> you (and I) so intensely believe in, find language that will not be
> misunderstood by the taxpayers and will not jeopardize our missions.
> Think about losing "esoteric" as a repeated word to characterize what
> we do.
> To call it scholarship and research surely cannot be offensive to you
> and will be better understood by folks in general. Ann

One can't please everyone. I am not at the moment writing texts for Joe Citizen, but for a somewhat more sophisticated constituency: Scientists, Scholars, Research Librarians, Scholarly Publishers.

I will try to find something in place of "esoteric" for talks to lay audiences, but "scholarship and research" does not convey the MESSAGE behind my esoteric terminology: that the (ONLY) literature for which I am advocating the non-trade, advanced-subsidy model is a no-market literature with only a few specialists qualified to and interested in reading it, yet with ALL of us -- scholars/scientists and the population as a whole -- the BENEFICIARIES of this free flow of esoteric research and information: Not because every citizen needs or wants to read the International Journal for Numerical and Analytic Methods in Geomechanics or the Journal of Pre-Raphaelite Studies, but because we are all better off if these specialists can read one another's work without having to pay for it as if it were a market commodity; the enhanced contributions the qualified specialists can consequently make to science, learning and culture are then everyone's reward.

I feel strongly that if we collaborate in the mentality that the only research worthy of public support is what can be "sold" to the taxpayer then we will all get exactly what we pay for...

Yours esoterically,

Stevan

P.S. Remember that some of the scholarly/scientific literature is NOT esoteric; it may have a wide intra- or interdisciplinary and general readership, even the occasional nonfictional best-seller. If I cater to the view that all or most of science and scholarship ought to be like that, then we may as well just stick to the trade model! Think about it... The real issue here is not public support for scholarly research, but public support for specialists' access to publicly supported specialized research. What's the point of pretending that's supposed to be of general interest?

Date: Tue, 23 Aug 94 12:57:20 EDT
From: "Stevan Harnad" <harnad>
Subject: Esoterica/Exoterica

> Date: Tue, 23 Aug 1994 12:34:01 +0500
> From: fred@brainmap.med.umich.edu (Fred Bookstein)
>
> You're just about to leave, so I'll be brief. In re the
> discussion of the word "esoteric" in your exchange with Ann
> Okerson, you might want to take advantage of a wonderful
> English word, "exoteric," that has precisely the opposite main
> meaning. "Exoteric" crops up in the anthropology of
> religion, the sociology of the professions, and similar
> places. I extract from the 1961 Merriam-Webster
> unabridged, 1981 printing, page 798:
>
>   "exoteric adj. 1a. suitable to be imparted to the public,
> readily comprehensible. 1b: belonging to the outer or less
> intimate circle. 1c: publicly known, popular. 2. relating
> to the outside.
>   "exoteric n. layman, outsider.
>   "exoterica n.pl. exoteric doctrines or works.
>   "exoterics n.pl. doctrines or discourses for the uninstructed
> or the general public."
>
> So I think we've got our word here. "Trade publications" =
> "exoterica"; what the discussion in who.payspiper is about is _esoterica_,
> which is, of course, the more frequently encountered term. Okerson
> may have been subliminally troubled by another connotation of
> "esoterica," namely, pornography, but better to direct the
> connotation via an opposition than to disallow the more
> frequently explored pole.
>
>
> Fred Bookstein

Many thanks for the flip-side term, "exoteric." I had not known it, but
"exoteric/esoteric" captures exactly the trade/nontrade distinction I had
in mind (with the qualification that there is nothing RARE about esoterica
in primary scientific and scholarly publication: it constitutes the bulk of
the corpus). I'll use it!

I think you are confusing esoterica and erotica in your second comment,
though... Ann was worried that the elitist connotations of esoterica might
have a bad effect on scholarly/scientific funding (and it just conceivably
might, but attempting to join the endless populist beauty contest that

politics has become would, I believe, leave all sides the losers: yes, most of primary scholarship is by the few, for the few; but the many are still the ultimate beneficiaries).

Stevan Harnad

XIII. E-Journal Costs and Editorial Costs

The question of costs returns to the fore, arising from a proposal for a specific project. The question is taken up of what and whether editors should be paid. A university press journals manager contributes some current, real-world information to the discourse on editors and editorial offices. One of the undoubted inefficiencies of the present journal system is the delay and redundancy introduced by a distributed and publication-linked practice of peer-review, resubmission, and limited acceptances.

Date: Sun, 24 Jul 94 15:26:49 EDT
From: "Stevan Harnad" <harnad>

Dear Andrew,

Below is a discussion of an important side-issue that has arisen in discussions regarding a confidential proposal concerning electronic publication. The side issue is: In what do the true residual costs of electronic-only periodical publishing actually consist?

I am circulating this to a wider group. At the request of the author of the proposal, the proposal itself is not circulated, and I have deleted below anything that refers to its content. Nothing hinges on what is removed, however. The present discussion concerns what the real functions and real costs of the editorial office of a peer-reviewed journal are.

I will try to itemize quite explicitly what comprises that residual "<25% of paper per-page costs" for quality control that will continue to need to be covered in electronic-only periodical publication. Apart from spelling this out explicitly, I also note in passing what might be some cross-disciplinary differences (especially between highly technical and symbolic texts, as in mathematics, and more prose-intensive disciplines -- the latter constituting the vast majority of the esoteric scholarly/scientific periodical corpus). In certain important respects, my own discipline of "cognitive science" (a mix of experimental psychology, theoretical psychology, brain science, biology, computer science, linguistics and philosophy) is perhaps better positioned than mathematics to provide a representative model that would apply to most of the rest of learned publication (though there may well be other views on this).

Andrew Odlyzko wrote:

ao> From: amo@research.att.com
ao> Date: Fri, 22 Jul 94 22:39 EDT
>
ao> Stevan,
>
ao> A few remarks on your comments on [the anonymous] proposal.
ao> I agree with you fully that the full [text of any published article]
ao> has to be certified, and that this certification has to be performed
ao> by the scholars who are editors and referees. I assumed that this is
ao> also what [the author] had in mind.
>
ao> I was a little confused by your discussion of what scholarly
ao> publishing ought to cost. Aside from the scholar's time
ao> in doing the research and writing a paper, we have
ao> the following stages in publishing it:
>
ao> (a) Typing or typesetting the manuscript. This essentially
ao> always takes place at the author's institution, and
ao> is increasingly being done by the author, since
ao> technology has made that alternative attractive.
>
ao> (b) Peer review. This is done by scholars who are editors
ao> and referees, and who are almost never paid. Secretarial
ao> assistance is usually provided by these scholars'
ao> institutions, and sometimes is reimbursed or provided
ao> by the publishers.
>
ao> (c) Typesetting, copy editing, printing, distribution, etc.,
ao> by the publishers after the peer review and author revisions
ao> are completed.
>
ao> It seems safe to assume that the costs of (a), which I estimated
ao> at $ 200-400 per paper, will continue to be shouldered by the
ao> authors' institutions in those increasingly rare cases that
ao> the scholars do not typeset their own paper.

Andrew,

I agree about (a) and its costs. But I have to point out that in over 15 years of editing Behavioral and Brain Sciences and 5 years of editing PSYCOLOQUY, I have never once encountered a paper where the author's final draft could be published verbatim! In any case, this is not the real issue, as you will shortly see; the real issue is the cost of generating a publishable peer-reviewed text, and that consists (relatively seamlessly) of all of (b) plus copy editing (i.e., one component of (c)).

ao> In discussing economics of future scholarly journals it seems
ao> worthwhile considering (b) and (c) separately. Here is where
ao> I do not fully understand what you advocate. Perhaps it is
ao> because our fields have different practices and different
ao> expectations. In one place in your message you say
>
sh> But what about the costs (and responsibility) of implementing peer
sh> review for the "free texts"? THOSE costs, plus some subsequent editing
sh> and copy-editing, are the only TRUE costs in electronic-publication...
sh> I estimate those true, essential costs of purely electronic quality control
sh> at (well) below 25% of per-page paper costs (i.e., current journal page
sh> costs).
>
ao> In that passage you seem to imply that in the electronic world
ao> both (b) and (c) should cost below 25% of the current figure.
ao> Later on, though, you say
>
sh> Copy-editing (which is what is really at issue here)
sh> is such a minor part of the function (and the cost)
sh> of publishing that it hardly seems worth talking about. (If that were all
sh> there was to it, Universities could easily hire a staff copy-editor
sh> to vet all final texts, and that would be the end of it.) It's the REST
sh> of the quality control (implementing peer review and substantive
sh> editing) that's the real work, and it's not clear from this proposal
sh> who is to see that that's done, who's to do it, and how its true expenses
sh> (a per-page cost I estimate at under 25%, but not zero) are to be paid.
>
ao> Here you seem to be saying the 25% is to go for peer review and
ao> "substantive editing." Perhaps what we need here is your definition
ao> of "copy-editing" and "substantive editing." Also, what do you mean
ao> by the costs of peer review? Your answers might clarify
ao> what you really have in mind in the passages above. In the meantime,
ao> I'll explain how I see the situation.
>
ao> Both of us agree that (b) is indispensable. The only part of (b) that
ao> I expect will continue to cost money is the secretarial assistance,
ao> which I estimate in my essay should cost a maximum of $ 100-200 per
ao> paper. In mathematics, computer science, electrical engineering,
ao> and the few other fields that I know, the only editing that is provided
ao> at this stage is what the referees and editors do gratis. Sometimes
ao> this editing is extensive, and might be called "substantive editing"
ao> by any reasonable definition of the term. I have had a few referees
ao> completely rewrite some particularly interesting papers by Chinese
ao> or Russian writers whose command of English was practically non-existent.

ao> We also have the example of Walter Gautschi, which I cite in my essay,
ao> who does extensive editing of manuscripts in his unpaid job as editor.
ao> (Most of his work is copy editing, but some I would classify as
ao> substantive.) In the overwhelming majority of cases, though, the editing
ao> at this stage is trivial, such as referees pointing out the most egregious
ao> mistakes. I expect this situation to continue, at least in my field.
>
ao> The editing in stage (c) that I am used to can be classified as
ao> copy-editing. This involves correcting typographical mistakes,
ao> formatting the paper, providing running heads, page numbers,
ao> making sure references follow the journal's standards and are
ao> actually invoked in the text, etc. I would not call any of this
ao> "substantive editing." Furthermore, neither I nor any of my
ao> colleagues that I have ever discussed this with would want anything
ao> more than what is provided. The risk of getting the mathematical
ao> substance of the paper damaged is just too great. There are all
ao> too many horror stories of newly hired employees at publishers
ao> trying to "improve" the presentation in a math paper only to
ao> mangle it hopelessly.
>
ao> What do I see in the future? Well, (b) will be carried out as
ao> before, primarily by unpaid scholars, possibly with some minor
ao> assistance from secretaries. This will cost $100-200 per paper.
>
ao> Stage (c) now costs $ 4,000 per paper. This goes for printing,
ao> distribution, and copy editing, but not (at least in the case
ao> of mathematics) for "substantive editing." When we move to
ao> electronic publishing, the only thing in stage (c) that
ao> I feel will be worth preserving will be copy editing. It is
ao> not all that minor a part of the publishing process, as it
ao> seems to account for the bulk of the present cost. The reason
ao> it is so costly is that it involves several layers of specialists.
ao> It used to be that publishing involved the extremely expensive
ao> steps of typesetting and printing, and it was not possible to
ao> lower their costs below a certain level. Thus there was
ao> an absolute floor under the cost of stage (c). In the future,
ao> when (c) consists basically just of copy editing, I expect we
ao> will be able to operate it at any price we choose, and my guess is
ao> that an expenditure of $ 200-600 per paper will provide adequate
ao> quality. Whether this function will be done at publishers or
ao> the authors' institutions, I am not sure.

Let us say we agree, roughly speaking, about copy-editing, the only
expense in (c) worth mentioning, once we move to electronic-only
publishing. But my estimate of < 25% of paper per-page costs in
electronic only periodicals was definitely NOT based only on the cost of

(c); (b) costs money too, and is far more important than copy editing.

First let me itemize what (b) entails (and I will argue that the copy-editing component of (c) is probably best assimilated seamlessly with (b), but not much hangs on that):

A journal has an Editor. Editing takes time -- time that would otherwise be devoted to research, teaching and publishing. Refereeing takes time too, but the difference is that refereeing is done on a voluntary, as-time-is-available basis, whereas someone who accepts the commitment to edit a journal (or to subedit a section of a journal) must give requisite time to process the entire manuscript flow. What does that time consist of?

(1) Submitted manuscripts must be processed; this is done by an editorial administrator and secretaries who report to the Editor (and must be paid by someone).

(2) The Editor (or Subeditor) must read or at least skim all submissions and select referees (sometimes with the help of an Editorial Board, sometimes even with formal weekly real-time meetings, for journals with high submission rates and large annual page-counts).

(3) The editorial administrator and secretaries must then see to it that the referees are invited, receive the manuscripts, submit the reports in time, get followed up, get replaced if delinquent, etc.

(4) For each manuscript, once the reports are in, the Editor (or Subeditor, or Board) must read or skim the manuscript (conscientiousness varies -- as does the rigor of the peer-review provided by a given journal) as well as the referee reports and prepare a disposition letter, indicating whether the manuscript is rejected, accepted (rare without revision, at least in my fields), conditionally accepted contingent on minor revision, or requires major revision and re-refereeing (if the latter, go back to (1) and start again when the revised draft is submitted).

(5) A conscientious Editor who may only have skimmed manuscripts until they reach the possibly acceptable stage, will become more actively involved in the manuscripts that are likely to be published, not only in making the substantive judgements about which referee recommendations need to be followed, and when they have been successfully met, but in the finalizing of the manuscript itself. This is what I call substantive editing (it is not the checking of format and references) and it is an essential part of the peer review process -- indeed, without it, the Editor is not really Editing but simply doing box scores on referee reports (and the quality of the journal will reflect this).

(6) Finally, when the Editor judges it is ready, the paper is accepted, with the prior and subsequent negotiations between Editor and author, then copy editor and author, and finally the proofing of the final text mediated by the editorial administrator and secretaries, all reporting to the Editor.

(1) - (6) is, in broad strokes, the relatively seamless stream that leads to a peer-reviewed publication. It takes time (the time of the Editor, editorial administrator, editorial office secretaries, and copy-editors; hence it also costs money. (Note that I have NOT reckoned in the time contributed by the referees, which is a voluntary service we all perform when we have time, and perform gratis; these are editorial, and hence publishing costs only).

There are many different ways that journal editorial offices are structured. One common model (the one used, for example, by the American Psychological Association, which publishes most of the leading psychology journals) is to have an Editor appointed for from 4-6 years who receives an honorarium and/or some of his time is bought from his University, and the editorial office receives a budget to pay for the editorial help (editorial administrator and secretaries -- copy-editing may be administered by the editorial office or the publisher, depending on which is more efficient).

In brief, I think your misconstrual of the true functions and costs of generating peer-reviewed publications is based on assuming that Editors and editorial office staff can be thought of in the same way as referees, donating their services gratis whenever time is available: They cannot be, however, because editing a journal is a calendar based, unrelenting, obligatory workload (and time-consuming in direct proportion to a journal's manuscript flow and annual page count) rather than a voluntary, ad lib function such as refereeing. It is an ongoing commitment that takes time from other things scholars and scientists do, and takes it systematically, on a daily, weekly basis.

Perhaps in some disciplines the Editor's function can be decentralized and distributed -- but some centralized entity still has to keep up with the manuscript flow without developing arbitrary lags -- and I for one think peer review, for better or for worse, is best filtered through an Editor's unitary judgment rather than an anarchic system with only local answerability (I could be wrong on this); but either way, SOMEONE has to make the commitment to exercise editorial judgment, a key component in peer review (peer review is not simply referees, voting).

Disciplines like mathematics may require less copy editing or less substantive editing than others; fine. If they needed less in paper, they'll likewise need less on the Net. But many (most) disciplines do need substantive editing and copy editing, and I'll bet my < 25% figure adjusts for this across disciplines: The less prose-intensive disciplines probably already had lower copy-editing costs, so their 25% of paper costs will simply be a smaller absolute figure (unless other special costs counterbalance it) than the 25% for more prose-intensive disciplines. In any case, as you see, I've stressed copy-editorial functions less than editorial ones in all of these considerations.

So there you have it. In my view, it's (1) - (6) that underlie the true per-page costs of electronic-only publication, and I think the < 25% figure will derive mostly from (1) - (5).

Best wishes, Stevan

From: amo@research.att.com
Date: Tue, 26 Jul 94 07:08 EDT

Various email discussions that involved Stevan Harnad and myself, as well as others, have uncovered an important question, namely, whether it is customary to pay scholars who work as editors. (Relevant payments might take the form of a stipend on top of the editor's regular salary or might be paid to the editor's university to lessen the editor's teaching duties.)

It appears that practices vary between fields. Harnad says that in his area, cognitive science (which he describes as "a mix of experimental psychology, theoretical psychology, brain science, biology, computer science, linguistics and philosophy"), such payments are common, and conjectures that his area is typical in its publishing practices. I have not seen any need to pay editors, because this is simply not done in the areas I know. I have served in the past, or am now serving, on the editorial boards of 18 different journals. These journals are published by several learned societies (AMS, IEEE, SIAM, etc.) as well as by some commercial publishers. Slightly over half are in mathematics (both pure and applied), and the others are in computer science, cryptology, electrical engineering, and one that is partially in physics. Not a single one of these jobs involved any financial compensation for me. The editors do work for free in these areas (*).

Are there any studies that address the question of how often editors are paid, and how much? Any information in this area would be helpful.

Payments to editors should be considered separately from paying for secretarial assistance. The latter is rather common, it seems. Information on how much it costs would be useful as well.

Answers to the questions posed here will be helpful in assessing the costs of future electronic journals. If it is customary in an area to provide substantial payments to editors, and this practice persists, this will alter calculations of how much scholarly journals will cost, and might restrict the choice among various models for future electronic journals.

Andrew Odlyzko amo@research.att.com

(*) I am aware that there are journals with paid editors. For example, Physical Review Letters, which I cite in my essay "Tragic Loss ...," has about four full-time senior physicists in charge of the peer-review process (which also involves unpaid volunteer editors). Other Physical Review publications have a mix of paid and unpaid editors in charge. Mathematical review journals, such as Mathematical Reviews, also have paid staffs of professional mathematicians. Such situations are easy to identify. The main question, though, is how often are scholars who work part-time as editors compensated financially? In the areas I know, this is uncommon, and when it occurs, is minor. (For example, one journal of whose editorial board I now serve is paying its two managing editors $1,000 per year each.)

From Stevan Harnad
Date: Mon, 25 Jul 94

My prediction is that the cost of Editor's services and editorial office staff will vary with:

(1) Discipline and specialty (and perhaps degree of interdisciplinarity)
(2) Journal size (annual published page count)
(3) Submission rate (and rejection rate)
(4) Journal prestige (perhaps)
(5) Subscribership and readership size (perhaps)
(6) Esotericity of contents (readership per ARTICLE as opposed to subscribership per journal)
(7) Prose-intensiveness of contents

Because refereeing is a volunteer, ad-lib service we all perform when we happen to have the time and interest for a particular paper or grant proposal, whereas Editing (and, a fortiori, editorial office work) is a fixed, timetable-bound commitment, I believe they will continue to be represent part (indeed most, along with copy-editing costs) of the true per-page costs of quality control in electronic-only periodical publishing (which I estimate will be < 25% of the per-page costs of paper periodical publishing). -- SH.

From: amo@research.att.com (Andrew Odlyzko)
Date: Mon, 25 Jul 94 08:18 EDT

Stevan,

I've sent out a request for information on the costs of peer review to several mailing lists and also a diverse group of individuals. If you have sent your message of yesterday afternoon to some other lists, please do forward my request for information to them as well. Since we are talking of concrete data, we should be able to obtain some estimates of what is going on.

Below I comment on a few of your remarks. It would be fascinating to study in detail why various fields differ so much in their publishing practices.

Best regards, Andrew

[Ed. Note: sh> indicates Stevan Harnad's message of Sunday, July 24, addressed to Andrew Odlyzko and several electronic mailing lists]

text that is left-justified: Andrew Odlyzko's comments of July 25

sh> Dear Andrew,
sh>
sh> I will try to itemize quite explicitly what comprises that residual
sh> " < 25% of paper per-page costs" for quality control that will continue
sh> to need to be covered in electronic-only periodical publication. Apart
sh> from spelling this out explicitly, I also note in passing what
sh> might be some cross-disciplinary differences (especially between highly
sh> technical and symbolic texts, as in mathematics, and more
sh> prose-intensive disciplines -- the latter constituting the vast
sh> majority of the esoteric scholarly/scientific periodical corpus). In
sh> certain important respects, my own discipline of "cognitive science" (a
sh> mix of experimental psychology, theoretical psychology, brain science,
sh> biology, computer science, linguistics and philosophy) is perhaps
sh> better positioned than mathematics to provide a representative model
sh> that would apply to most of the rest of learned publication (though

sh> there may well be other views on this).

Yes, the differences do seem to be related to the different disciplines that we operate in. As to which is more representative of scholarly publishing, that is something that we should ascertain. My experience is based not just on mathematics, but also computer science and parts of engineering, as I will explain later.

sh> I agree about (a) and its costs. But I have to point out that in over
sh> 15 years of editing Behavioral and Brain Sciences and 5 years of
sh> editing PSYCOLOQUY, I have never once encountered a paper where the
sh> author's final draft could be published verbatim! In any case, this is
sh> not the real issue, as you will shortly see; the real issue is the cost
sh> of generating a publishable peer-reviewed text, and that consists
sh> (relatively seamlessly) of all of (b) plus copy editing (i.e., one
sh> component of (c)).

I agree with you about the real issue. However, while you have never once encountered an author's final draft that could be published verbatim, I have even seen a few initial drafts that were published essentially verbatim (aside from minor copy editing that turns a reference listed as "7. S. Harnad, ..." into "7. Harnad, S., ...", say). Further, in the areas I know, it is very common for final drafts (after revisions requested by editors and referees) to be published verbatim (again subject only to minor copy editing).

sh> Let us say we agree, roughly speaking, about copy-editing, the only
sh> expense in (c) worth mentioning, once we move to electronic-only
sh> publishing. But my estimate of < 25% of paper per-page costs in
sh> electronic only periodicals was definitely NOT based only on the cost of
sh> (c); (b) costs money too, and is far more important than copy editing.

This seems to be the crucial difference in our views. In my fields, (b) costs very little, and (c) is where almost all the cost resides. (Note that my cost estimate of $ 4,000 per article was for mathematics and computer science, although it seemed to be consistent with the data I had for physics as well. We might need to get cost data for other areas.)

sh> First let me itemize what (b) entails (and I will argue that the
sh> copy-editing component of (c) is probably best assimilated seamlessly
sh> with (b), but not much hangs on that):

As a slight distraction, let me say that I feel that the copy-editing component of (c) is probably best assimilated seamlessly with (a), not with (b). If we are going to move to the kind of electronic journals that I foresee, with a continuum of publication and refereeing, it will make sense for authors to devote more effort into making their preprints easy to read.

sh> So there you have it. In my view, it's (1) - (6) that underlie the true
sh> per-page costs of electronic-only publication, and I think the < 25%
sh> figure will derive mostly from (1) - (5).

Broadly speaking, I accept your description of steps (1) - (6) as describing the peer-review process. (I have some minor quibbles, but they are not worth bothering about.) I also agree on the desirability of having secretarial assistance for editors. In my essay, "Tragic loss ...," I estimated this can be provided at a cost of $100-200 per published paper in the electronic world (where less time will be needed, since all the physical work of making copies, sticking correspondence into envelopes, etc., will be eliminated). With present print journals, this type of assistance is likely to cost $200-400 per paper, if it were provided to all editors.

The big difference in our views is on the issue of costs of scholar editors. As I said in the message I sent out a few minutes ago, my experience is very different from yours. We'll have to gather some data to decide which model is more common. If we don't obtain good enough information from the message I sent out, I propose that we do a quick survey. Since Princeton is likely to be much more representative of the broad spectrum of scholarly activities than Bell Labs, how about contacting the department chairs at Princeton and asking them what the common practices in their fields are? I would be happy to help in this work.

Do unpaid editors produce acceptable quality? They seem to, at least in my areas. Moreover, this is achieved in various ways. One way is by having small journals. Mathematics has slightly under 1,000 journals, as I recall, and many are small, publishing perhaps 400 pages per year. Thus the editors do not have too heavy a load. However, there are also large journals. Some, such as Proc. AMS, used to have a totally decentralized approach when I was on their board. There were a large number of editors, each with an associated specialty that was listed in the journal, and authors sent their papers to the editor covering the area of the paper. Simplifying a bit, each editor could accept a paper on his or her own. A still different approach is in force at Math. Comp., where all submissions go to the Managing Editor, who then decides which of the associate editors is most appropriate for that paper, and forwards the paper for handling to that paper.

Andrew Odlyzko

From: Stevan Harnad (harnad@princeton.edu)

Dear Andrew,

I only circulated the "Itemized Costs" posting to the lists to which you sent your query (and they are also the lists most actively involved in these questions, hence perhaps best posed to answer them): vpiej-l, serialst, globalsci. I now send this to one further list, my own internal alias list of individuals who are interested in electronic publication. Some will be on the big lists, but just in case, could you please re-send me your survey and I will branch it to them.

A systematic survey across disciplines certainly needs to be conducted -- and I wish I had the time to do it, but I'm about to move myself and my lab to the UK (University of Southampton) to take up the Directorship of a new Cognitive Sciences Centre and a Professorship in Psychology, so in the next couple of months I will not even be able to do the Princeton survey you suggest below, unfortunately. (If there were a Departmental Chairs email list, I could do it quickly, but there isn't, and I unfortunately haven't the time or the staff to do it piecemeal right now, or to process the results).

> From: amo@research.att.com
> Date: Mon, 25 Jul 94 08:18 EDT
>
> I've sent out a request for information on the costs of peer review
> to several mailing lists and also a diverse group of individuals.
> If you have sent your message of yesterday afternoon to some other
> lists, please do forward my request for information to them as
> well. Since we are talking of concrete data, we should be able
> to obtain some estimates of what is going on.

Your survey is an excellent idea. I too would like to have real data on these questions. Besides discipline differences, you'll probably also find differences as a function of the size/page-count of the journal, whether it is narrow-specialty or multi-specialty, and perhaps even as a function of the size of its readership (esoteric vs. broad spectrum).

> Below I comment on a few of your remarks. It would be fascinating
> to study in detail why various fields differ so much in their
> publishing practices.
>
> Yes, the differences do seem to be related to the different disciplines
> that we operate in. As to which is more representative of scholarly

> publishing, that is something that we should ascertain. My experience
> is based not just on mathematics, but also computer science and parts
> of engineering, as I will explain later.

I suspect that my distinction between ad-lib and fixed, clock-linked commitments will be an important variable, as will the submitted and accepted manuscript-page counts.

> I agree with you about the real issue. However, while you have never
> once encountered an author's final draft that could be published
> verbatim, I have even seen a few initial drafts that were published
> essentially verbatim (aside from minor copy editing that turns a
> reference listed as "7. S. Harnad, ..." into "7. Harnad, S., ...",
> say). Further, in the areas I know, it is very common for final
> drafts (after revisions requested by editors and referees) to be
> published verbatim (again subject only to minor copy editing).

I suspect this will vary with the prose-intensiveness of the field.

> This seems to be the crucial difference in our views. In my fields,
> (b) costs very little, and (c) is where almost all the cost resides.
> (Note that my cost estimate of $ 4,000 per article was for mathematics
> and computer science, although it seemed to be consistent with the data
> I had for physics as well. We might need to get cost data for other
> areas.)

My experience is that the lion's share of the cost is (b) rather than (c), and that that cost is fairly well predicted by the number of hours called for from the Editor(s), the Editorial Administrator and the secretaries. If you include (c), you just add in the hours of the copy-editor(s). Don't worry too much, though, because I continue to hold to the < 25% figure for all these costs together.

> As a slight distraction, let me say that I feel that the copy-editing
> component of (c) is probably best assimilated seamlessly with (a), not
> with (b). If we are going to move to the kind of electronic journals
> that I foresee, with a continuum of publication and refereeing, it
> will make sense for authors to devote more effort into making their
> preprints easy to read.

Authors can be relied on for a lot, but no author can be a self-referee, editor, or copy editor. Even if (as I think they should and will), academic departments take on staff copy-editors to help with this, the individual needs to be someone other than the author. With journal publication, though, I suspect that some centralized monitoring will continue to be necessary, over and above the enhanced role of author, word-processor and house copy-editor. I think this is true of all human quality-control enterprises: People cannot be relied upon to do their own quality control in any sphere -- and there will always be a (marked) difference between relying on someone else to ensure that certain quality standards are met or instead leaving this up to each individual. (Andrew, you cannot get a sense of this from introspection on your own conscientiousness, or that of particular colleagues; we are talking about a Gaussian population of frail mortals here; quality control means answerability.)

> Broadly speaking, I accept your description of steps (1) - (6) as
> describing the peer-review process. (I have some minor quibbles,
> but they are not worth bothering about.) I also agree on the
> desirability of having secretarial assistance for editors. In my
> essay, "Tragic loss ...," I estimated this can be provided at
> a cost of $100-200 per published paper in the electronic world
> (where less time will be needed, since all the physical work
> of making copies, sticking correspondence into envelopes, etc.,
> will be eliminated). With present print journals, this type
> of assistance is likely to cost $ 200-400 per paper, if it were
> provided to all editors.

Remember, our estimates of the orders of magnitude (by proportion) are about the same; we just seem to be itemizing it differently.

> The big difference in our views is on the issue of costs of scholar
> editors. As I said in the message I sent out a few minutes ago,
> my experience is very different from yours. We'll have to gather
> some data to decide which model is more common. If we don't obtain
> good enough information from the message I sent out, I propose that
> we do a quick survey. Since Princeton is likely to be much more
> representative of the broad spectrum of scholarly activities than
> Bell Labs, how about contacting the department chairs at Princeton
> and asking them what the common practices in their fields are?
> I would be happy to help in this work.

Alas, my move leaves me too overloaded to undertake this now (and especially to process the replies). By the way, I did not say that editorial honoraria and/or time-buy-outs were large, just that they were non-zero. But it is really in the administrative and secretarial back-up support (which you describe as "desirable" whereas I would call it absolutely essential) that the significant expenses occur.

> Do unpaid editors produce acceptable quality? They seem to,
> at least in my areas. Moreover, this is achieved in various
> ways. One way is by having small journals. Mathematics
> has slightly under 1,000 journals, as I recall, and many

> are small, publishing perhaps 400 pages per year. Thus
> the editors do not have too heavy a load. However, there
> are also large journals. Some, such as Proc. AMS, used
> to have a totally decentralized approach when I was on their
> board. There were a large number of editors, each with
> an associated specialty that was listed in the journal,
> and authors sent their papers to the editor covering the
> area of the paper. Simplifying a bit, each editor could
> accept a paper on his or her own. A still different approach
> is in force at Math. Comp., where all submissions go to
> the Managing Editor, who then decides which of the associate
> editors is most appropriate for that paper, and forwards
> the paper for handling to that paper.

There are many variants; page-counts are important. One cannot legislate that there should be many small journals (that may not even be a good idea). And the question of centralization is also partly a practical one: In principle, one could divide all submissions into 6-paper modules and assign them to a different "Editor," but what would that do for the reliability of quality overall, and for that journal's "imprimatur" when people are trying to calibrate their reading and browsing on the basis of reliable quality-tagging?

Managing Editors (I've avoided the term) are another matter; usually they are involved in the business end of the journal. But where they professionalize the Editor's traditional functions (referee selection, referee report assessment, dispositions, revision assessment) another risk is run, namely, that of taking quality control out of the hands of the peers themselves. In my view, an Editor should be a Primus Inter Pares rather than a professional Manager of some sort. It would be interesting to hear statistics here too.

Stevan Harnad

Date: Mon, 1 Aug 94 20:44:12 EDT
From: "Stevan Harnad"
harnad@princeton.edu

Responses to Andrew Odlyzko's Questionnaire about Electronic Editorial Costs follow below. -- S.H.

Date: Fri, 29 Jul 94 08:34:56 EDT
From: Janet Fisher <FISHER@MITVMA>
Subject: Editorial Costs
To: Andrew Odlyzko <AMO@RESEARCH.ATT.COM>
Cc: Stevan Harnad <HARNAD@Princeton.EDU>

Thanks for sending me a copy of your questions about editorial payments. I agree with Stevan's description of the process that an editor (and support staff) go through to review papers. Yes, it is common for publishers to pay a portion or all of the expenses of the editorial office. In the humanities this is less the case, but it varies tremendously depending on the editor, the editor's institution, and the competition for the journal. When publishers compete for a journal, this is where the deal can either be made or broken. These costs have increased dramatically for a large percentage of our journals in the last five years due to tightening funds at universities. We now have editors wanting us to buy them computer equipment and software, editorial tracking packages, etc.

In addition to editorial office support, some editors do indeed receive royalties (in our case, usually after the journal has reached a break-even position and the Press has recovered its initial deficits). Or the bottom line can be split with the editor and/or the editor's institution (if they own the journal). Patricia Scarry (U of Chicago Press) and Jill O'Neill (Elsevier) gave a presentation on editorial office costs at the last Charleston Conference. Perhaps they might have copies of their presentations to share.

We have a diverse list of journals in disciplines from humanities to social sciences to computer and cognitive science, with a diverse range of arrangements across disciplines. Many, many disciplinary and institutional factors come into play in the way journals are supported and financed. There is no single formula.

The other point I would make is that most journal editors accept between 25% and 35% of the papers actually received. Possibly 10% are rejected outright, but the rest of the rejected do go through the review process and possibly through a revision stage also. These take up the time of the editor and the editor's staff also, and this time has to be paid for too. Only in a very few fields (like economics) are submission charges common.

(Note from S.H.: The acceptance rate varies greatly from discipline to discipline. The acceptance rate in physics and mathematics is more like 75-80% and author page charges are less uncommon there.)

Most of our editors have at least a half-time assistant to handle the clerical parts of the editorial tasks (acknowledging manuscripts, contacting potential reviewers, sending manuscripts out for review, dogging reviewers, writing authors, etc.), and if the assistant is a "managing editor type" and also does copyediting, this is more likely a full-time position. These costs can be anywhere from $12,000 to $30,000 per year just for that staff position. (Not including equipment, phone, fax, postage, office space, university overhead [yes, really!] that universities often try to recuperate.)

Editorial board members are usually not paid, but this doesn't mean that Editors are not. A few of our journals given token payments to Associate Editors (the usually three top people under the editor) but not to editorial board members. The fact that you have been a member of the editorial board of 18 journals and never been paid is consistent with our experience. But you cannot conclude from that fact that editors are not paid and editorial offices are not paid for by the journal or publisher.

I would also argue that there will still be some "typesetting" cost with electronic journals. I do not believe that authors -- even in the most highly sophisticated fields -- will ever do all the formatting required to take manuscripts directly without some intervention. "Typesetting" will really become formatting, I guess, but there are costs associated with this. We should know more about what these are once _Chicago Journal of Theoretical Computer Science_ begins publication.

I guess that's all for now. Let me know what editorial costs you are interested in and if you have questions -- or disagreements -- over anything in this message.

JANET H. FISHER
ASSOCIATE DIRECTOR FOR JOURNALS PUBLISHING
MIT PRESS, 55 HAYWARD STREET, CAMBRIDGE, MA 02142
FISHER@MITVMA.MIT.EDU
PHONE (617) 253-2864

Date: Tue, 26 Jul 94 12:51:25 EDT
From: VMONTY@VM2.YorkU.CA (Vivienne Monty)

Hi: I shall look for harder data but in Library Science and History, two fields that I am familiar with, I have never known a scholar/editor to be directly paid. It is mostly in terms of release time or such remuneration that I have known. Even these release time arrangements are hard to get now in Canada at least.

Often the scholar/editor however has a "bureaucracy" to call on at the Association sponsoring the journal or the publisher who take care of the day to day administrative operations. The key word is often and NOT always however.

As stated earlier in your discussions, the world of academe "sponsor" academic publishing to a large degree through the granting release time, research leaves and the personal time of scholars. Universities have a tremendous dollar value investment in editorships, writing etc. whether some realize it or not. And some count such time as zero.

Date: Tue, 26 Jul 94 13:02 CDT
From: Jack P Hailman <JHAILMAN@macc.wisc.edu>
Subject: Re: Odlyzko Editorial Survey

Things might be changing on the subject of paid editorships, at least my own views have changed. I served as editor of Animal Behaviour for three years (or was it five?), and never again would I devote that much of my life uncompensated. I wonder if other former editors of major international journals feel the same way?

Date: Tue, 2 Aug 94 11:30:00 EDT
From: "Stevan Harnad" <harnad>

From: amo@research.att.com (Andrew Odlyzko)
Date: Tue, 2 Aug 94 06:07 EDT

> I cannot speak about physics with any confidence, but the acceptance
> rate for a typical journal in mathematics is usually considerably
> lower than 75-80%. Judging from my own experience in serving on
> a variety of editorial boards, I would estimate that rate is perhaps
> around 50%. The rate of acceptance to all the journals in mathematics
> is higher, and might easily approach 75%. If a paper is rejected
> because of a serious mistake, or else because the results had been
> published previously, then that usually ends the matter. However,
> when a paper is rejected because of the much more subjective judgement
> that it is not of sufficient quality, the author typically submits
> it to another journal.

It would be extremely useful to get exact figures across disciplines. Apart from the social science acceptance rates (25%) cited by Janet Fisher and the physical science rates (75% in physics, perhaps 50% in math), there are the biomedical sciences (low acceptance rates), the humanities (probably varied), and interdisciplinary journals (Science, Nature, etc.) with very low rates. And the acceptance rates probably rise as one descends in the prestige hierarchy (except where self-selection keeps submissions to prestigious journals at a high level of likely acceptability, as in the top physics journals). All these data would be useful to have. The articles I cited (Cichetti, Hargens) report some of it.

> In evaluating the costs of running a journal, it is the 50% acceptance
> rate that is the significant one, not the 75% rate. The work involved
> in handling a rejected manuscript is usually comparable to that of an
> accepted one.

I agree completely. And another figure that needs to be calculated field by field is the ULTIMATE (cross-journal) acceptance rate: It is my belief that in one form or other, just about EVERYTHING gets published eventually, if the author is persistent enough, even if it's in the unrefereed vanity press. Having approximately the same manuscript refereed repeatedly for different journals is a drain on resources, but I'm not sure how to get around it: the prestige hierarchy is based in part on (intellectual) competition.

> The other remark is that page charges have essentially disappeared
> in mathematics. They have been bringing in less and less revenue,
> and the American Mathematical Society, for one, has eliminated them
> completely.

This has to be re-thought. Page charges made little sense in paper publication, since the publisher needed to take copyright and charge subscribers anyway. Author page charges were usually just a voluntary supplement, sometimes offered as a way of speeding publication. But in the electronic medium, where total page costs would be so much lower (75% lower) and reader access would be so rapid, global and free, it should be re-thought whether it would not in fact be to EVERYONE's benefit (especially the author's) if the requisite advance subsidy to cover the FULL minimal costs per electronic "page" came from a combination of learned society, university, library, and author-publication-grant sources.

Stevan Harnad

From: Ann Okerson <ann@cni.org>
Date: Tue, 2 Aug 1994 12:19:03 -0400 (EDT)

About the topic of acceptance rates:

There is not a great deal of real data published about this particular question. There are a lot of general, informal speculations and assertions. The acceptance rates for individual journals are certainly *not* the same as the overall acceptance rates across *all* journals in a field.

According to a presentation I heard a couple of years ago from the Editor of the PMLA, a major journal in the modern languages area published by the Modern Languages Association, the rejection rate for PMLA is in the low 90% range. The journal is relatively small, highly prestigious, and has not grown commensurately in physical size with the growth in the size of the literature of the field. The editorial board works diligently to select the small proportion of submitted articles that can be published, but the Editor-in-Chief affirmed that "much" of the work that is rejected is of high calibre, and "the great majority" of it ends up published elsewhere, often in more specialized journals. He presented no data beyond that.

According to figures from Louise Addis, formerly Librarian at the Stanford Linear Accelerator, slightly over 70% of the high energy physics preprints that are accessible via SLAC's major database of same, are eventually published somewhere in the print physics literature. That is, the finished products are recognizably close to the original preprint and thus the librarians can indicate with the preprint record that the work has appeared in Journal XYZ with a standard citation to it in its "finished" form.

In attendance at many, many meetings of societies, publishers, and libraries on the topic of scholarly journals and communication, I have heard many generalizations about the rejection and acceptance rates in the sciences, social sciences, and humanities. Yet in each of these broad areas, the range of acceptance/rejection across journals must be very, very great, for the "averages" rarely resemble the specific data quoted for any individual title, such as the PMLA.

Absent real data, this suggests that one should be careful of making generalizations. What does seem true is that a great majority of work is eventually published somewhere. In high energy physics, we know it's close to at least 3/4 of all submissions. I've always thought that passing an article through two or three or more editor's or publisher's hands wastes some of the time of the system overall. (Note that this competitive process is also the way that book submissions, particularly in the trade market, work and the mechanism by which work is rewritten, revised, and improved.) I hope, possibly naively, that some of the current duplication of editorial and reviewing effort can be reduced as the process of scholarly communication is more and more electronically supported.

Ann Okerson/ARL
ann@cni.org

From: amo@research.att.com (Andrew Odlyzko)
Date: Tue, 2 Aug 94 12:46 EDT

I just realized that I did not express myself clearly in the message I sent early this morning. (I'll blame this on a rush job, as I am leaving on a trip this afternoon.) The 50% acceptance rate I estimated for mathematics was for the average journal. The 75% rate was an estimate of what you call "the ULTIMATE (cross-journal) acceptance rate," namely the fraction of all preprints that ever get published. In mathematics, a substantial fraction of papers are discovered to be incorrect or not to be novel, so that not everything gets published.

The problem of papers going from journal to journal and referees having to redo each other's work is one reason I was proposing making referee reports public (possibly after some modifications by referees), and also having referees assign significance grades to papers, so that there might in effect be only a few journals. However, this might not be acceptable psychologically.

From: AJ Meadows <A.J.Meadows@lut.ac.uk>
Subject: Electronic Journal Costs
Date: Wed, 3 Aug 94 13:38:25 BST

I have been following with interest your discussion of this topic. Just one or two minor comments:

(1) The best source I know for data on journal use and economics is: D. W. King et al., Scientific Journals in the United States (Hutchinson Ross Pub Co; 1981). It refers to print journals only and is a little out of date, of course.

(2) Comparative data on journal rejection rates was published a good many years ago by R. K. Merton at Columbia. My colleagues and I have looked at these from time to time and they still seem to give comparative

rates fairly well.

(3) We are experimenting with an electronic journal that assumes distribution via a library. From this viewpoint, you have to add on the costs of the library getting ready to receive such journals. We estimate that, for the first such journal, the cost is of the order of $3,500.

Jack Meadows

XIV. Journal Publishing Systems and Models

Bernard Naylor, who entered the correspondence with a paper he wrote for another forum, now offers extended remarks that take up the issues of the whole series. His new contribution views the journals publishing system holistically and takes up issues such as prestige, pressure to publish, conservatism of authors and publishers, and the prognosis for acceptance of electronic publications by all the players in the current academic information chain.

From: harnad@clarity.princeton.edu
Date: Tue Aug 9 17:12:03 1994
To: gs@reagan.ai.mit.edu (UNESCO List EJ LIB), serialst@uvmvm.bitnet (Lib Serials list), vpiej-l@vtvm1.bitnet (Pub-EJournals)
Subject: On Trade vs. Esoteric Publication

The following remarks by Bernard Naylor, Director, University of Southampton Library, are followed by comments from Stevan Harnad.

From: "B.Naylor" <B.Naylor@soton.ac.uk>
Date: Thu, 4 Aug 94 17:38:16 BST

A SMALL CONTRIBUTION TO THE SUBVERSIVE DISCUSSION

Bernard Naylor

Director, University of Southampton Library

1.   Having quite a large department to run, I've only been able to keep one ear so far on the progress of your interesting discussions. I'm now snatching a few moments to make a comment or two which I hope you will find constructive.

2.1 The model which divides scholarly communication into "trade-scholarly" and "esoteric" is conceptually tidy, but I'm not convinced it takes full account of the actual state of affairs. While we are locked (for the time being) into the commercial and paper mode, I believe that journal articles can actually be described as lying at different places on a long and seamless spectrum rather than falling neatly into two groups. Often, the actual place where a journal is located on the spectrum is hard to define, and it may change with time as an article becomes hot or loses heat. Hence we have to imagine that there will be confusion in an indeterminate, but probably large, central area of the spectrum if the model to which you are working is to emerge. This will be while "journals" (or, more precisely, the communications they contain) follow through the process of being assigned to one of the two groups. And even then, any given article may show a tendency to migrate from the group to which it has become assigned.

2.2 The journals of highest prestige (which are most often the ones with the fewest apprehensions about the present financial situation for journals) will continue to be the magnets for people who think their work is of the highest quality and deserves the widest scholarly attention. Hence, the division of scholarly communication into two sets is likely to be seen as having connotations about quality of content. (I.e. "publish trade-scholarly" equals higher quality and relevance. "Publish esoterically" equals lower quality and relevance.)

2.3 Scholars here are already under heavy pressure from their departments to publish in highly-rated outlets and I cannot see that pressure easily letting up. It can have very serious financial consequences in the UK for a department if its members don't achieve that, because the process of awarding them money on account of their research makes that an important criterion. I cannot imagine any scholar readily saying to his/her head of department: "Actually, my work is of relatively low scholarly quality and relevance so I do not propose to try to get it published in any of the journals which our profession ranks highest" - even though, in practice, that may be where it will end up.

2.4 Money is also relevant here. I doubt whether a discussion about the altruism of the members of academe would get us very far. I just think that any scholar who could get some money for publication -- as well as transmitting ideas -- is quite likely to be attracted by that possibility. The attraction of that will become even stronger if the author perceives someone else (e.g. an information broker) making money out of something the scholar has made available free. It could be argued that the activities of the information broker should be stopped, but I think that would break down because for some people information brokers provide a very useful service, enabling them to use their own time in other, more productive ways.

2.5 I therefore think that the possibility I raise in my "Future of the Journal" paper, namely that the electronic (and esoteric) sector could feature for some time as the sink for the material of lesser quality, could quite likely emerge.

3.1 I've found the debate about where the costs of publication really lie very interesting. It may turn out to be true that the "ordinary" publishers are exaggerating the costs which the network will not substitute, by a factor of about three (their "over 70 per cent" as against your "less than 25 per cent"). If it does, I shall be a bit surprised since most of them depend, for earning their living, on being more or less right abut that kind of thing.

3.2 I think one reason for their caution about electronic substitution is because they find speculation about alternative cost-recovery models very complex and difficult. But one of the two main purposes of substitution is to address a perceived economic problem -- the other being to introduce one further industry to the IT revolution. The road from yesterday contains enough litter from high-tech disaster projects to suggest some caution, at least, on the economic/costing front. Remember; the conclusions reached are for testing in settings where red faces are the least of the penalties for being proved wrong.

4.1 On the question of technology, I am reasonably confident that I have not come across any technological problems which I don't think can be solved. There are still important questions as to: how soon? and by whom? and at what cost? At present, the "information superhighway" itself does not exist internationally in a form which could cope with the information traffic currently carried (not very efficiently) by print on paper (the "fat pipe" under the Atlantic at 1.5 Mbps is surely hopelessly inadequate?) and the other problems I referred to in my paper are also with us and have to be resolved if an electronic solution is to operate satisfactorily. Print on paper is currently carrying a colossal amount of information into all sorts of unlikely academic places.

4.2 An important additional consideration on this point, in my view, is what I might call "the mental preparation of the sector." The academic sector, in my view, has been right to point to the serious mistakes made in some industries where technological advance has been implanted without adequate preparation of the work force, in the form of reorientation of work processes and training of working people. We are now seriously contemplating the most dramatic change in the working habits of scholars for some centuries, but I look in vain for convincing signs that our sector appreciates this and is collectively bending its mind to preparing for the consequences. There is far too much "Throw the technology at them and they'll get on with it". A change of this magnitude is going to cause confusion and muddle anyway for a time, but we ought to be doing far more to minimise that. Our present approach, in my view, is asking for trouble. One of the biggest drags on the introduction of advanced technology solutions lies in the attitude of the people for whom we consider them to be intended. It's crucial that a much better effort is directed to changing that. When I had to cancel some physics journals a few months ago, our physicists gave me the impression that I was bringing the roof down on their department, and Paul Ginsparg wasn't mentioned once in their remonstrations -- though I've no doubt they're well aware of what he's doing.

4.3 I recently asked a group of about twenty chief university librarians (that is, about 20 per cent of the total UK cohort) "by what date do you expect your present number of current subscriptions to print-on-paper journals will have been reduced by 80 per cent." The extremes were "1995" and "2050" with 2010 by far the favourite prediction (2010 was mine as well -- honestly). (I said I thought that might be a way, for some of them, of saying "after I've retired".) There is some belief out there that the present system will collapse and change suddenly quite soon but it's not very widespread -- though it may be right. Otherwise, it implies that Southampton University Library must shed 300 print journals every year from now till 2010. At present, that does not look very likely and this means the process will have to accelerate substantially (and I expect it will) later in the period.

4.4 Re-reading some of what you and Andrew have written makes me wonder whether we are really that far apart. My job is to cope with today's reality (which is largely, like it or not, both papyrocentric and commercial) and try to anticipate the next few years' (say, five or at most ten) changes reasonably intelligently. You and Andrew appear to be speculating about a revolution which I am satisfied will come -- though I seriously doubt your present economic assumptions -- and I sometimes get the impression that Andrew might not disagree strongly with my speculation and the speculation of my librarian colleagues as to the time scale. I'm less sure, Stevan, about your views as to likely time scales.

5.1 One of the points I'm trying to underline in pointing out that journal publishing is an industry is that it will not sit quietly by and let itself be subverted. We must assume that, if a concerted plan emerges to cut major traditional publishers out from the knowledge communication business, they will fight very strongly for their "share of the action." Commercial publishers will have revenue streams to defend, not least in the interest of the people they employ and of their shareholders, and even learned societies and academic presses could face massive upheaval if revenue-earning titles (which are also circulated gratis to some as a privilege of membership) appear to be in danger of complete substitution, and they will fight to prevent that.

5.2 One of the main points that publishers are likely to raise in this country, and probably in Western Europe generally, will be to question (to put it no more strongly) the propriety of academic institutions using public money (all UK universities bar one very small one are funded by the taxpayer) in order to drive a viable industry (as they see it) to the wall. Perhaps the government will be happy to see the publishers as resembling the toll bridge owners of past centuries whose bizarre privileges were bought out or set aside with the growth of the road network. But the mood in the UK, even among universities themselves, is to press for more and more activities to go down the "charging" road. Our government believes passionately in markets -- I think it claims it got its predilection for them from the United States! -- and I can see it saying: "You must allow commercial academic publishers onto the academic superhighway on terms which allow them to compete fairly for the survival of their role". I don't think this necessarily means that it should always be carried out in the same way as now -- but they must be given a reasonable chance to adapt. I'm genuinely surprised that you appear to think that it will be politically acceptable in the United States to make most scholarly information a non-tradeable commodity. I don't think it will be here.

6.   Maybe these few remarks have irrevocably confirmed my typecast for you! They are among the reasons why I think evolution is a better mode than revolution and why I think that the economic problems which libraries and others face in the scholarly communication field are unlikely to be resolved by an agreement that it should all be for free in an electronic setting.

Comments by S. Harnad:

> 2.1 The model which divides scholarly communication into
> "trade-scholarly" and "esoteric" is conceptually tidy, but I'm not
> convinced it takes full account of the actual state of affairs... I
> believe that journal articles can actually be described as lying at
> different places on a long and seamless spectrum rather than falling
> neatly into two groups... there will be confusion in an indeterminate,
> but probably large, central area of the spectrum...

There is indeed a continuum from trade (scholarly) publishing to esoteric (scholarly) publishing, but the lion's share of the kind of periodical publication that I and most publishing scholars and scientists are concerned with falls quite safely within the unequivocally esoteric region of that continuum. The gray area is not at issue, nor is it an issue.

At the root of our disagreement is your identification of the factors you apparently think determine a journal's place in the continuum. You think they have to do with the prestige of the journal, whereas I think they are much bigger factors than that, and that they eclipse the relatively trivial differences between high and low prestige esoteric journals (they're ALL esoteric, compared to journals whose individual articles actually have a nontrivial readership size). More below.

> 2.2 The journals of highest prestige (which are most often the ones with
> the fewest apprehensions about the present financial situation for
> journals) will continue to be the magnets for people who think their
> work is of the highest quality and deserves the widest scholarly
> attention. Hence, the division of scholarly communication into two sets
> is likely to be seen as having connotations about quality of content.
> (I.e. "publish trade-scholarly" equals higher quality and relevance.
> "Publish esoterically" equals lower quality and relevance.)

Here is the root of our disagreement. Of course the highest prestige journals are the ones with the fewest financial worries (because they are the last ones likely to be cut from library budgets), and, by definition, they are also the ones that authors and readers value the most highly. But this has NOTHING to do with the trade/esoteric continuum! The high prestige journals, like their lowlier cousins are ALL esoteric if one takes the proper measure of esotericism. This proper measure is NOT:

(1) how much a journal costs,
(2) how many libraries subscribe to the journal, or
(3) how likely libraries are to drop the journal.

Nor is it:

(4) how eager authors are to publish in the journal, or
(5) how heavily publications in the journal weigh with promotions committee.

It is not even:

(6) how much weight readers assign to articles in that journal,
(7) how many individual subscribers there are to that journal, or even
(8) how many readers browse that journal.

We are closer, but not quite there yet, with:

(9) how many readers READ a particular article in that journal

and even closer with

(10) how many readers CITE that article.

But even with the last two measures, the relevant comparison is not between the more and less prestigious journals in a given field (it is a foregone conclusion that prestige will correlate positively with (9) and (10)). What one must look at is the average readership per article in relation to the true cost of producing that article. An even more dramatic way to depict it would be as the RATIO OF THE PER-PAGE READERSHIP TO THE PER-PAGE COST. That ratio may differ a little if one compares high- and low-prestige journals within a given field, to be sure, but if one compares it with the ratio for pages that really DO have a market -- either popular scientific and general intellectual periodicals or the magazine market in general (with or without adjusting for the contribution of advertising revenues, wherever they kick in), then the true locus of most of scholarly/scientific publication along the trade-esoteric continuum will, I suggest, become plainly and unequivocally apparent. And once we scale up to this broader sample of the continuum, the relatively trivial differences between high and low prestige journals will be altogether eclipsed.

Let's be more specific. Though it's risky to resort to figures from hearsay (and that is all I must confess I have so far), I am confident enough in what I am about to point out that even if I am wrong by one or two orders of magnitude, the upshot is the same: The average published scientific article has fewer than 10 readers and no citers; I'll bet the same is true for the average piece of scholarship in the humanities.

You aren't speaking of average work? Alright, let's move up to the top end of the Gaussian distribution and consider just the top 5% of the articles in a given field: How much higher do you think those figures are likely to be for them? (And don't forget that this excludes 95% of what is published, and is reckoned on a per-article, not a per-journal basis: not even the most prestigious journals produce exclusively, or primarily, winners.)

So what are the figures for a winner likely to be? Twenty readers, two hundred, two thousand? Suppose it's two thousand. We all know that in paper those rare articles that generate a huge demand are supplied mostly in the form of preprints and reprints, because a journal certainly cannot calibrate its print run by banking on occasional individual articles. (Journals print issues and volumes, whereas "citation classics" are relatively rare individual papers, exceptional by definition.)

But citation classics and the best-sellers among the separata are not what the economies of scholarly publishing are based on. Even if we restrict ourselves to the single journal in each academic specialty that is by consensus the most prestigious one, the per-page readership ratios for most of its pages will be off-scale compared to the periodical literature that actually has a market.

Why has this never come up before? Because no matter how absurd the per-page ratios were in scholarly periodical publication, there was nothing anyone could do about it (and they certainly weren't going to give up the reporting and reading of scholarly research), because the economies of paper were such that the only way to recover the true costs of making the research available at all was by levying reader-access charges. Yet of course it was never the (on average less than 10) readers who actually paid the costs per page; it was the vast infrastructure (mainly University libraries) that was set up to SUBSIDIZE the minuscule demand there really was for any particular page of this esoteric (sic, I now state without trepidation) corpus. The nonreaders (all of us) subsidized the readers (each of us) of any particular article.

Well that is simply no longer necessary; or, rather, the subsidy can now be set up in a much more sensible way, matching the true demand structure and the nature of the service provided by the publisher: not by continuing to treat a no-market commodity as if it were a viable trade item and benightedly trying to sell it to the vanishingly small number of scholars who may ever want to see it, but by charging the much lower true per-page costs of esoteric publication at the point where it is the most sensible to charge them: At the point of access to the peer community's eyes and minds. That much more modest per-page cost will be the price of the service that esoteric publishers perform for AUTHORS (and their institutions and research support agencies) in making their work available to their fellow-specialists, globally, in perpetuum, and, of course, for free. And we will all be the better off for it.

> 2.3 Scholars here are already under heavy pressure from their
> departments to publish in highly-rated outlets and I cannot see that
> pressure easily letting up .... I cannot imagine any scholar readily
> saying to his/her head of department: "Actually, my work is of relatively
> low scholarly quality and relevance so I do not propose to try to get it
> published in any of the journals which our profession ranks highest" -
> even though, in practice, that may be where it will end up.

But this point is only pertinent if one accepts your assumption that high-prestige journal = paper (= trade) and low-prestige journal = electronic (= esoteric).

Whereas, as I have tried to argue, I think that assumption is incorrect. Currently ALL journals, low prestige and high, are paper. The trade/esoteric dichotomy, as I have tried to argue above, has nothing to do with prestige. And it will continue to have nothing to do with it as journals become electronic; prestige will continue to depend on the rigor of the peer review and the quality of the authors and submissions, not on the medium.

It is true that today's high-prestige paper journals are likely to be the last to be cancelled by libraries for economic reasons, and it may even be true that this irrelevant side-factor will affect the initial conditions among electronic journals (the first new ones, and the first ones to migrate, will not be the high-prestige ones), and that will of course be regrettable, and will retard the inevitable, for reasons that are NOT to scholarship's advantage. But that still has nothing to do with the trade/esoteric continuum, and hence does not provide a rational basis for drawing conclusions about the applicability and appropriateness of the trade model to no-market papers, whether high prestige or low.

> 2.4 Money is also relevant here. I doubt whether a discussion about the
> altruism of the members of academe would get us very far. I just think
> that any scholar who could get some money for publications -- as well as
> transmitting ideas -- is quite likely to be attracted by that possibility.
> The attraction will become even stronger if the scholar perceives someone
> else (e.g. an information broker) making money out of something the scholar
> has made available free. It could be argued that the activities of the
> information broker should be stopped, but I think that would break down
> because for some people information brokers provide a very useful
> service, enabling them to use their own time in other, more productive
> ways.

This passage is rather complicated, and again involves some assumptions and contingencies that I think are erroneous: First, one of the marks of the esotericity of most of scholarly and scientific periodical publication is that the author does NOT make a penny from the sale of his text, and does not, and never has expected to. (It is an instant signal that one is in the trade rather than the esoteric region of the continuum if this is not true, and the author expects and does receive royalties for those pages. This happens in popular and general-audience scholarly/scientific writing. OF COURSE most of us would jump at the opportunity to make a few bucks from publishing our words, but how often do we get a chance to do that?) Trade publishing is medium-independent. When there is a potential paying readership, one can and should charge, whether on paper or on the airwaves. It's just that this contingency is absent in the region of the continuum I am concerned with; no author is making money there on paper, and no author will make money there on the Net either.

So whereas I agree that scholars are not altruists -- if there were money for them to make from the sale of their words (and if this were not too much at odd with their scholarly mission, if any) -- then they would certainly be happy to collect it; but the fact is that for the overwhelming majority of the scholarly/scientific corpus there IS no money to be made from the sale of their words -- at least not money for THEM (the author/scholars). Money is being made, to be sure, but it is being made exclusively by the paper periodical publisher, not the author.

Which brings me to the second (in my view incorrect) assumption: To show why this assumption is incorrect, I must first re-introduce what I have come to refer to as the "Faustian Bargain" that esoteric authors have reluctantly entered into with paper publishers -- and let me stress that in this metaphor it is PAPER that is the devil, not paper publishers, for they too are victims of the tyranny of the true costs and technology of that unfortunate medium. This bargain is ONLY Faustian in the case of esoteric publication -- publication in which the market for most papers is virtually zero, the author does not make a penny, and the sole motivation is to reach the eyes and minds of one's peers and posterity with one's findings. To have to treat that special transaction on the same model as the quite normal and un-Faustian bargain between a paper publisher and an author who makes a living by selling words is very close to absurd, yet for centuries there was no choice: The only hope an esoteric author had of reaching the tiny potential non-market of peers was to allow the publisher to charge for access to the writing, even though the author would not make a penny, because that was the only way that the expenses and a fair return could be paid for the true and sizeable per-page costs of the technology and logistics of paper periodical production and distribution.

To repeat: The Faustian bargain was reluctantly accepted, despite containing an essential internal conflict of interest between the esoteric author's desire to reach as many interested peers as possible and the publisher's need to restrict access with a price-tag to defray the substantial per-page costs and a fair return for investment and effort, BECAUSE THERE WAS NO OTHER CHOICE.

So if the first incorrect assumption was that esoteric authors can and do make money from selling their articles, the second one was that their Faustian symbiotic relationship with the paper publisher would somehow carry over to his "information broker" counterpart in the electronic medium. But what are we imagining here? The true per-page costs (if my estimate is right) are now down to less than a quarter of what they were in paper, so there is no longer a Faustian dependence on a technology whose sizeable costs need to be recovered by blocking access to esoteric work that already has virtually no market; the author, the author's institution, library, scholarly/scientific societies and research (publication) grants can with a little perestroika EASILY collaborate to subsidize life-long published page quotas as needed, thereby allowing access to be free for all (as it always should have been).

So who is this "information broker"? The editor of the electronic journal and the editorial staff (their services are already reckoned as making up most of the remaining < 25% per-page costs)? The (unpaid) referees? The author's own word-processing budget? The copy-editors/proofreaders (the rest of the < 25%)? Or the classifiers and maintainers of the electronic archive (these are currently called "librarians" and they do not normally get a cut from the sale of the author's text in any case).

So what is it that the "information broker" is doing that allows the author to get on with scholarly life instead of being a jack of all trades? In paper, this was clear: The author did not have to spend time printing, disseminating and archiving the work for all; the publisher did it for that author (but unfortunately had to charge admission in exchange). Where is the counterpart of this in the electronic medium that would warrant reincarnating the Faustian bargain yet again, now that there is clearly no need for it?

> 2.5 I therefore think that the possibility I raise in my "Future of the
> Journal" paper, namely that the electronic (and esoteric) sector could
> feature for some time as the sink for the material of lesser quality,
> could quite likely emerge.

Even within the paper medium itself, new journals always have to struggle initially to establish a niche (and many fail, or fail to attain a high level of prestige). This is true in spades when it is not just a new journal that is at issue, but a new medium. So the prediction that the Net will carry material of lower quality than paper initially is quite a safe one to make (I myself have described the Net as a "Global Graffiti Board for Trivial Pursuit" till not that long ago), but this has nothing at all to do either with esotericity or the nature of the medium itself. The initial disparity is simply due to history, demographics and initial conditions. Paper currently holds virtually all the scholarly cards (and the hearts and habits of the major card-players) and the Net is a haven for the young and unscholarly or not-yet-scholarly.

But don't bank on it. The house of cards is also poised to collapse. All that's needed is something that will overcome the primarily MENTAL obstacles that exist currently: mainly superstitious habits and beliefs about correlations between paper and quality, correlations that are there, to be sure, but for arbitrary historical reasons rather than functional ones -- indeed, as I am trying to suggest, these reasons are becoming increasingly DYSfunctional, and THAT will be what finally makes the paper house of cards collapse.

> 3.1 I've found the debate about where the costs of publication really
> lie very interesting. It may turn out to be true that the "ordinary"
> publishers are exaggerating the costs which the network will not
> substitute, by a factor of about three (their "over 70 per cent," as
> against your "less than 25 per cent"). If it does, I shall be a bit
> surprised since most of them depend, for earning their living, on being

> more or less right about that kind of thing.

Indeed. But the PREMISE of such livelihood-preserving calculations is that one must continue to earn one's living essentially the same way. (As I suggested, those who have calculated the true per-page costs as 75% rather than 25%, as I do, have only been reckoning what electronic processing will save from a system that is designed to produce PAPER pages, as they do; let them redo it for a system designed solely to produce electronic pages.)

If I am right, publishers will have to be prepared to do a major restructuring (and reconceptualizing) of their role in esoteric scholarly publishing or else this anomalous portion of the symbiotic author/publisher system will simply break off and start anew, as an autonomous form of publication. The key factor is that the Faustian Bargain is no longer necessary; the true per-page costs (and a fair return) for esoteric publication can be recovered on a page-subsidy model. There is no longer any need to charge admission to a show that virtually no one wants to see.

> 3.2 I think one reason for their caution about electronic substitution
> is because they find speculation about alternative cost-recovery models
> very complex and difficult.

Indeed; but that does not make those models wrong, or impossible. Nor does it support your suggestion that publishers must be doing the calculations correctly because that's what they do for a living...

But there are (and there inevitably will be) publishers who DO understand the arithmetic (MIT Press seems to be one such publisher), and it is my hope that their efforts will eventually lead in a direction that serves the interests of all, without Faustian conflict, and without heroic efforts to preserve the unstable and far-from-optimal status quo.

> But one of the two main purposes of substitution is to address a
> perceived economic problem - the other being to introduce one further
> industry to the IT revolution. The road from yesterday contains enough
> litter from high-tech disaster projects to suggest some caution, at least, on
> the economic/costing front. Remember; the conclusions reached are for
> testing in settings where red faces are the least of the penalties for being
> proved wrong.

By all means. But I don't see esoteric scholarly/scientific publishing as a potential cash cow for any big IT ventures (perhaps for popular and wide-spectrum scholarly/scientific publishing, but not for the esoteric region of the continuum). This no-market form of publishing is essential to us all -- it's what keeps human learned inquiry going. But the trade model just does not fit it (and never did).

Besides, most of us are talking about shrinking and restructuring rather than big, risky investments; that's mostly what the migration from paper to the Net entails (see Andrew Odlyzko's paper).

> At present, the "information superhighway"
> itself does not exist internationally in a form which could cope with
> the information traffic currently carried (not very efficiently) by
> print on paper (the "fat pipe" under the Atlantic at 1.5 Mbps is surely
> hopelessly inadequate?)... Print on paper is currently
> carrying a colossal amount of information into all sorts of unlikely
> academic places.

This is an empirical question, and not in my domain of expertise, but I have heard that, once we decide to make a commitment to carrying the (scholarly/scientific) information that way, the Net will be ABUNDANTLY able to bear the weight. In any case, it is not clear to me who should be worrying about capacity problems these days, when people are passing vast quantities of, for example, porno-graphics, freely back and forth on the Net. Metaphors, of course, settle nothing, but my own image of the full corpus of esoteric periodical publishing (see Andrew Odlyzko's essay for some sample figures) as the flea on the tail of the dog, insofar as the Net's carrying capacity is concerned, especially in the future, when more and more of the rest of the traffic will be commercial and paid for (because it DOES have a market).

Humanity will be better served by granting that flea a free ride in perpetuum, rather than treating it as if it were another commercial traveller.

It's odd, by the way, that the "Net Capacity" and "Net Highway Toll" alarms are so often sounded by individuals who are no better informed than you or I are, but in whose interests it would be if there WERE an awkward capacity limitation or a prohibitive toll...

> 4.2 An important additional consideration on this point, in my view, is
> what I might call "the mental preparation of the sector." The academic
> sector, in my view, has been right to point to the serious mistakes
> made in some industries where technological advance has been implanted
> without adequate preparation of the work force, in the form of
> reorientation of work processes and training of working people. We are
> now seriously contemplating the most dramatic change in the working
> habits of scholars for some centuries, but I look in vain for
> convincing signs that our sector appreciates this and is collectively

> bending its mind to preparing for the consequences. There is far too
> much "Throw the technology at them and they'll get on with it". A
> change of this magnitude is going to cause confusion and muddle anyway
> for a time, but we ought to be doing far more to minimise that. Our
> present approach, in my view, is asking for trouble. One of the biggest
> drags on the introduction of advanced technology solutions lies in the
> attitude of the people for whom we consider them to be intended. It's
> crucial that a much better effort is directed to changing that.

I agree with this completely. Authors, readers, librarians, etc. do need to be prepared, informed, etc. But that's not an argument for the status quo, or even for slowing down (the pace of the move toward electronic journals is already excruciatingly slow, to my tastes: 99.9999% of the esoteric scholarly periodical literature is still in paper, after all; hence there is no precipitous hurtling toward an unknown doom going on here!). Preparing the populace should be undertaken pari passu with the migration itself, but certainly not prior to it, or instead of it...

> When I had to cancel some physics journals a few months ago, our
> physicists gave me the impression that I was bringing the roof down on
> their department, and Paul Ginsparg wasn't mentioned once in their
> remonstrations - though I've no doubt they're well aware of what he's
> doing.

This is not surprising, and I don't think it is evidence of anything more than that no one has a rational command yet over what is happening and what is about to happen. It is because of this irrational factor that I never make predictions about WHEN it will all happen; I simply affirm THAT it will happen (and the sooner the better)...

> There is some belief out there that the present system will collapse
> and change suddenly quite soon but it's not very widespread - though it
> may be right. Otherwise, it implies that Southampton University Library
> must shed 300 print journals every year from now till 2010. At present,
> that does not look very likely and this means the process will have to
> accelerate substantially (and I expect it will) later in the period.

I suspect it will be a critical-mass effect: After a slow linear phase, consisting mostly of new electronic journals rather than migrations of established paper journals (though you are probably right that, unfortunately, the weaker paper journals make take to the skies first) as well as regressive "hybrid" projects (paper journals offering a double deal: paper plus electronic version, but to subscribers only, aimed eventually at developing an electronic-only subscriber base), a critical mass of free-access refereed electronic journals will form and demonstrate that they can be as rigorous as refereed paper journals, but with the added advantage of (1) universal searchability and access as well as (2) interactivity (peer commentary). That -- with the help of subversive projects like Paul Ginsparg's HEP Archive and Public Preprint/Reprint Archives created by authors -- will trigger a relatively rapid and dramatic restructuring that will end with most or all of the esoteric periodical corpus airborne.

> 4.4 Re-reading some of what you and Andrew have written makes me wonder
> whether we are really that far apart. My job is to cope with today's
> reality (which is largely, like it or not, both papyrocentric and
> commercial) and try to anticipate the next few years' (say, five or at
> most ten) changes reasonably intelligently. You and Andrew appear to be
> speculating about a revolution which I am satisfied will come - though
> I seriously doubt your present economic assumptions - and I sometimes
> get the impression that Andrew might not disagree strongly with my
> speculation and the speculation of my librarian colleagues as to the
> time scale. I'm less sure, Stevan, about your views as to likely time
> scales.

Ah, I refrain from committing myself to numbers when it comes to time scale. I stick to (1) editing and adapting PSYCOLOQUY as a model and to (2) trying to describe what is actually happening, what is possible, and what is rational in talks and papers. Chronology must fend for itself. (But if it's my 'druthers you're inquiring about, it can't happen too soon for me.)

> 5.1 One of the points I'm trying to underline in pointing out that
> journal publishing is an industry is that it will not sit quietly by
> and let itself be subverted. We must assume that, if a concerted plan
> emerges to cut major traditional publishers out from the knowledge
> communication business, they will fight very strongly for their "share
> of the action." Commercial publishers will have revenue streams to
> defend, not least in the interest of the people they employ and of
> their shareholders, and even learned societies and academic presses
> could face massive upheaval if revenue-earning titles (which are also
> circulated gratis to some as a privilege of membership) appear to be in
> danger of complete substitution, and they will fight to prevent that.

No doubt. But what will eventually prevail, I hope, is what is in the best interests of scholars/scientists and Learned Inquiry itself. As most of our intellectual wares (99.9999%, as I said, and add more 9's for the retrospective literature) are currently on the paper flotilla, it is in ALL of our interests to ensure that that flotilla does not sink prematurely. I believe a benign solution is possible to effect an orderly transition to the skies, one that will be fair to all; publishers simply need to be flexible and innovative, and not be tempted to adopt the short-sighted strategy of filibustering in favor of some version or other of the status quo. It just won't fly.

> 5.2 One of the main points that publishers are likely to raise in this
> country, and probably in Western Europe generally, will be to question
> (to put it no more strongly) the propriety of academic institutions
> using public money (all UK universities bar one very small one are
> funded by the taxpayer) in order to drive a viable industry (as they
> see it) to the wall. Perhaps the government will be happy to see the
> publishers as resembling the toll bridge owners of past centuries whose
> bizarre privileges were bought out or set aside with the growth of the
> road network. But the mood in the UK, even among universities
> themselves, is to press for more and more activities to go down the
> "charging" road.

You will not be surprised, perhaps, that this scenario evokes little empathy. I hope the motivation on all sides will be more constructive than this. Esoteric scholarly publishing is motivated by something far more important to us all than the money to be made from selling its texts.

> Our government believes passionately in markets - I think it claims it
> got its predilection for them from the United States! - and I can see it
> saying: "You must allow commercial academic publishers onto the
> academic superhighway on terms which allow them to compete fairly
> for the survival of their role." I don't think this necessarily means that
> it should always be carried out in the same way as now -- but they must
> be given a reasonable chance to adapt.

This makes it sound as if the only problem is access to the Internet: But there WILL be a lot of toll-way traffic on the Internet. That is absolutely irrelevant to the issue under discussion here. Unless publishers are planning to re-tool themselves as telecommunications companies, they are not the ones for whom those bells would toll in any case! (This is a red herring, just as the capacity argument is.)

Paul Ginsparg's HEPnet currently gets 35,000 "hits" per day -- 35,000 physicists the world over retrieving articles. It is simplistic to conceptualize Net use as a finite resource (dramatic increases in Net capacity can be gotten for relatively small investments in money and material; and it makes little sense to tax the number of bits received or the time spent receiving them in an interdigitating network with varying transmission times, especially if the Net is far from saturation), so it is a mistake to imagine a toll on each "hit."

But suppose things did go in that direction: If the Net were privatised (and apparently it is about to be), AND if the Universities chose to pass on to their user communities the 10% increase in costs this would entail over their current flat connection costs, this still would not be reckoned on a "per hit" basis, but as a flat rate. Users would pay their own flat rates for unlimited sending and retrieval, and the rest would depend on WHAT they were retrieving: If it was a commercial newspaper or magazine, they would be prepared to pay a further toll, as they do now (and the writers of the material, and their publishers) would make a fair profit from that toll.

But what if it was a scholarly article that only ten people would ever want to read, and from which the author would never make a penny? Even on this commercial tollway model there is no way to make it rational to squeeze a further fee out of the would-be esoteric reader. It's a foregone conclusion that the author, eager to be read, would happily spring in advance for ten complimentary tickets for those few who will ever want to see the show. In short, the trade model makes no sense for esoteric publication EVEN ON A COMPLETELY COMMERCIALIZED NET, and there is still no money for the publisher to make for the sale of words no one wants to buy!

The real service that esoteric publishing provides is to authors, their institutions and their research funding sources: The "product" they provide is not the author's words for those who want to buy them but the means of access to the eyes and minds of the author's fellow-specialists. Hence that's the natural place to seek to recoup the true expenses of providing that service. I hope it is becoming evident by now how hopelessly Procrustean a trade model is for a product/service/market like this.

> I'm genuinely surprised that you appear to think that it will be
> politically acceptable in the United States to make most scholarly
> information a non-tradeable commodity. I don't think it will be here.

The United States has little to do with this. The question is: Why and for whom do scholars publish? The answer is radically different from the answer to the question of why an author who makes a living by writing publishes. The esoteric market will simply reflect this, once it has been released from its Faustian bonds to the commercial market. "Trade" there will still be, but it will be the selling of the services (25% of paper costs per page) of the esoteric publisher to the esoteric AUTHOR and his institutions rather than to the esoteric READER and his institutions, as it was under the Faustian model. There is a "subsidy" in both cases: Institutions provided it through their library subscriptions the old way; the new way, much less expensive, the (25%) subsidies will be up front. And apart from the Institutions having to pay much less for the availability of the esoteric scholarly corpus, individual scholar/readers will be the greatest beneficiaries, now able to search, browse and read one another's work in the Virtual Library to their hearts and minds content, never having to worry about paying a toll to go where virtually no one cares to go anyway.

What possible objection (or role) could the United States have in something like that?

> 6. Maybe these few remarks have irrevocably confirmed my typecast for
> you! They are among the reasons why I think evolution is a better mode
> than revolution and why I think that the economic problems which
> libraries and others face in the scholarly communication field are
> unlikely to be resolved by an agreement that it should all be for free
> in an electronic setting.   -- Bernard Naylor

For the record, I'm for evolution rather than revolution too, and I have my fingers crossed for a peaceful, fair and orderly evolution rather than a revolution that produces casualties to anyone. And I'm also for paying the true costs of refereed electronic periodical publishing (they are low, but they are not zero); I am simply opposed to having them paid (and/or surcharged) on a completely inappropriate trade/subscription model (subsidized by University Libraries). Everyone's interests would be better reflected and served if they were paid an author/subsidy model.

Stevan Harnad

—————————————————

Date: Wed, 10 Aug 94 11:45:34 -0600
From: Paul Ginsparg 505-667-7353 <ginsparg@qfwfq.lanl.gov>
Subject: Re: On Trade vs. Esoteric Publication

stevan, (i know i promised e-mail blackout, but i found myself with a bunch of networkphilic physicists so it became reasonable to restructure the local environment with a lan and internet feed...)

just a few comments on the most recent (as usual from my pragmatic and non-visionary approach -- in current commercial parlance "just do it"):

>From: "B.Naylor" <B.Naylor@soton.ac.uk>
>Date: Thu, 4 Aug 94 17:38:16 BST

> 4.1 On the question of technology, I am reasonably confident that I
> have not come across any technological problems which I don't think can
> be solved. There are still important questions as to: how soon? and by
> whom? and at what cost? At present, the "information superhighway"

> itself does not exist internationally in a form which could cope with
> the information traffic currently carried (not very efficiently) by
> print on paper (the "fat pipe" under the Atlantic at 1.5 Mbps is surely
> hopelessly inadequate?) and the other problems I referred to in my
> paper are also with us and have to be resolved if an electronic
> solution is to operate satisfactorily. Print on paper is currently
> carrying a colossal amount of information into all sorts of unlikely
> academic places.

i have always been perplexed by what goes into other people's calculation of bandwidth. finally i realized that they are talking about transmitting uncompressed bitmaps: an 8.5" x 11" page scanned at 300 dpi is roughly a Mb. but remember that all the white space compresses extremely well so this is already a grotesque overestimate. moreover in an earlier segment of this thread, we pointed out that the "scan and shred" technique was backward-looking, just adding additional expense with network distribution an ad-hoc afterthought. the savings are enormous if one avoids the paper stage entirely, instead retaining the electronic form the documents typically *already* possess.

(for comparison a page of ascii is 3-4kb, and less than half that after compression -- so we typically gain a factor of 500 over the raw bitmap. using a sophisticated page markup language such as compressed postscript [or preferably its successor [Adobe's pdf] with full font and graphics capability, the savings remain dramatic.) yes it will be a major task to render all the currently existing "print on paper" to network distributable form if that is desired, but we need to point out repeatedly that the issue of costs under discussion centers on a medium that is text from inception to final distribution. even the "fat pipe" as a bottleneck is a red herring in any event, one can always run mirrors (as i run in italy and japan) to ensure adequate bandwidth -- that way only a single transfer across the weakest link is necessary.

and speaking of "unlikely academic places", i am currently organizing a physics summer school in the french alps (les houches, next to chamonix -- i had expected to be out of network range but found an old hp 715 here and together with some other stone age implements forged a 64 kbit/s internet link -- say goodbye to minitel) and the students are from all over the world. the most common comment regarding the physics archives is how much they have *already* improved the situation in developing and former eastern-block countries, where the "colossal volume of print on paper" does not penetrate due to cost and other issues. at lanl, the systems i'm running still consume less than .01% (i.e. .0001) of the lanl.gov backbone capacity so we really do realize stevan's "flea on tail" metaphor.

> When I had to cancel some physics journals a few months ago, our physicists
> gave me the impression that I was bringing the roof down on their
> department, and Paul Ginsparg wasn't mentioned once in their
> remonstrations - though I've no doubt they're well aware of what he's
> doing.

well it is still premature. note that the current physics archives branched out from high energy particle physics and do not yet cover close to the whole of physics. this was primarily due to lack of resources (i.e. zero) at my end, a situation recently rectified, and when i get back to the u.s. in mid sept there will be a dramatic horizontal expansion. (but even so it may be a couple more years before you can cut physics journals without complaint.)

> 4.3 I recently asked a group of about twenty chief university
> librarians (that is, about 20 per cent of the total UK cohort) "by what
> date do you expect your present number of current subscriptions to
> print-on-paper journals will have been reduced by 80 per cent". The
> extremes were "1995" and "2050" with 2010 by far the favourite
> prediction (2010 was mine as well - honestly). (I said I thought that
> might be a way, for some of them, of saying "after I've retired".)

your colleagues are incorrect. the driving force will not only be economics but the enhanced functionality of the electronic medium. there are many things that the new medium supports (see, for example, http://xxx.lanl.gov/hypertex/), including the overall fluid nature (on-line annotations, continuously graded refereeing, automated hyperlinks to distributed resources including non-text based applications, etc., etc.) that simply have no analog in print. it will be more or less like moving from radio to television -- radio remains for those things for which it's better optimized, but the majority of new material will move to the new medium.

> 5.1 One of the points I'm trying to underline in pointing out that
> journal publishing is an industry is that it will not sit quietly by
> and let itself be subverted. We must assume that, if a concerted plan
> emerges to cut major traditional publishers out from the knowledge
> communication business, they will fight very strongly for their "share
> of the action". Commercial publishers will have revenue streams to
> defend, not least in the interest of the people they employ and of
> their shareholders, and even learned societies and academic presses
> could face massive upheaval if revenue-earning titles (which are also
> circulated gratis to some as a privilege of membership) appear to be in
> danger of complete substitution, and they will fight to prevent that.

this will proceed quickly. the subversion is that their bottom line will be removed.

formerly we were at their mercy because we needed their production and distribution facilities. now we can outdo them on both counts, at dramatically reduced cost. at the same time, we expose how little intellectual added value they provide in general (i mean the validation and identification of significant research which can only come from within the community.) sure they could remain in the game if they were willing to scale down to the more efficient operation enabled by the fully electronic medium, but the bottom line will not be there for them and they will have little ability to compete with a streamlined operation organized by researchers in alliance with their research libraries (and perhaps non-profit professional societies).

> 5.2 One of the main points that publishers are likely to raise in this
> country, and probably in Western Europe generally, will be to question
> (to put it no more strongly) the propriety of academic institutions
> using public money (all UK universities bar one very small one are
> funded by the taxpayer) in order to drive a viable industry (as they
> see it) to the wall.

but why is it currently viewed as appropriate to use gov't funds to sponsor this same "viable" industry in the form of overhead on grants that eventually makes its way to research libraries for transfer to them???

re:

>> Date: Tue, 9 Aug 94 17:12:04 EDT
>> From: "Stevan Harnad" <harnad@Princeton.EDU>

>> Paul Ginsparg's HEPnet currently gets 35,000 "hits" per day -- 35,000
>> physicists the world over retrieving articles.

one small clarification: actually it is just over 20,000 users (and more than just physicists since it has branched out into other fields including computational linguistics and economics). the 35,000 "hits" per day include all variety of searches, etc., not each an article retrieval.

Paul Ginsparg

From: amo@research.att.com (Andrew Odlyzko)
Date: Sun, 14 Aug 94 06:57 EDT
To: Bernard Naylor <B.Naylor@soton.ac.uk>
Subject: Balance Point and the economics of ejournals

Bernard,

Thank you very much for your comments, and please excuse the delay in responding to them, but I was away on a trip when they arrived. In the meantime, Stevan Harnad and Paul Ginsparg have responded to your message. I agree with what they say, and have only a few minor comments to add.

1.   Inadequacies of present networks:

You are right that the present 1.5 Mbps pipe over (or under) the Atlantic is inadequate for full-scale scholarly communication. It can carry about 5 TB (tera-bytes) in a year. In my article I estimated that just the mathematical literature alone requires about 1 TB to store (with fax compression). However, network speeds are increasing at dramatic rates, and soon we will have an adequate infrastructure in place.

As an aside, we can obtain much higher quality of material and lower communication burdens by converting the old documents into TeX, say. This is not as hard as it might seem. In mathematics there are about 20 M pages of printed material. At the rates that skilled typists in the US command, it would cost $ 200-400M to typeset them into TeX. By going to the Third World we could lower this to the $ 50-100 M range. (Obviously there aren't enough skilled typists in the Third World or even in the industrialized world to do this quickly, but the conversion could be done over 5-10 years, which would offer opportunities to train the necessary labor force.) For comparison, the existing mathematics print journals cost about $ 200 M per year. Thus a fraction of the annual cost of today's system would suffice to convert all the literature to a modern format. I expect similar estimates apply to other fields. The trouble would be in organizing this conversion effort.

2. Time scales:

Here are some comments on what you wrote:

> 4.3   I recently asked a group of about twenty chief
> university librarians (that is, about 20 per cent of the
> total UK cohort) "by what date do you expect your present
> number of current subscriptions to print-on-paper journals
> will have been reduced by 80 per cent". The extremes were

> "1995" and "2050" with 2010 by far the favourite prediction
> (2010 was mine as well - honestly). (I said I thought that
> might be a way, for some of them, of saying "after I've
> retired".) There is some belief out there that the present
> system will collapse and change suddenly quite soon but
> it's not very widespread - though it may be right.
> Otherwise, it implies that Southampton University Library
> must shed 300 print journals every year from now till
> 2010. At present, that does not look very likely and this
> means the process will have to accelerate substantially
> (and I expect it will) later in the period.

I am rather surprised that so many of these librarians picked 2010 as the date for a major change. I would have expected them to be much more conservative.

I agree fully with you and Stevan that the drop in paper journal subscriptions will be very nonlinear. The most dramatic part of the drop is likely to occur between 2000 and 2010. I would be surprised if it occurred this decade, since networks and computer capacities are not adequate yet, and there is tremendous inertia in the system. On the other hand, it's hard for me to imagine print journals surviving more than 15 years in large numbers, as by 2010 the world will be fully "wired."

> 4.4   Re-reading some of what you and Andrew have written
> makes me wonder whether we are really that far apart. My
> job is to cope with today's reality (which is largely, like
> it or not, both papyrocentric and commercial) and try to
> anticipate the next few years' (say, five or at most ten)
> changes reasonably intelligently. You and Andrew appear to
> be speculating about a revolution which I am satisfied will
> come -- though I seriously doubt your present economic
> assumptions -- and I sometimes get the impression that
> Andrew might not disagree strongly with my speculation and
> the speculation of my librarian colleagues as to the time
> scale. I'm less sure, Stevan, about your views as to
> likely time scales.

You are right, we are not that far off in our opinions. My essay looked at the future about two decades from now, when all the novel features should be in place. Its aim was to show people what will be available then, and why the present system is bound to collapse. It dealt hardly at all with how to get there from here. That is a thornier issue, and one I now have to devote some thought to, as I am on some committees that are supposed to make recommendations for near-term actions.

The transition to electronic publishing is likely to be turbulent, and I do not wish to make it sound too easy. As just one example, it is likely that various administrators will seize on the projections of low-cost electronic publishing of scholarly journals and decide that this will allow them to save the bulk of their libraries' costs. However, while electronic journals can easily eliminate or at least drastically lower journal subscription costs, these costs are at most one third of the total cost of running research libraries. Since conversion of libraries to digital formats is going to be a long process, immediate savings are likely to be considerably smaller than such administrators might hope for.

Best regards,
Andrew Odlyzko

XV.   Brief Discussions -- Format, Economics, Submissions

Several messages pick up various topical threads that arose earlier in the discussion.

Date: Sun, 21 Aug 94 10:59:24 -0600
From: Paul Ginsparg 505-667-7353 <ginsparg@qfwfq.lanl.gov>

> Date: Sat, 13 Aug 94 18:25:38 EDT
> From: "Stevan Harnad" <harnad@Princeton.EDU>

> The generality and adaptiveness of the www superset is impressive!
> But ftp/gopher also has a PROVIDER-side argument: In text-only,
> non-tech (non-Tex) disciplines the probability of a successful
> subversion knocking down the paper house of cards is MUCH higher
> if authors need merely store their ascii texts rather than convert
> them or learn html (trivial as it is). -- S.H.

i wasn't clear enough, and this is an important point: of course, OF COURSE, www can be used to transmit plain text (this is a trivial corollary of my statement that it is a superset of gopher). after all, i'm using it to transmit .tex, .dvi, .ps, etc. -- it can transmit anything, bytes are bytes. more specifically, if an http server sees a file with e.g. a .txt (or other unrecognized extension), it tells the client that plain text is on the way and the client presents it unformatted (i'm surprised you haven't encountered this before). that is why gopher is dying out worldwide (indeed it is only naive confusion and misinformation on the above issues responsible for keeping it afloat even this long). everything gopher does, www does just as well or better (including automatic indexing of pre-existing directories). anyway, just a matter of time -- makes little difference to worry about it on way or another.

> Once the subversion has had its effect, we can convert them to the
> virtues of hypertext, etc. (But your point on the generality of www
> is taken!).

and now the point of the hypertext project becomes clear -- we do transmit all this non-html via www, but these have all been network dead-ends. so rather than wait forever for some group of ncsa undergrads or whomever to reproduce a satisfactory typesetting environment within these primitive html browsers, we've taken the shortcut of adding html capabilities to our preferred medium and its browsers. (in particular that means i've been able to reprocess all pre-existing tex source in the new mode, and internal linkages are produced automatically, with no modification of the underlying .tex)

Paul Ginsparg

Date: Tue, 23 Aug 1994 08:27:14 EDT
Subject: Re: ftp vs. gopher vs. www
From: Rich Wiggins <WIGGINS@msu.edu>
To: Multiple recipients of list VPIEJ-L <VPIEJ-L@VTVM1.BitNet>

> that is why gopher is dying out worldwide (indeed it is only naive confusion
> and misinformation on the above issues responsible for keeping it afloat
> even this long). everything gopher does, www does just as well or better
> (including automatic indexing of pre-existing directories).

This claim is not quite true. The Web does not embrace the Gopher+ extensions, which have never been popular among HTTP/HTML aficionados, and are not implemented in Mosaic and its descendants.

Gopher+ provides a mechanism for alternate typing of documents. The theory is that information providers might offer documents in a variety of ways and intelligent clients might help users select among them. Web folks feel that multiple document types are handled just fine "their way" and that alternate views can be coded as part of the HTML.

But Gopher+ also provides a mechanism for named attributes of documents -- the sort of stuff like the date of the last update, author's e-mail address, etc. This is the sort of "meta-information" that is talked about interminably in IETF and Web discussion groups. Gopher+ included a mechanism for adding such attributes as of early 1993. Even in the Gopher community, though, it seems it isn't widely exploited. There are conventions for some meta-information in HTML, and no doubt discussions will lead to real standards.

The "yes there is Gopher+ but it is useless" discussion has been carried out elsewhere, and probably wouldn't be helpful here. Most new announcements of online services seem to be coming from the Web side. In general, I view Gopher as part of a progression from FTP to hierarchical menus with nice titles to Web-style hypermedia. Mosaic paved the way for the Web; now we need is bandwidth to deliver all those inline logos.

Rich Wiggins, CWIS Coordinator, Michigan State University

Date: Tue, 23 Aug 94 13:45:43 -0600
From: Paul Ginsparg 505-667-7353 <ginsparg@qfwfq.lanl.gov>

> I agree the gopher/www quibbling is trivial

as was pointed out in message you just forwarded -- that whole discussion has been carried out through a multi-hundred message thread on comp.infosystems.gopher and comp.infosystems.www (probably still continues).

(although again misses that "in-line" logos are not necessary to www servers, they are a choice -- and i was careful to make them purely elective for everything i did, which included checking that everything worked fine from a vt100 using lynx, so that my less well-off colleagues are not left behind).

but it all remains irrelevant to the issue of costs of journals that we try to focus on -- whatever the final delivery protocol (and it may in five years be something other than what we have now, though most likely some generalization that encompasses it). but as you frequently point out, i'm here "preaching to the converted."

Paul Ginsparg

Date: Mon, 22 Aug 94 08:45:39 EDT
From: Janet Fisher <FISHER@MITVMA.BitNet>
Subject: Odlyzko on Net Capacity and Citation Frequency

It has been interesting to read Bernard Naylor's responses to the "Esoteric Publication" discussion, as well as the comments on his comments. They triggered some questions in my mind which I would like to pose.

If authors were to be charged for access to the eyes of the audience rather than readers for subscriptions, where would this money come from? The university's research budget? The library's materials budget? The government? If the university, how much publication would the available money allow for the university's faculty members? Would it be enough? It would be interesting to take some sample universities of various sizes, look at the relevant budget areas that might be applied to publication of "esoteric" research and determine if that amount would cover the amount of publication being done by that faculty. How much per page would that allow?

Regarding the lack of information about number of times an article is cited, I wonder if there is information from Paul Ginsparg about how many times articles in HEPnet are looked at, and how many times they are downloaded? What are the typical numbers? What is the pattern of usage? What percentage occurs in the first year of publication, and what percentage occurs in the second and third years after "publication"? What do we know about long-term usage?

I believe that the number of times cited is not entirely a measure of the article's usefulness or interest to the community. It seems like often researchers would review an article but not cite it in their own research because it is not exactly on point to the current argument. That doesn't mean the article is of no use to that researcher. Maybe I'm being naive...

I think it would be helpful to get as much concrete data as possible. Especially about where the money for these author charges is likely to come from if subscription charges are done away with for "esoteric" publications. Is that money there? If not, will authors pay out of their own pockets?

Janet Fisher
MIT Press

Date: Wed, 24 Aug 94 19:25:47 EDT
From: "Stevan Harnad" <harnad@princeton.edu>

Here is another long-distance reply from Paul Ginsparg at Les Houches. Henceforth I will refer to his archive as the "Los Alamos Physics E-Print Archive," because, as he indicates, "HEP" (high energy physics) is now far too narrow a descriptor for the scale it has reached in physics. Below, Paul replies to Janet Fisher's questions about usage levels. One VERY important point to note is that these statistics are for what readership levels in esoteric research WOULD be if they were not constrained by the admission price imposed by paper publication and its associated costs and practices.

Stevan Harnad

Date: Wed, 24 Aug 94 16:37:25 -0600
From: Paul Ginsparg 505-667-7353 <ginsparg@qfwfq.lanl.gov>
Subject: Re: Author-Side Electronic Page-Cost Subsidy for Esoteric Publication

> Date: Mon, 22 Aug 94 08:45:39 EDT
> From: Janet Fisher <FISHER@MITVMA.BitNet>
> Subject: Odlyzko on Net Capacity and Citation Frequency

> Regarding the lack of information about number of times an article
> is cited, I wonder if there is information from Paul Ginsparg about
> how many times articles in HEPnet are looked at, and how many times
> they are downloaded?

what is the difference between "look at" and "download"? (in any politically correct client/server environment, one must download in order to peruse -- note that one does not do remote logins, that's why these servers have no problem handling large amounts of traffic)

> What are the typical numbers? What is the
> pattern of usage? What percentage occurs in the first year of
> publication, and what percentage occurs in the second and third
> years after "publication"? What do we know about long-term usage?

indeed i have statistics going back to aug '91 when the original hep-th started (by the way HEPnet is a misnomer [not my terminology], since the e-print archives cover far more than just high energy physics; and moreover HEPnet is the name of the [completely unrelated] high energy physics DECnet that started in the early 80's.)

these statistics are subtle to assess for a variety of reasons. for example, there are places that simply download everything either for local printing or local caching; so there's an automatic lower bound on the number of times these things are accessed, which is not necessarily a measure of readership. but on the other hand this distributed access (including remote photocopying) means that many papers are significantly undercounted. then there are papers whose initial submission may have had some technical processing problem, corrected by a quick replacement, and hence had many 2nd requests for a viewable version. and many people tend to use these papers as a substitute for memory -- i.e. they know a paper with a particular equation so get it just for that equation then delete it (does that count as reading?). and so on.

nonetheless some trends emerge. the bottom line paper gets about 50 requests -- we can call that the noise level. then there are the typical popular papers which get a few hundred requests, and finally there is the extremely popular ("delta function" papers that appear once every month or so, i.e. at the < .5% level, typically review or other submissions of broad cross-disciplinary interest) that instantly get a few hundred requests (i.e. in the first day after submission) and asymptote in the many hundreds or near a thousand.

finally, and perhaps most surprisingly, is that papers back to '91 (i.e. long since published) remain frequently accessed (i.e. roughly 75% of the submissions dating to '91 were accessed at least once in '94 -- and a quick check just indicated that many of these were accessed in the past two months), another indication that people find the electronic format an easier means of access than physical access to a library. (and why the vilification of high energy physicists as interested in papers at most a few nanoseconds old is so absurd).

but for the aforementioned reasons, it is dangerous to try to read too much from this data (in particular as well due to continued growth of these systems, and attendant change in habits). finally it is awkward for me to go into much greater detail since i am accessing from remote (still in french alps) til mid-sept.

Paul Ginsparg

XVI.   The Collapse of Traditional Journals

Frank Quinn, a mathematician at the Virginia Polytechnic Institute and State University and a member of various American Mathematical Society decision-making committees, adds a further voice foreseeing radical change to the discussion.

Date: Thu, 25 Aug 1994 11:46:16 -0400
To: cpub@math.ams.org
From: quinn@math.vt.edu (Frank Quinn)
Subject: electronic pub. in physics

Consequences of Electronic Publication in Theoretical Physics

Frank Quinn
quinn@math.vt.edu

The development of electronic scholarly communication as a whole is still impossible to forecast. Theoretical physics, however, is further along in this development and definite trends are taking shape. The purpose of this note is to describe some of the trends, and some things to watch for in the future. Some of the changes, and some of the mechanisms, are special to physics. Nonetheless this is an illuminating "natural experiment" with important lessons for science and scholarship in general.

===The collapse of traditional journals ===

It is widely expected that by 2010 the bulk of scholarly communication will be electronic. The wild success of new access tools suggests it may happen sooner (note 1). But in any case it will definitely happen much sooner in physics: a powerful mechanism is set to act. There is steady erosion of journal subscriptions due to pressure on library budgets. Cuts have to be made, and librarians are very concerned that they cause as little damage as possible. They are aware of the physics preprint databases, and at the first sign of weakness in the defense of physics journals they will beginning cutting them preferentially. The argument will be: "you really don't use the paper versions, and you have other, easier, access to the information. It is appropriate that we cut physics in order to protect backward areas which would really be disadvantaged by the loss of paper." (note 2)

   This argument suggests a sudden decline in subscriptions in the next two to five years (depending largely on library financial problems). Some journals may reconfigure in electronic form, but the termination of the revenue stream will mean most of them will just die. After this happens most transactions in physics will take place through the preprint databases. These databases should remain essentially the same as they are now, except for advances in access tools. (note 3).

=== The advent of hypertext ===

A very significant new development is the addition of hypertext capabilities. Paul Ginsparg and others have developed tools which, with very little additional effort for authors, allow active references: selecting the reference on screen immediately calls up a copy of the other paper (note 4). For this the paper being referred to must reside in an electronic database, and the URL must be added to the reference. This is a dramatic and very attractive increase in functionality (note 1), and will have many consequences.

The first consequence of the new functionality is that papers not in the database will be cited less frequently, and citations will obviously result in less-frequent retrieval of the paper. This reinforces the motivation to put papers into the database, so use will become more universal. There may also be a "filling out" of the archive as authors add older papers to encourage citation and to use self-citation as a way to lead readers to them. Both of these trends will accelerate the collapse of the paper journals.

Another consequence of hypertext citation is that readers will access papers without knowing where they are, or whether or not they have been published. Even if they have been published the hypertext link will frequently be to preprints, and any modifications made to final printed versions will be lost. In particular the prestige and quality filtering aspects of the traditional publication process will be hidden or lost. These factors will certainly reduce interest in, and benefits of, the traditional process.

A final consequence of hypertext citations has not yet arrived, but will provide another big advance in functionality. This is automatic forward referencing. It will be trivial to invert citations, and for each paper maintain a list of the papers which cite it. This will be a powerful tool for exploring the literature. To some extent this can be done now with the Science Citation Index. But it will be far superior to SCI in many ways: data will be available faster; it will give instant access to the citing papers (by hypertext links, if they are in the database); and it will be higher quality since citations containing a URL will not be "lost" because the cited paper cannot be located.

=== Sociological consequences ===

So far there is only anecdotal information about sociological fallout, so the following discussion is more forecast than observation. But it is important to watch this development very closely. It will give us the first glimpse of upheavals soon to be visited on all of science.

The first thing to watch for is a decline in average quality of papers. There already seems to be a trend in this direction (in theoretical physics). It should accelerate as writers no longer worry about being subjected to a refereeing process (note 5). Inevitably, also, cranks and "flamers" will find the databases. Some filtering may be instituted to eliminate the worst offenders, but it will have to be minimal since there is no mechanism to pay for careful review.

The reactions to the decline in quality will be very revealing. With the loss of peer review as the first line of defense, the main literature-level opportunities for quality control will be selective citations and review articles. At present the custom is to cite all (known) previous work on a subject. Will this change? Will authors refuse to dignify defective papers with a citation? Or will they give a "dead" reference which does not link to the defective work, and does not show up in citation data? Review articles which sift and consolidate the primary literature are likely to become more important for quality control. "Acceptance" for citation in a major review article may serve as a replacement for acceptance in a journal.

The next thing to watch is the impact on the "reward structure." Currently there are still plenty of submissions to physics journals, presumably because "credit" is still attached to formal publication. Candidates for promotion are certainly still concerned about this. What will happen when the journals have thinned out enough so that fewer than 50% of physics papers can be published? Probably new "impact indicators" will emerge (note 6). The best candidates for such indicators are citation data, though this will bring a new set of problems (note 7).

Other adaptations to watch for are changes in work habits. Some of this is specialized to theoretical physics, and lessons from it will not be universal. Many theoretical physicists think of themselves more in terms of analytical skills than a specific subject. They are not anchored to a specific topic (by equipment, for instance), and from time to time change to different topics accessible to their skills (note 8). On a social level this shows up as "fads" in which areas are tremendously popular for a while and then are abandoned. Will lower quality mean that fads pass more quickly (note 9)? Or will the overhead of having to sort through more trash slow down the process?

=== Conclusion ===

Bernard Naylor has written:

> "We are now seriously contemplating the most dramatic change in the
> working habits of scholars for some centuries, but I look in vain
> for convincing signs that our sector appreciates this and is
> collectively bending its mind to preparing for the consequences."

These words may haunt us in the next decade. It seems to be too late for theoretical physics to "bend minds and prepare," and this is somewhat foreign to the physics mind-set anyway. But the rest of the scholarly enterprise has much to learn by watching these bold pioneers, and may yet be able to prepare for the consequences.

NOTES

1) The new tools, particularly http and Mosaic, seem to be dramatically more attractive to users, and usage is exploding. See Science v.265 (12 August 1994) pp.895-901.

2) Bernard Naylor (Univ. Librarian, U. Southampton) has noted that so far physics journals are still being defended against cuts. (He is obviously watching, though). Paul Ginsparg (LANL) replied that it is still a bit early, but he expects a shift in the next few years. It may also be that Naylor is not distinguishing between theoretical and experimental physics: the change of attitude will come first in the theoretical areas.

3) Naylor has suggested that the impending demise of journals may trigger changes in the Net to "level the playing field" and allow commercial journals to compete "on an equal footing." This is unlikely to make any difference. Ginsparg has already demonstrated that it is politically impossible to close down the preprint database. The argument against closure will strengthen as journal numbers and access declines. Access charges might conceivably be instituted, but since there are no processing expenses in a preprint database, the charges would be far below what would be required to support a traditional journal. In fact access charges would accelerate the process. Subscriptions to the database would certainly be necessary and this would make it even less attractive to also pay for journals containing essentially the same information.

4) For information about the hypertext tools see the following URL: http://xxx.lanl.gov/hypertex/

5) Stevan Harnad refers to good-quality writing resulting from the anticipation of being reviewed as the "invisible hand" of the reviewing process. In other words, reviewing is a "pump" as well as a "filter."

6)   Theoretical computer scientists seem to have had some success in convincing deans and employers to accept non-traditional indicators of impact.   In particular an abstract in the right conference proceedings is more prestigious than a refereed paper in a journal.

7)   We may see promotion documents offering "245 total citations, including 33 from the Institute for Advanced Study, and two in a review article written by a Harvard professor" as evidence of quality.   Unfortunately there are enormous and obvious opportunities for abuse of any such system.

8)   There is concrete evidence that this characterization by skills rather than subject is correct: financial institutions have found that PhD training in theoretical physics is very effective preparation for sophisticated economic analysis.

9)   Quality problems probably play a role in the "fad" phenomenon. As errors and guesses accumulate in theoretical analysis a point is reached where further work is pointless.   The area is then abandoned by theorists until it can be cleaned up by more compulsive life-forms like experimentalists, mathematicians, and "distillers" (see Herring, "Distill or drown: the need for reviews," Physics Today 21 No.9 (1968) pp. 27-33).

[My comments on Frank Quinn's "Consequences of Electronic Publication in Theoretical Physics" are followed by some comments by Paul Ginsparg. -Stevan Harnad]

> Date: Thu, 25 Aug 1994 11:46:16 -0400
> To: cpub@math.ams.org
> From: quinn@math.vt.edu (Frank Quinn)
>
> Some [paper] journals may reconfigure in electronic form, but the
> termination of the revenue stream will mean most of them will just die.
> After this happens most transactions in physics will take place through
> the preprint databases. These databases should remain essentially the
> same as they are now, except for advances in access tools. (note 3).

I must unfortunately disagree entirely with both of these predictions. The termination of paper publication need NOT mean the death of many or most refereed paper journals. These need only reconfigure (at much lower cost, and on the author-side subsidy model, rather than the trade model) as refereed electronic journals. There are already many ab ovo refereed electronic journals starting up currently; there is no reason to believe that taking to the skies will not be a preferable option to being interred for paper journals that can no longer make ends meet in paper. It is hard to imagine, in this era of information explosion in science and scholarship, that information-sources will prefer to implode rather than simply switch media!

The second point is related to this (and "peer review" is the key word linking the two): I am an enormous admirer of the electronic preprinting initiative in physics (mostly arising from the efforts of Paul Ginsparg), but I have to keep reminding everyone that this initiative is COMPLETELY PARASITIC at the present time on the (so far intact) paper flotilla, for which all these prepublication goods are ultimately intended. It is what I have called the "Invisible Hand" of that flotilla, namely, peer review, under which virtually all of these papers are destined to pass, that ensures the quality of what appears in the electronic archives -- and not just AFTER it has been refereed (when the authors of course quietly swap the refereed reprint for the preprint in the e-print archive) but even BEFORE, for all these papers are written with the expectation and intention (and necessity) of being submitted to peer-reviewed journals.

Human nature is such that if you were to pull that peer-control mechanism out from under this system quality would drop radically (just as Quinn predicts it would), but Quinn is simply wrong that peer review will be absent from the Net: Why on earth should it be? It is a completely medium-independent means of controlling the quality of human output. Just as the papers themselves migrate to the Net, so will peer review.

Having now challenged these two predictions (that the literature will simply shrink as paper journals die, rather than migrating to the Net, and that papers on the Net will just constitute a vast, unrefereed preprint archive, rather than the usual hierarchy of refereed journals, as in paper), let us see how the rest of the analysis fares.

> There may also be a "filling out" of the archive as authors add older
> papers to encourage citation and to use self-citation as a way to lead
> readers to them. Both of these trends will accelerate the collapse of
> the paper journals.

The electronic archive will indeed "fill out" with the rest of the retrospective paper corpus that is worth recreating electronically, but not because of citation and self-citation motives but for scholarly/scientific reasons: I want and need the prior literature at my beck and call on the Net just as I want and need the current literature. All those incommensurable "value-added" features that the Net, with its speed, scope, interactivity and global interwebbing, provides for preprints, it can also provide for reprints, and offprints (and out-of-prints) of paper provenance.

> Another consequence of hypertext citation is that readers will access
> papers without knowing where they are, or whether or not they have been
> published. Even if they have been published the hypertext link will
> frequently be to preprints, and any modifications made to final printed
> versions will be lost. In particular the prestige and quality filtering
> aspects of the traditional publication process will be hidden or lost.
> These factors will certainly reduce interest in, and benefits of, the
> traditional process.

This, if I might be permitted to point it out, is a rather circular prophecy: Once one has prophesied that peer review will not migrate to the Net (without giving any reason why not), it quite safely follows that quality and discriminability will decline. But is it not much more reasonable to suppose that peer review WILL migrate to the Net along with the journals themselves, and that it is trivially easy to devise a CODING system that will not only distinguish whether a paper is a preprint or a refereed reprint, but exactly where in the journal prestige hierarchy (corresponding to the rigor of the peer review each journal can be counted on to provide) a particular article is located? Such a prestige hierarchy currently exists in paper: Is there any reason it cannot take to the skies too?

> The first thing to watch for is a decline in average quality of papers.
> There already seems to be a trend in this direction (in theoretical
> physics). It should accelerate as writers no longer worry about being
> subjected to a refereeing process (note 5). Inevitably, also, cranks and
> "flamers" will find the databases. Some filtering may be instituted to
> eliminate the worst offenders, but it will have to be minimal since there
> is no mechanism to pay for careful review.

These are excellent Darwinian reasons why, if the Divine Hand of peer review does not (for some reason) see fit to rise with it as the paper flotilla takes to the skies, then It will simply have to be re-invented up there.

> The reactions to the decline in quality will be very revealing. With
> the loss of peer review as the first line of defense, the main
> literature-level opportunities for quality control will be selective
> citations and review articles... "Acceptance" for citation in a major
> review article may serve as a replacement for acceptance in a journal.

I do not believe for a minute, even in our absurdly populist age, that a popularity contest and box scores can or will replace the systematic scrutiny administered by editors and referees (imperfect as that is; see bibliography appended to these comments). Powerful electro-bibliometric analysis is a supplement, not a substitute, for peer review.

> The next thing to watch is the impact on the "reward structure." Currently
> there are still plenty of submissions to physics journals, presumably
> because "credit" is still attached to formal publication. Candidates for
> promotion are certainly still concerned about this. What will happen when
> the journals have thinned out enough so that fewer than 50% of physics
> papers can be published? Probably new "impact indicators" will emerge (note
> 6). The best candidates for such indicators are citation data, though this
> will bring a new set of problems (note 7).

The present "impact indicators" are certainly insufficient, and the Net will indeed provide many valuable and informative supplements, including dynamic citation analysis, forward and backward, and probably even more sophisticated bibliometric measures of "air time" and "mileage" in the increasingly transparent and measurable embryology of knowledge. But up there with the other indicators will be the perfectly classical one, inherited from bygone paper days, namely, the altitude in the prestige hierarchy of the peer reviewed journal in which the paper was accepted. And the busy, rational lector will always be able to calibrate that all too finite reading time -- the difference will be that that that quality-tagged information will now be infinitely more easily accessible, once the lector has decide how to set those information filters.

> 3) Naylor has suggested that the impending demise of journals may trigger
> changes in the Net to "level the playing field" and allow commercial
> journals to compete "on an equal footing". This is unlikely to make any
> difference. Ginsparg has already demonstrated that it is politically
> impossible to close down the preprint database. The argument against
> closure will strengthen as journal numbers and access declines. Access
> charges might conceivably be instituted, but since there are no processing
> expenses in a preprint database, the charges would be far below what would
> be required to support a traditional journal. In fact access charges would
> accelerate the process. Subscriptions to the database would certainly be
> necessary, and this would make it even less attractive to also pay for
> journals containing essentially the same information.

I continue to preach, patiently, that the trade model is not, and never was appropriate for no-market esoteric writing and reading. The true per-page costs of a fully quality-controlled (edited, peer-reviewed, copy-edited) ELECTRONIC literature will be so low compared to paper (less than 25% according to my estimate -- which of course becomes no more accurate by dint of my repeating it) that it will make much more sense for the institutions (Universities, Research Funding Agencies, Research Libraries) that currently support and subsidize scholarly and scientific research by paying huge research library costs to instead subsidize these minimal electronic page-charges up front, making the product -- the esoteric corpus -- free for all. There is absolutely no reason for many journals, or for peer review itself, to disappear in this transition. Quality control need only be re-implemented in the new medium. (And there is no reason at all why the traditional scholarly publishers should not likewise reconfigure to make them themselves skyworthy too, in this new, rescaled, nontrade model for esoteric scholarly publishing.)

> 5) Stevan Harnad refers to good-quality writing resulting from the
> anticipation of being reviewed as the "invisible hand" of the reviewing
> process. In other words, reviewing is a "pump" as well as a "filter".

Not just good quality writing, but also good quality research, and reports you know you can trust (or trust as much as you could in paper).

Stevan Harnad
Professor of Psychology
Director, Cognitive Sciences Centre
Department of Psychology
University of Southampton
SO17 1BJ UNITED KINGDOM

harnad@ecs.soton.ac.uk harnad@princeton.edu
phone: +44 703 592582

Date: Thu, 25 Aug 94 16:16:53 -0600
From: Paul Ginsparg 505-667-7353 <ginsparg@qfwfq.lanl.gov>

> From: quinn@calvin.math.vt.edu (Frank Quinn)
> Subject: electronic pub. in physics

> A final consequence of hypertext citations has not yet arrived, but will
> provide another big advance in functionality. This is automatic forward
> referencing. It will be trivial to invert citations, and for each paper
> maintain a list of the papers which cite it. This will be a powerful tool
> for exploring the literature.

actually this has already been on-line for a while, courtesy of the spires-hep database maintained by the slac library. if you bring up the abstract view of an e-print from one of hep-th et al on the www interface, there is a link to "cited by" which brings up a list of papers that cite it (and the ones that are available electronically -- typically almost all for papers submitted in the past two years -- automatically appear as hyperlinks into the database).

> === Sociological consequences ===

my main comment here is that my stance re the utility of peer review is frequently misunderstood. we are aiming for a system in which much *more* stringent standards are applied, so that the truly significant is easily distinguished from the very good, average, irrelevant, and just plain wrong. my point has long been that the current journal system with its all-or-nothing accept or reject does not play that role, and hence we manifestly lose nothing by abandoning it. (i speak here of course of the much-maligned theoretical physics literature, and speaking of subversion many of its practitioners are as critical of its overall quality as is frank q.) the ultimate plan is to adopt a much more flexible system, with far more precise tools for extracting signal from noise. since this "experiment" is being conducted in a global goldfish bowl, details will be visible before too long (but not til i'm back from abroad).

Paul Ginsparg

XVII. Systemic and Structural Costs -- Networks & Connectivity

A wider context for costs is invoked. How cheap will the infrastructure be? How expensive is a good network? Will universities and scholars have to pay more? How much?

Date: Mon, 5 Sep 1994 11:21:30 EDT
From: Ann Okerson <ann@org.cni>
To: Multiple recipients of list VPIEJ-L <VPIEJ-L@BITNET.VTVM1>

The 12 August 1994 issue of the prestigious journal SCIENCE (of the AAAS organization in Washington, DC) carries a special section of articles on electronic networks/computing and science (pp. 879-914). It's worth a look for its generally upbeat overview of the kinds of important activities that broad-based network communications are facilitating and enhancing.

It is the lead article, "Culture Shock on the Networks," that reminds one of the recent "subversive" discussions here, though. The subtitle is, "An influx of new users and cultures could threaten the Internet's tradition of open information exchange, while commercialization is raising fears that pricing changes will squeeze e-mail and database browsing." The article expands on these themes and what it says is true: large economic and political forces *and* enormous growth are pressuring the system we have known, a system which is beginning a period of great change. We do not know what the future NII will look like.

Quoted is Rick Weingarten, executive director of the Computing Research Association here in DC and a strong advocate of the public interest. "What's the life expectancy of the culture of open information exchange if users have to pay a toll for every byte they send [NB: which, btw, is indeed the position of a number of publishing spokespeople]? ... We have to make sure that some public space is preserved. Otherwise, research, education, museums, and libraries really could get trampled."

"There is tremendous distrust and worry in the community about how this all working out," says Scott Shenker of the Xerox Palo Alto Research Center (PARC), who feels that some sort of usage pricing is inevitable.

The period of transition does indeed raises many such concerns and makes me, for one, less than sanguine that the indefinite continuation of the freely accessible world that Harnad, Ginsparg, Odlyzko, etc. imagine is much assured. If such access is not continued, then things will simply cost a whole lot more than all the projections -- which I want to believe but feel are somewhat unrealistic. It is important that we not only *use* the Internet for new ways of communicating research and scholarship and ideas, but that we also participate, however we can, in the telecommunications policy debates at whatever level we are able, so that widespread, cheap use can easily continue. The government doesn't just do things on its own -- it R US and the more voices that keep saying it, the better for the education, science, scholarly and library community.

Ann Okerson/Association of Research Libraries
ann@cni.org

Date: Mon, 5 Sep 1994 13:01:44 -0400
From: quinn@edu.vt.math.calvin (Frank Quinn)

Dear Andrew,

Thanks for your comments. I would like to reply to two of your remarks. First, you write:

> . . . you neglect the countervailing trends that are already visible. Peer
> review evolved to meet a real need. This need will continue to exist,
> and some mechanism will be set up to meet this need on the Net. The
> only question, in my opinion, is what this mechanism will be.

I quite agree with this. Our difference is in time scales. You have remarked that you tend to think of what the future might look like in 20 years. I concentrate on the next 10. I have no doubt that some mechanism will evolve. But if we simply let nature take its course there will be an unpleasant period AFTER the present system has declined, and we become acutely aware of the needs met by peer review, and BEFORE a replacement is in place. Two comments: the simple fact that it is unclear what mechanism will develop means it will be at least 10 years before it can be in place and credible. Maybe more like 20. The other comment is that evolution is a response to a change in environment. Relying on evolution commits us to feeling the pain before we begin to adapt. So my point is that we should be proactive to try to minimize the discomfort of the transition.

You also write:

> A final point I would like to make is related to Paul [Ginsparg]'s comment
> that with electronic publications we should aim "for a system in

> which much *more* stringent standards are applied." It is hard
> to overemphasize the inadequacies of the present system.

and go on to discuss some of these inadequacies. Please remember that not all areas are the same in this regard. Paul has been quite open that the peer review system in his area has no credibility, and is so weak that dispensing with it would be little loss. I have had some contact with his area, and this is also my impression. So indeed ANYTHING he can do will be "much *more* stringent." This is certainly not the case in topology, and is really wrong in the most stringent area I have had contact with, algebra. These areas have a whole lot to lose.

I wonder, from your comments, if your field is more like theoretical physics than algebra in the effectiveness of quality control. Or perhaps you have not had enough contact with physics literature to appreciate what a real breakdown looks like. Anyway I urge you not to generalize too much from experiences in physics and psychology.

Best regards, Frank

From: "B.Naylor" <B.Naylor@uk.ac.soton>
Date: Mon, 5 Sep 1994 18:15:21 +0100 (BST)

I'm interested to see that the question of charging for the use of the INTERNET has popped up again. I have to say that if it does once again go away it will only be temporary. I don't think that the argument about the flea on the tail of the dog will eventually carry decisive weight. From the way that dogs behave, I get the impression that they're well aware that fleas are about and they're going to "make them pay," in their case by some pretty fundamental disturbance.

One of the reasons why some librarians are perhaps more phlegmatic about this prospect is that we have been paying for online access to some journals (namely, secondary sources such as indexing and abstracting tools) for twenty years or more. We have already made the migration from an exclusively pay as you use or just in time tariff framework, to one which (via CD-ROM etc) allows us to mix pay as you use and pay up front (just in case) in accordance with what we perceive as our best interests, and the best interests of our users. We have even been paying for some information sources (e.g., in the field of law) which are crucial primary sources and not available in any other form except the electronic form, for about fifteen years. It's not clear to me why the growth (dramatic, I agree) in our ability to access information over the networks should be predicated on an assumption of a change in cost recovery practices which are already quite well established over more than a decade, albeit in a relatively small (but very important) part of the sector.

While I am on the ether, could I revert to the question of esoteric versus trade-scholarly, on which there has been some previous discussion? One factor making for differences in the debate between those on the two opposite sides of the pond is the great difference in the number of current journals taken. For example, the University of Wisconsin takes something like seven or eight times as many journals currently as the University of Southampton (something like 45,000 as against 6,000 according to the most recent figures I have seen). And many other big American research libraries are in the twenty odd or thirty odd thousand current subscriptions range. So it wouldn't surprise me if they carry a lot more esoteric material by comparison with their trade-scholarly accessions than we do. Certainly, not all our journals are used as heavily as the protestations of some of our scholars at the prospect of their cancellation might imply. But we are too inclined to forget this pretty stark difference between the big American research libraries (like Princeton I would guess, though they didn't cite their number of current journals in the source I used).

Another important concept that has to be weighed in this discussion (as I have mentioned in previous papers I have given) is the concept of redundancy. One simple way of pointing it up runs as follows: "If all papers worth publishing are to get published, it is inevitable that some papers not worth publishing will get published." The redundancy principle works in lots of walks of life (hospital beds, seats on trains etc etc); it is a factor of the human condition. The point that follows is that the esoteric papers should not be in any way separated off from the others; they constitute an essential part of the whole scholarly context. One should no more do that than one should say: "We'll have two constituencies of theatre, one where only the plays that are going to survive down the years will get mounted, the other for the rest."

One of the essential filtering processes will be: what are people prepared to pay for?

Bernard Naylor

From: Stevan Harnad (harnad@soton.ac.uk

I disagree with Bernard on the same points that have come up before, so I will try to put it differently so as not to repeat myself:

> From: "B.Naylor" <B.Naylor@uk.ac.soton>
>
> One of the reasons why some librarians are perhaps more phlegmatic
> about this prospect is that we have been paying for online access to
> some journals (namely, secondary sources such as indexing and
> abstracting tools) for twenty years or more... It's not clear to
> me why the growth (dramatic, I agree) in our ability to access
> information over the networks should be predicated on an assumption of
> a change in cost recovery practices which are already quite well
> established over more than a decade, albeit in a relatively small (but
> very important) part of the sector.

The fact that we are in the habit of paying for things when we have no
choice is hardly relevant to what we will be inclined to do when we do
have a choice. But I must repeat: text for which there was a paying
market in paper (such as indexing/abstracting tools, which become even
more valuable in electronic form) will continue to have a paying market on
the Net, and there is no reason it should not continue to be sold, on the
classical trade model. (Hence the above example, besides being a
minoritarian outlier in its proportion of the paper corpus, is also highly
unrepresentative.) The issue is text for which there is no paying market,
even on paper; text that the libraries and universities are ALREADY
subsidizing now (but in a highly RubeGoldberg way, with hostage library
budgets).

> "If all papers worth publishing are to get published, it is inevitable
> that some papers not worth publishing will get published." The
> redundancy principle works in lots of walks of life (hospital beds,
> seats on trains etc etc); it is a factor of the human condition. The
> point that follows is that the esoteric papers should not be in any way
> separated off from the others; they constitute an essential part of the
> whole scholarly context. One should no more do that than one should
> say: "We'll have two constituencies of theatre, one where only the
> plays that are going to survive down the years will get mounted, the
> other for the rest."

Unfortunately, as pointed out when this same kind of inference was
made by Frank Quinn, this reasoning is circular. There is very little
correlation between the market-value of scientific/scholarly writing and
its scientific/scholarly value. Hence "esoteric" does not mean of lesser
epistemic value, it just means of lesser MARKET-value. Nor are
redundancy and esotericity that tightly coupled. Most of it may be chaff,
but what's not chaff is not measured by whether it's bought, but by
whether it breeds: whether further knowledge is built on it. And the
principle (if it's true, and it probably is) that we must be prepared to
countenance a high chaff/wheat ratio in all fields of human endeavor in

order to ensure the inevitable proportion of wheat -- again suggests that something other than market indicators might be desirable here.

> One of the essential filtering processes will be: what are people
> prepared to pay for?

Indeed; and the likes of myself will always be looking out for the fate of what people are NOT prepared to pay for. Fortunately, we have in the skies a much stronger potential ally than in the Faustian medium of the paper trade...

Stevan Harnad

From: amo@com.att.research (Andrew Odlyzko)
Date: Mon, 5 Sep 94 20:52 EDT
Subject: Science article

I agree with [Stevan Harnad's] three claims, all of which say that Ann Okerson's alarm is not justified. The article in the August 12 issue of Science that Ann cites is rather confused on the two factors that are leading to changes in the way Internet is run: (a) participation of commercial organizations, and (b) growth of multimedia services (including Mosaic usage as well as the more exotic videoconferencing). It is factor (b) that is much more likely to force institution of a pricing scheme because of its dramatically higher bandwidth requirements. A better discussion than in the Science article of why this is so, and what kind of pricing schemes might be adopted can be found in

> MacKie-Mason, J.K. and H. R. Varian, Some economics of the
> Internet, in "Networks, Infrastructure and the New Task for
> Regulation}, W. Sichel, ed., to appear. (Available via gopher or
> ftp together with other related papers from
> gopher.econ.lsa.umich.edu in /pub/Papers.)

Some simple back-of-the-envelope calculations show that the fears that Ann and some of the experts quoted in Science express about the Internet being priced out of the reach of scholars are baseless. Reasonable videoconferencing systems run at about 400 kilobits per second. This is about 50,000 bytes per second, or 200 MB (megabytes) per hours. Now a typical paper is somewhere between 250,000 bytes (uncompressed PostScript) and 20,000 bytes (compressed TeX). In any case, the transmission of a one-hour videoconference takes about as much capacity as the transmission of between 1,000 and 10,000 papers. Further, as the Science article does point out, the videoconference transmission cannot tolerate any significant delays, whereas paper transmission can. Thus any rational pricing scheme will require substantially higher payments per byte for videoconferencing with a service guarantee than for a "best-effort" paper transmission that might be delayed by minutes. Thus we can expect that transmitting a paper might cost 1/10,000 or even 1/1,000,000 of the cost of a one-hour videoconference. (Some of the schemes discussed in [MacKieV] involve fees only for services with a service guarantee, which would let most scholarly communication go through for free.) However, videoconferencing cannot cost too much, or else it won't be used. Therefore scholarly electronic communication will have trivial costs.

We might have charges based on bytes transmitted, as opposed to capacity of the link to the Internet, but if so, the charge per byte will be so small as not to merit attention, at least for the kinds of transmissions that are required for publishing of today's scholarly literature (*). If your department gets charged for each word you write with a pen the department provides, would it affect how much scratch paper you filled with your jottings, if the total charge for a few months' work still came to the $1 cost of a cartridge refill?

Andrew Odlyzko

(*) The arguments above apply only to traditional publications, since that is all that is relevant in evaluating the feasibility of electronic versus print journals. Scholars will surely avail themselves of the novel services, such as videoconferences, and presumably their usage of such will be rationed by price. We can already see substantial loads on the network generated by genetic and astronomy data. Even mathematicians are becoming bandwidth hogs. For example, I cited the average paper as being 20,000 bytes in compressed form. However, my colleague David Applegate has now made available on the Internet proofs of the optimality of some Traveling Salesman Tours (an important combinatorial optimization problem he has been working on with collaborators across the country) that are 20 MB each, even in compressed form! (These proofs are not made to be checked by people, only by computers.) There will surely be many more such cases, as scholars do things electronically that are not possible in print. Technical and economic constraints will always be present, it's just that they have moved far enough away to enable print journals to be replaced by electronic ones at much lower cost.

From: amo@com.att.research (Andrew Odlyzko)
Date: Mon, 5 Sep 94 21:51 EDT
To: quinn@edu.vt.math.calvin
Subject: Re: electronic pub. in physics

I don't think [Frank Quinn and I] differ much on what should be done. I agree with [Frank] completely that "we should be proactive to try to minimize the discomfort of the transition." However, the picture [Frank] presented in "Consequences of electronic publication in Theoretical Physics" seemed to be too bleak. Even if indeed the trends [Frank] describe[s] do continue uninterrupted in theoretical physics, without any counter-vailing forces coming into play, it's not clear how much that means for other areas, such as mathematics. [Frank himself] says that the refereeing system in theoretical physics is broken. If we accept that, then it is no wonder that there is no great rush to set up a rigorous system for electronic publication in that field. I do not think that mathematicians, say, should allow that to happen, and I have been arguing for an even more rigorous standard for e-journals.

I will spend a bit more time on [Frank's] second point:

ao> A final point I would like to make is related to Paul [Ginsparg]'s
ao> comment that with electronic publications we should aim "for a system
ao> in which much *more* stringent standards are applied." It is hard to
ao> overemphasize the inadequacies of the present system.

fq> and go on to discuss some of these inadequacies. Please remember that
fq> not all areas are the same in this regard. Paul has been quite open
fq> that the peer review system in his area has no credibility, and is so
fq> weak that dispensing with it would be little loss. I have had some
fq> contact with his area, and this is also my impression. So indeed
fq> ANYTHING he can do will be "much *more* stringent". This is certainly
fq> not the case in topology, and is really wrong in the most stringent
fq> area I have had contact with, algebra. These areas have a whole lot
fq> to lose.

fq> I wonder, from your comments, if your field is more like theoretical
fq> physics than algebra in the effectiveness of quality control. Or
fq> perhaps you have not had enough contact with physics literature to
fq> appreciate what a real breakdown looks like. Anyway I urge you not to
fq> generalize too much from experiences in physics and psychology.

It is true that I have not had too much contact with physics literature, but what I had did not inspire me with any confidence in its editorial and refereeing system. However, all the areas I have worked in (and there are quite a few, such as number theory, cryptology, probability theory, combinatorics, and a few others) have very stringent standards as to correctness. I would venture to guess their standards are at least as high as for algebra, at least for journal articles. (Some of these areas do use conference proceedings extensively, but those are recognized as not being as reliable as journals, even when they do become the dominant mode of communication.) The journals I cited as examples ("Discrete Mathematics," "J. Combinatorial Theory," and "Codes, Designs, and Cryptography") are all in discrete mathematics, and all have stringent refereeing standards. Very few of their papers are incorrect. When I complained about "the inadequacies of the present system," I chose these journals precisely because they contain rigorously checked results. My point was that they fail to provide the signals as to significance of their results that are often touted as a great advantage of print journals (this claim is usually followed by the non-sequitur claim that therefore e-journals cannot replace print ones). Because of specialization (journals engage in "monopolistic competition," as economists call it), it is seldom that two journals are strictly comparable, and so the information that one can derive from where an article is published is "noisy."

Andrew Odlyzko

From: Ann Okerson <ann@org.cni>
Subject: Re: Network Management
To: amo@com.att.research
Date: Mon, 5 Sep 1994 23:00:31 -0400 (EDT)

Andrew [Odlyzko wrote:]

> I agree with [Stevan Harnad's] three claims, all of which say that Ann
> Okerson's alarm is not justified. The article in the August 12 issue of
> Science that Ann cites is rather confused on the two factors that are
> leading to changes in the way Internet is run: (a) participation of
> commercial organizations, and (b) growth of multimedia services
> (including Mosaic usage as well as the more exotic videoconferencing).
> It is factor (b) that is much more likely to force institution of a
> pricing scheme because of its dramatically higher bandwidth
> requirements.

The SCIENCE article made both points, but with respect to [Andrew's] (a) it is not participation of commercial organizations but the fact that the government/NSF is getting out of the network support business pretty much. They are continuing the process of handing the networks over to commercial organizations, a move which will be finished by next April. Both (a) and (b) will be influential, or at least that is a view widely shared by policy makers and folks throughout the public interest sector here. SCIENCE is reporting that, not creating the concern.

Ann Okerson

From: Stevan Harnad (harnad@soton.ac.uk)

Steve Goldstein can correct me if I am wrong about this, but my understanding is that the NSF is now supplying only 10% of the cost of the backbone; when the Universities, which now pay 90% take this on, it will accordingly amount to 10% more than what they pay now. Because of the nature of network transmission, they have not found it necessary to pass on these costs to individual users so far, and I doubt that the additional 10% will change matters. It is indeed, as Andrew Odlyzko has aptly suggested, somewhat analogous to charging for ink used per word...

Stevan Harnad

From: Stevan Harnad <harnad@ecs.soton.ac.uk>
Date: Tue, 6 Sep 94 18:31:34 BST
Subject: Re: Naylor on Paying the Piper

Bernard Naylor <B.Naylor@uk.ac.soton>, quoting me, wrote:

> Subject: Re: Naylor on Paying the Piper
> Date: Tue, 6 Sep 1994 09:58:17 +0100 (BST)
>
sh> The issue is text for which there is no paying market, even on paper;
sh> text that the libraries and universities are ALREADY subsidizing now
sh> (but in a highly Rube-Goldberg way, with hostage library budgets).
>
bn> This is an interesting use of the concept of "subsidy". I doubt whether
bn> the purchase of academic journals by libraries has any elements
bn> amounting to subsidy which economists could not point out are readily
bn> perceivable in other settings where goods with "value" are acquired in
bn> return for payment. If academe has a false sense of values in respect
bn> of journals (or some journals), then it should set about correcting
bn> that - as there are some tentative signs it is in the process of
bn> starting to do.
>
sh> There is very little correlation between the market-value of

sh> scientific/scholarly writing and its scientific/scholarly value.
sh> Hence "esoteric" does not mean of lesser epistemic value, it just
sh> means of lesser MARKET-value.
>
bn> I think the marketeers (who are my paymasters) would not
bn> entertain this assertion for a moment. They would say: "If it's
bn> worth having, it's worth paying for. People who try to deny the
bn> links between valuing something enough to want it and being
bn> prepared to pay for it are just trying to have their cake and eat
bn> it." No doubt, they wouldn't claim that everything is correctly
bn> valued in the market place, but they wouldn't see that as any
bn> reason for not letting markets work. On the contrary; they would
bn> say that the operation of the market should be reviewed in order
bn> to make it work better. As you say, the wheat/chaff ratio is a
bn> fact of life in so many areas. Paying for things (or not being
bn> prepared to pay for them) is one way of sorting out the one from
bn> the other which is well established. Naturally, people who write
bn> articles for scientific journals might like to think that this
bn> one area is so different that different processes should apply.
bn> I just don't think the case has been made.

I regret that I must keep disagreeing with my new Southampton colleague before we have even had a chance to meet nonvirtually, but there are two crucial points that are either being systematically misunderstood or have so far managed to escape notice:

(1) I have not for a moment suggested that, when there is something that people want and need that they can and must pay for, they should not or will not. What I am saying is that whereas a circumstance conforming to this did indeed obtain in the case of paper (esoteric scholarly/scientific) periodical publication, it no longer obtains in the electronic-only medium (and to keep speaking or thinking of it as if it did does not make it so; it is simply a failure to take a proper measure of the radically new circumstances): To spell it out: it is the "must" that no longer applies (given the true per-page costs of electronic-only scholarly periodical publication, which I estimate at below 25% percent of the per-page cost in paper). There is now a CHOICE available to the consumer that never existed before. Say whatever you want about market forces, if there is a way to get something (practically) for free, there is nothing (except duress or opacity that will make consumers continue to pay for it. And that brings me to the second crucial point:

(2) Even NOW, in paper, the consumers (i.e., the readers) of the esoteric periodical corpus are NOT the ones paying for it (hence it is with justification that I say that their consumption is ALREADY "subsidized" -- by the university libraries, for the most part). All I am proposing is

that this subsidy would be much more sensibly placed up-front, once the per-page charges shrink to their electronic scale: Let esoteric AUTHORS be subsidized for publishing, rather than esoteric readers for reading. The consequence will be more (and, if properly peer reviewed, better) esoteric publishing and a GREAT deal more esoteric reading (currently constrained by both the cost and the inconvenience of paper). And the entire scholarly/scientific community (as well as humanity as a whole, if you believe that learned inquiry is a good thing) will be the beneficiaries.

Ceterum censeo: market-value is not the proper measure of scholarly value (it's NOT just a matter of weeding out the bad buys among libraries' current periodical acquisition lists!). The essential esotericity of human inquiry is fundamentally at odds with mass-market thinking.

Stevan Harnad

From: amo@com.att.research (Andrew Odlyzko)
Date: Tue, 6 Sep 94 06:52 EDT
To: ann@org.cni (Ann Okerson)
Subject: Network Management

As Stevan has already mentioned in the message he posted a couple of hours ago, the fact that "the government/NSF is getting out of the network support business" does not matter much. Too little money came from that source for it to be the dominant factor. If the Internet were to be occupied just by academic researchers, and there were no dramatic growth in the demand for new services, the present service providers would continue the existing policy of charging by the capacity of the link to the Internet that they provide. The costs of implementing tolls are considerable; the regionals have been doing well with old policies.

The two factors influencing the evolution of the Internet are (to quote from my earlier message)

(a) participation of commercial organizations,
(b) growth of multimedia services (including Mosaic usage as well as the more exotic videoconferencing).

Each is leading to changes. Factor (a) yields a much higher growth rate than would prevail if only academic organizations were involved. It also leads to incidents such as the immigration lawyers' flooding news groups with ads for their services. To prevent that, some sort of access controls might be needed. However, the growth rates for traditional text transmissions from these new commercial entrants to the Internet are not all that dramatic, and might have been accommodated with traditional pricing schemes (by capacity size, or, in terms that librarians use, "just in case"). On the other hand, factor (b) appears to force the introduction of a pricing scheme soon. This would be so even if only academic researchers were involved. The reason is the dramatically higher bandwidth requirements of the new services. The videoconferencing example I cited in last night's message requires 0.4 Mbs (megabits per second). The Internet backbone operated until recently at 45 Mbs and the trans-Atlantic link at 1.5 Mbs (although they have probably both been upgraded by now). Relatively rich institutions have T1 links at 1.5 Mbs, and many poorer ones only 0.056 Mbs. Clearly the infrastructure we have now is not adequate to support videoconferencing on a large scale, and so some sort of control is needed. (There are also fascinating technical issues about congestion controls on networks with multimedia traffic, which require new routing schemes to be developed, but that is another issue.)

I referred to the Science article as "confused" because it did not point out the relative importance of factors (a) and (b) to the changes that are taking place and are likely to occur soon. For example, when researchers talk about "loss of innocence," they often mean only the troubles with lawyers advertising on news groups, which is part of (a).

Here is one final argument that should allay the "dollars for every byte" concerns about prices for Internet services. According to that August 12 issue of Science, the Internet traffic is around 13 terabytes per month (tera here is 10^{12}), or around 150 terabytes per year. The total charges for running the backbone and the regional service providers seem to be around $200 M per year, with about $20 M coming from the explicit NSF subsidy that is being phased out. (There is also indirect government support for development as well as for access charges to the regionals, which often come at least partially from the overhead on government grants and contracts, but we'll ignore those, as they are being threatened with cutoff.) Hence if we tried to recover present costs by charging a uniform price for each byte, the charge per byte would be $ $1.5*10^{(-6)}$. A typical email message of 2,000 bytes would then cost all of $0.003. A paper of 50,000 bytes would be more, $0.075. When I sent out the latest draft of the "Tragic Loss ..." essay, which was almost 200,000 bytes, my mailing list had around 300 addresses, so this giant mailing of 60 MB would cost $90.00. Given the rapidly decreasing prices for networks, I feel it is safe to conclude that tolls on the NII are not going to be large enough to impede scholarly communication.

Andrew Odlyzko

Date: Tue, 6 Sep 1994 11:33:16 EDT
From: ghermanp@edu.kenyon (Paul Gherman)
Subject: Cross subsidy
To: Multiple recipients of list VPIEJ-L <VPIEJ-L@BITNET.VTVM1>

[Andrew Odlyzko] suggests that we need not worry about the cost of transmitting text over the internet because the cost will be so much lower than the cost of transmitting video. He postulates that the cost of video will need to be kept low, and therefore the cost of text will be proportionately lower. Past practice would suggest quite the opposite, that the cost of text transmission will be close to the cost of video transmission, and the differential will cross subsidize the cost of video, keeping video affordable. The telcos see the real profits in video not text, so I suspect they will bump up the price of text to lower the cost of video.

Paul Gherman

Date: Tue, 6 Sep 1994 11:33:41 EDT
From: "James O'Donnell" <jod@edu.upenn.sas.ccat>
Subject: esoteric fleas
To: Multiple recipients of list VPIEJ-L <VPIEJ-L@BITNET.VTVM1>

I've been reading the debate on this list with interest, and while my heart is with those who look to a future of free information, my head is cautious. NSF privatizes the backbone, as Ann points out. What happens then if Rupert Murdoch decides to buy the company that supplies the backbone? Are we going to depend on the FCC to come in and *remember* that there are academics out there and cut us a special break? This isn't just marginal business news we're talking about, this is the biggest new money-making playground opened up since Japan reindustrialized after the war: the big boys are going to be taking this game very seriously, and they will gladly squeeze every esoteric flea for every penny we've got. We may be able to resist, we may be able to get some special breaks: but it won't come easily or automatically, and we *must* not be blase about it.

Jim O'Donnell
Classics, U. of Penn
jod@ccat.sas.upenn.edu

Date: Tue, 6 Sep 94 15:29:12 -0400
From: Hal Varian <hal@edu.umich.lsa.econ.alfred>

Sorry to butt in on the discussion, but I've been doing lots of work in this area and thought that I might be able to help. Those of you with Mosaic might want to look at my page on the "Economics of the Internet" at http://gopher.econ.lsa.umich.edu. The "Economic FAQs about the Internet" available there is especially relevant.

ghermanp@edu.kenyon (Paul Gherman) suggests:

> Past practice would suggest quite the opposite, that the cost of
> text transmission will be close to the cost of video transmission,
> and the differential will cross subsidize the cost of video,
> keeping video affordable. The telcos see the real profits in video
> not text, so I suspect they will bump up the price of text to lower
> the cost of video.

The problem is that there is no way to do this: bits is bits. The current Internet treats all packets the same. Future protocols will probably want to treat different types of data differently, but whatever pricing scheme is invoked will have to be (warning, economics jargon coming) "incentive compatible" since it is trivial to disguise data: if video is subsidized, I can just create "video packets" that contain text.

"James O'Donnell" <jod@edu.upenn.sas.ccat> asks:

> What happens then if Rupert Murdoch decides to buy the company that
> supplies the backbone?

There are currently 4 backbone suppliers ANS, Alternet, PSInet, and SprintLink and more entry is expected. In fact, all that it takes to enter the business is some money to rent a telephone line, a few routers, and--- most importantly---some engineering expertise.

Hal.Varian@umich.edu   Hal Varian
voice: 313-764-2364   Dept of Economics
fax: 313-764-2364   Univ of Michigan Ann Arbor
                       MI 48109-1220

Date: Sat, 10 Sep 1994 14:43:59 -0400
From: quinn@edu.vt.math (Frank Quinn)

This is another reply to the questions about charges for internet use. It seems to me that there are actually several similar questions being asked, and the answers suggested don't always address the intended question. Maybe this is why the issue keeps coming up. Anyway three variations are discussed here.

First, charges for use of the internet itself, without regard to the content of the message. Such charges may be coming, but I believe the right perspective is provided by thinking of them as postage, rather than subscriptions. Right now it looks free because our institutions have "bulk mail" arrangements. But even if it changes to a per-piece charge it will be small (note 1).

The second variation concerns charges related to the content. These are in the form of site licenses, individual connect charges, or delivery fees. None of these seem likely to become widespread. Individual charges shift the expense from libraries to the individuals, and the individuals I know will have no enthusiasm for this. Use would plummet since browsers won't pay. The "subversive proposal" mechanism would also take a toll: People would find other, free, ways to offer and obtain the information. As for site licenses, it has already been observed that the market for new journals in any format has collapsed. Expensive electronic startups (e.g. Online Journal of Clinical Trials) have not fared well for this reason if no other. This narrows the possibilities down to paper journals converting to electronic format and trying to retain the subscription base. Does anyone know of a successful example (scholarly journal)? The ones I know about (e.g. "TULIP") are still piggy-backed on paper subscriptions. In any case there is no mass movement in this direction, and publishers (at least) don't seem to have any confidence in it.

The third variation on the question is not so sharply formulated. Currently we pay a lot for access to information, through journal subscriptions. Soon, we are led to believe, we will have nearly free access to it all. Surely this is too good to be true, and someone will find a way to re-institute charges? Even if the arguments above are correct, isn't something else we can't forsee bound to happen?

Put this way we see good news and bad news. The good news is that yes it really will be essentially free. The bad news is that we will get what we pay for: the old system is expensive partly because it adds value during the transmission process, and the new system doesn't. As far as I can tell nothing has been improved by being sent out over the net. The problem is not that they will find another way to charge us. The problem is that the added value we used to buy, and were willing to pay for, may no longer be available for sale. (note 2)

=== notes ===

Note 1) I do NOT, however, buy the argument that, since the market will be driven by video-on-demand, our relatively insignificant bandwidth requirements must be almost free. The video-on-demand idea is shaping up in an unattractive way: see "Dreamnet," Charles Piller, Macworld October 1994. Some proposals have nearly all the center-to-user bandwidth dedicated to video, and the user-to-center bandwidth so spread out that it will scarcely match current internet capabilities. A very poor medium for scholarship! Maybe there is a bit of comfort though: with such poor functionality in the commercial versions the academic network will probably stay intact and separate for a long time.

Note 2) Most people feel some substitute will evolve for the value added by print publication (particular quality control via peer review). Paul Ginsparg, for instance, seems to agree that the total "archive" will be of lower quality without quality control at the front end of the process. He suggests that instead of CONTROL, we will have GUIDES which will develop as an "overlay" on top of this archive, and point us toward the good stuff in it. "Overlay guides" already exist in the form of review and survey articles, and selective bibliographies. It is an attractive and hopeful idea that this activity should increase and diversify. But incentives and a support mechanism (eg. a way to redirect current subscription budgets to pay for it) are still missing. Conyers Herring in 1968 (Physics Today) argued strongly that more reviews were needed even then. The situation is worse now, 26 years later, but reviews have failed to materialize in the necessary quantity. Why should this trend reverse itself when the literature goes electronic?

Date: Sun, 11 Sep 94 07:56 EDT
From: amo@com.att.research (Andrew Odlyzko)

Here are some more matchbox estimates for you. The current traffic through NSFNet, the heart of the US part of the Internet, is about 15 TB (terabytes, or 10^{12} bytes) a month. It is often claimed there are around 20 M denizens of the Net, but that seems to be an overestimate, and in any case, many Net users seldom use the US portion of the Net, or else have poor connections to it. However, there ought to be at least 5 M users with decent access. Now 15 TB divided by 5 M users yields average traffic per user of 3 MB per month. This is good for quite a lot of email messages and even a few file transfers, but not much more. A single serious "surfing the Infobahn" session with Mosaic, looking at some graphics, etc., can easily require the transfer of more than 3 MB of data all by itself. This suggests that:

(a) The Net in its present form could accommodate scholarly publishing only in a bare-bones form, without use of modern tools such as Mosaic. We do need a few more years of growth in its capacity before scholars' needs can be accommodated and yet still be just "a flea on the dog's tail."

(b) We do not need to await the arrival of videoconferencing to bring the Net to its knees. Wider usage of Mosaic will do that by itself. In particular, there may be a crisis on the Net in the near future. Traffic on NSFNet has been doubling every year for the last few years. However, WWW/Mosaic traffic is growing at astounding rates, doubling every 3 months or so, and already amounts to 5-10% of all Net traffic. Hence we may soon see serious congestion, followed by usage restrictions and tolls. This does not alter the long-term outlook that scholarly publication will be accommodated easily on data networks, but will surely be used by nay-sayers as a sign that we can't rely on communication to stay cheap.

My feeling is that a crisis caused by rapidly growing use of Mosaic can only be good in the long run. It will show that there is a lot of demand for electronic information that is presented in decent form, and will lead to more capacity. The more traffic on the Net, the lower the costs will be. We really do want the hoi polloi on the Net, to cover up our usage.

Even in the short term, imposition of tolls and different grades of service is likely to be useful, in that it might even out the traffic. I've been corresponding with Hal Varian in the last few days on the question of Internet traffic, and it appears that the main Internet links in the US are on average utilized at only 5% of capacity (judged on a monthly basis), although there are shorter measuring times when the utilization reaches 50% (and clearly there are bursts when it is at 100%). It should be easy to increase that usage by factors of 3-5 by charging fees for immediate transmission, and allowing free transit for traffic that can wait an hour or a day.

Andrew Odlyzko

[Ed. Note: the message that follows was not part of the discussion but it surfaced about the same time as the messages above were being distributed and was seen by a number of players. We include it with permission, for it casts light in some murky corners.]

Date: Tue, 13 Sep 1994 09:25:06 -0700 (PDT)
From: BOBG@u.washington.edu
Subject: Slightly revised--Latest version of Cost memo Q/A
To: ann@cni.org

Robert G. Gillespie

NSFNET Pricing/Costs

1.   Many people appear to use the Internet for free regardless of the distance or the amount of use. Who does pay?

Faculty members and others in institutions that have connections to the Internet through their regional networks ordinarily do not see any charges because most institutions have not chosen to recover their costs through usage charges to the end-user. The institutions are paying for the connections and services in these categories:

1)   The institutions are investing in their local infrastructure (networks, workstations, operations, training, software, routers, etc.).

2)   The institutions pay for access (connectivity) to the NSFNET through their regional networks (NWNET, SURANET, CICNET,...). Those fees are usually membership fees that provide operations, training and access. In addition the institution usually is paying the regional telephone company for the high speed line that connects the campus network to the regional network.

3)   The institution may be also paying for the use of information services (commercial data bases) from an information service provider. In some circumstances those are flat fees governed by a maximum number of users.

4)   NSF has been paying for the cost of the national backbone (to ANS, MERIT, MCI and others) that has interconnected the regional networks (and others) and also has paid for a portion of the regional network costs. Total costs for networking include local computer support and local network infrastructure, in addition to the wide area services. It is estimated that NSF's support defrays less than 10% of the overall networking costs spent by institutions.

For institutions that do not have direct connection and are using dial-up connections, faculty members and others may be already paying usage fees to Internet service providers. Of course those fees can be usage based or flat rate depending on their service provider's approach (and competition). Currently there are about one thousand out of thirty six hundred institutions of higher education that have direct connections to the Internet. A recent NCLIS survey of a sample of public libraries indicates that approximately 21% of public libraries have Internet Connections, but many of these use dial-up connections.

2) How can a message that is sent across the world with a million bytes be treated the same as one sent in the state with a few lines?

There are several reasons for this. The major cost for lines and routing remain independent of the volume of use until it is necessary to add more bandwidth. Also, because of the way that packets may be routed through different elements and subnetworks, it would be very difficult and costly to keep track of the actual paths and use.

However, growing traffic because of increased use (more users, more bandwidth intensive applications--video, mosaic, etc.) means that the network bandwidth must increase or congestion and delays will occur. Other approaches to avoiding congestion involve establishing priorities or setting different rates for different types of service.

The costs of increasing bandwidth are closely related to the costs of switching (which track the computer chip costs). It may be possible to match the demand for bandwidth without increasing costs as the technological improvements in switching speeds lower costs for bandwidth. However, since there are other factors involved---for instance, regulatory oversight--there are no guarantees!

3) Who sets the policy for the way that persons connected with an institution or library pay?

The institution/campus/library determines how the cost should be recovered or not (just as for telephone costs or computer costs). Neither NSF or the telephone companies set the rates for Internet services. Those are set by Internet service providers which are either nonprofit (like most regionals) or commercial.

4) How will transition to the new NSFNET affect charging to the faculty members and others connected with institution?

The faculty members and others are unlikely to see any changes. Charging is a policy decision for the local institution or library.

Institutions may see an increase in the cost of connection (in their membership fees for regional networks). This is not expected to be more than 10% but there may be anomalies. While NSF has assumed that institutions will be able to absorb these cost increases at this level it is also providing transition funds for the regionals over four years to cushion the impact of those changes. The new architecture replaces the current single national backbone, NSFNET, which currently carries the traffic between regional networks, with a new architecture where traffic between regional networks will be carried by commercial network providers. NSF is funding interconnection points (Network Access Points --NAP) which will provide interconnection for all Internet network service providers.

5) What are the some of the difficult issues ahead?

Guiding the Internet through another order of magnitude of growth and yet providing the stability and increased services necessary will be difficult. Some good questions that were discussed at the recent FARNET Workshop on the Transition from the NSFNET included:

1. How and who will ensure that interconnection is ubiquitous?

2 . How will cost and charges be handled?

3. How will "seamless problem solving" be achieved?

4. Who will set the ground rules for technical interactions?

5. What is the attitude toward providing enhanced privacy and security?

6. What kind of policy framework/governance needs to be established? What are the policy framework options for disputes and resolution of issues? How will policy issues and resolution of disputes be handled for users?

7. What resources are need to achieve interruption-free service?

8. How will the positive aspect of the Internet culture be preserved? What are they? Can they be scaled up?

XVIII. Citations and Citation Frequency

The measure of use that is most easily quantified on a national or international basis is "citation frequency." This group of messages began during the net-wide subversive proposal discussion and then some of the discussants picked up the topic about two months after the main body of the conversation ended, for further probing. Not every message in the sequence went to the public lists directly; there was more discussion among individuals, with some of the postings occasionally being referred to the wider audience. In this regard, a rudimentary kind of editing and peer review is already taking place.

Date: Thu, 11 Aug 1994 08:57:37 EDT
From: David Stodolsky <david@arch.ping.dk>

Stevan Harnad <harnad@Princeton.EDU> writes:

> field by field is the ULTIMATE (cross-journal) acceptance rate: It is
> my belief that in one form or other, just about EVERYTHING gets
> published eventually, if the author is persistent enough, even if it's
> in the unrefereed vanity press. Having approximately the same
> manuscript refereed repeatedly for different journals is a drain on
> resources, but I'm not sure how to get around it: the prestige
> hierarchy is based in part on (intellectual) competition.

Moving the arena of competition from publication rates to citation rates is one way. Since almost everything gets published, why not just abandon this competition? There is no economic justification for prior review in electronic publication. Various preprint archives have already demonstrated that direct publication is viable.

Even with traditional publication, citation rates are given more weight than publication rates. Trying to move the old mechanisms of accreditation on-line is domed to failure, in the long run. We need more powerful methods of evaluating citations. The old system of just counting them has always been recognized as inadequate. Networking tools allow us to see whether a citation supports or opposes a given publication.

This can reflect back upon the "publication rate." If an author sees that his/her article is being devalued by numerous bad reviews, then it would be wise to take it "out of circulation".

David S. Stodolsky, PhD
Internet: stodolsk@andromeda.rutgers.edu, or
Internet: david@arch.ping.dk
Peder Lykkes Vej 8, 4. tv.
DK-2300 Copenhagen S, Denmark
Voice + Fax: + 45 32 97 66 74

From: amo@research.att.com (Andrew Odlyzko)
Date: Sun, 14 Aug 94 08:40 EDT
Subject: citation frequency

Stevan,

In your comments on Bernard Naylor's "A SMALL CONTRIBUTION TO THE SUBVERSIVE DISCUSSION," one passage caught my eye, namely

> Let's be more specific. Though it's risky to resort to figures from
> hearsay (and that is all I must confess I have so far), I am confident
> enough in what I am about to point out that even if I am wrong by one or
> two orders of magnitude, the upshot is the same: The average published
> scientific article has fewer than 10 readers and no citers; I'll bet the
> same is true for the average piece of scholarship in the humanities.

I expect that your figure for no citers for the average scientific article is ultimately derived from the same source that I have seen quoted on many other occasions, namely the Science Citation Index (SCI). As I recall, the SCI figures indicated that only a couple of mathematics journals achieved an average of more than one citation to one of their articles, and most were well under one. Now if the average number of citations per article is below 0.5, then it certainly follows that most articles are not cited at all.

I have long been suspicious of the SCI figures, based on my own experience with them. It seemed that only a small selection of mathematics journals was covered, since often references that I knew existed would not be included in the SCI listings. However, your comment stimulated me to do some more thinking and research, and I believe I can show by a simple argument that the SCI estimates are bogus.

I have just picked up the latest issues of three mathematics journals that have accumulated on my stack of correspondence during my recent trip.

They were from several areas of mathematics, and all were primary research journals, not survey ones. They contained 35 articles, and these 35 articles had a total of about 630 references, for an average of 18 references per article. (The range of number of references was from 3 to 51, and 18 seemed to be close to the median as well.) It seemed that of those typical 18 references, about 4 were to books, so there were usually about 14 references to research papers. This is a small sample, but it seems to me to be typical of the papers I see in mathematics, and so I did not bother to collect more data. It would be interesting to obtain similar estimates for other fields.

The figure of 14 backward references in a research paper is sufficient all by itself to show that the SCI figures are far from the truth. Since the scholarly literature is growing, the average number of references to a paper MUST BE IN EXCESS OF 14. To see this, consider a simple model in which papers published in a given decade reference only papers from the previous decade. In mathematics, about 250,000 papers were published during the 70s. Had there been only 250,000 papers published during the 80s, and each one referenced an average of 14 papers, each of the papers from the 70s would on average be referenced 14 times. However, the 80s saw the publication of 500,000 research articles in mathematics. Had they referenced an average of 14 papers from the 70s each, it would necessarily follow that the average number of citations per paper from the 70s would be 28. Thus it seems reasonable to estimate that the average number of citations to a mathematics paper is in the 15-30 range.

Comments:

1. This argument does not have much bearing on the discussion of electronic journals. However, it might be important in terms of general policy issues. If the typical scholarly paper does get cited 30 times, as opposed to disappearing without a trace in the vast scholarly literature, then it is much easier to argue that public support for the original research and subsequent publication is warranted.

2. The above argument can be used only to estimate the mean number of citations of a paper. For many purposes the median is a more useful figure, and it would be nice to obtain the complete distribution.

3. As long as only the mean number of citations is of interest, it is possible to obtain a much better estimate than that presented above with only a little more work. It would suffice to take the 35 papers that I used and note the year of publication of each of the 630 references. Since we do have good data for the total number of mathematics papers published each year (from the reviewing journals Math. Rev. and Zentralblatt), we

could then obtain a much better estimate for the total number of citations that a paper attracts, as well as the distribution of the time after publication that a paper is cited most often. This would provide much better data than that of SCI at a tiny fraction of the cost.

4. The procedure suggested above, of sampling backward references, would not provide information on the variation in the impact that individual papers have, at least not without large sample sizes that would provide information about repeated references to a particular paper.

5. In my article I used the figure of 20 serious readers per article. I don't think this is inconsistent with the estimates above, since scholars often reference papers that they do not know in detail. In mathematics, for example, a specialist in one area will often cite a result from another area without verifying it. By a serious reader in mathematics, I mean one who actually checks the technical details of the proofs at least to some extent. Clearly there are many more readers who just glance at papers to see what is in them.

6. The SCI figures might be useful for gauging the relative merits of various journals within a given field.

Have you seen any arguments like this, debunking the SCI estimates?

Best regards,
Andrew

From: Stevan Harnad (harnad@clarity.princeton.edu)
To: Andrew Odlyzko

Dear Andrew,

Very interesting analysis, and we certainly need a lot more like this. I don't know of further literature, but perhaps those who read this posting will. Three comments:

(1) I don't think we need to prove that the average article has many readers or citers to justify esoteric research. First, some important contributions may be based on the work of very few people, who read and cite only one another. And second, as in all areas of human endeavor, there will always be the usual Gaussian cream-to-milk ratio: To skim of the top .01% cream, you need to allow the full volume of milk. Let 1000 flowers bloom...

(2) It is not clear whether your sample of articles was a random sample (i.e., whether they were average articles). This may not matter much, but what certainly matters is the point you note: Are they mostly citing one another or the cream of the crop (the rare "citation classics")? If so, the latter, this would still leave the average article (i.e., most) uncited and unread.

(3) There will no doubt be great variability in the answers to these questions from field to field (and subfield). What I think you don't contest is that, give or take an order or two of magnitude above and below 10, the vast bulk of the scholarly corpus is still ESOTERIC: It is a no-market literature. That's the key to the rationale for abandoning the trade model.

Stevan Harnad

From amo@research.att.com Sun Nov 20 19:19:01 1994
Message-Id: <9411210019.AA11083@a.cni.org>
From: amo@research.att.com
Date: Sun, 20 Nov 94 18:54 EST
To: BERGE@guvax.acc.georgetown.edu
Cc: amo@research.att.com, ann@cni.org, garfield@aurora.cis.upenn.edu, ginsparg@qfwfq.lanl.gov, harnad@ecs.soton.ac.uk, jlang@smtpgwy.isinet.com
Subject: how often are scholarly articles read

Stevan Harnad forwarded your query and his reply to me. The estimate that the average scholarly article is read fewer than 6 times is part of the folklore, but I don't know of any solid studies that support it.

One of the main difficulties is in defining what it means to read a paper. In "Tragic Loss...", I use the figure of 20 instead of 6, and cite it as an gross overestimate, but this is in reference to a thorough study, not browsing. If you include browsing, the correct number is on the order of several hundred. This is supported by the data from Paul Ginsparg's preprint server (we had some email discussion on this topic a few months ago) for electronically available preprints, as well as various older studies of print journals, such as those in:

D. W. King, D. D. McDonald, and N. K. Roderer, "Scientific Journals in the United States. Their production, use and economics," Hutchinson Ross, 1981.

Citations are a different matter. There the folklore is that the average paper receives no citations at all. This is often supported by the journal impact factors from the Journal Citation Reports from ISI (the publishers of Science Citation Index). However, that bit of folklore is based on a misinterpretation of what the impact factors measure. In some email correspondence a few months ago, I showed that in mathematics, the average number of citations to a paper is around 20 to 30. Other fields are likely to have different figures.

What will happen when most papers are available electronically is a fascinating question. There will be at least three different influential developments:

(1) For one thing, we are likely to have many more curious outsiders poking around. I do not believe that the general public will ever want to read most of my research papers in mathematics, but there are lots of amateurs as well as people who did get advanced training in mathematics but are working in other areas who like to look around. Nowadays they are limited by lack of convenient access to good libraries, but that barrier will disappear on the Net. Such people are likely to raise the amount of browsing that takes place.

(2) The scholars who do most of the browsing today are likely to do somewhat more in the future, since it will be so much easier. People are not going to read faster, but faster and more convenient access to information will mean they will be able to scan more in the same amount of time they do now.

(3) The most important development is likely to be the emergence of intelligent agents. Scholars and amateurs alike are likely to rely on software that will perform customized searches based on their interests. What this may mean is that people will look at a smaller number of papers, but their agents may go through vast numbers of papers to come up with that selection. This will require new techniques to deduce anything about how widely a paper is read, since most of the accesses will be by automated program that will make the raw access data unreliable.

Andrew Odlyzko

From ginsparg@qfwfq.lanl.gov Sun Nov 20 21:07:42 1994
Date: Sun, 20 Nov 94 19:06:20 -0700
From: Paul Ginsparg 505-667-7353 <ginsparg@qfwfq.lanl.gov>
To: amo@research.att.com, ann@cni.org, garfield@aurora.cis.upenn.edu,.
harnad@ecs.soton.ac.uk, jlang@smtpgwy.isinet.com
Subject: RE: how often are scholarly articles read

> From: Stevan Harnad <harnad@ecs.soton.ac.uk>
> Date: Sun, 20 Nov 94 14:05:39 GMT
> To: "Zane Berge, Ph.D." <BERGE@guvax.acc.georgetown.edu>
> Subject: Re: Your FAQ regarding Electronic Publishing
>
> But if the figure is confirmed, I still think the database is too tiny
> and unstable to make comparisons yet -- except for the physics preprint
> archive. (And note that the paper data could not possibly monitor the
> paper BROWSING figures, which is what a lot of the electronic "hits"
> are: Remember, I share your intuition that the convenience and reach of
> the Net will raise the browse/read rate appreciably, but it won't be
> easy to make objective comparisons initially; only after a few years of
> use, when perhaps a sample of readers could be asked to systematically
> monitor their own "hit" rates in the two media.)

indeed the data here continues to collect (and usage, especially on the
www interface http://xxx.lanl.gov/, had a dramatic increase after the
summer -- i need to collect some revised figures on # of hits / day, etc.).
the "browsing rate" remains high -- almost no paper on hep-th gets fewer
than 50 hits the more popular ones instantly get a few hundred, and then
there are the "megahits" -- typically review articles, that get thousands of
requests. (most recently, for example, there was hep-th/9411028, posted
only two weeks ago, that already has over a thousand requests. it's a 153
page set of lecture notes "what is string theory?" delivered at les houches
in september that is also linked from my dedicated page
http://xxx.lanl.gov/lh94/ (i.e. the summer school proceedings i'm
editing).

another positive virtue of that electronic version is that one late
contributor no longer holds up the production -- things go on-line as they
come in [actually i have two more contributions to post today or
tomorrow as soon as i go over them just to verify the formatting]. also
these proceedings have traditionally had b&w photos interspersed, but
since i deal with a computer-literate community, i've been receiving them
this year electronically as color jpegs and posting [the compression
scheme gives reasonably good 24 bit quality at about 50-75kb per
photo].)

stevan's comment that "the database is too tiny and unstable" for the time being remains correct, and interpretation of the data will not be entirely straightforward even when it is more complete.

> From: amo@research.att.com
> Date: Sun, 20 Nov 94 18:54 EST
> To: BERGE@guvax.acc.georgetown.edu
> Subject: how often are scholarly articles read
>
> This will require new techniques to deduce anything about how
> widely a paper is read, since most of the accesses will by automated
> programs that will make the raw access data unreliable.

not sure i agree with this. automated programs will be required to respect an identification protocol -- this is already the case, for example, for all of the better www "robots" and "spiders" that identify themselves as such in the "user-agent" field for each requests. so things could in principle be set up to filter them out of the raw data if desired. automated programs are also fairly easy to detect dynamically when necessary -- i had some problems early on (see http://xxx.lanl.gov/RobotsBeware.html) and now when some automated program starts foolishly trying to index gigabytes of compressed postscript in violation of posted guidelines it gets blasted out of existence after only very few requests (remember these silly things have to open up a socket to read the data at their end... --- there was a period last spring when a new neophyte seemed to be born every week, and after getting something added to the official comp.infosystems.www faq about the problem, decided it was still useful to demonstrate that servers too could run automated programs).

on the other hand, it will remain impossible to distinguish browsing from reading (much less understanding...). the only way to gauge reading would be to adapt andrew's citation methodology, though in this case it would mean asking selected "typical" researchers to keep a diary over some period of time to keep track of papers they claim to read, and then scale from that to the size of the community and divide by total number of papers produced. in the electronic future, someone will undoubtedly try to enlist nielsen-like volunteers to have their electronic reading monitored automatically, but this will be subject to same deficiencies as current ratings (for example, statistics would be skewed by those scholarly members of nielsen families who insist on reading their esoteric scholarly publications while watching television (perhaps in a split screen display).

pg

From amo@research.att.com Sun Nov 20 22:47:14 1994
From: amo@research.att.com
Date: Sun, 20 Nov 94 22:04 EST
To: ginsparg@qfwfq.lanl.gov
Cc: amo@research.att.com, ann@cni.org, garfield@aurora.cis.upenn.edu,.
harnad@ecs.soton.ac.uk, jlang@smtpgwy.isinet.com
Subject: RE: how often are scholarly articles read

Paul,

Thanks a lot for your comments.

Concerning the issue of automated programs, the problem is not that they could not be distinguished from human beings in accessing the database. Instead, what is likely to happen is that just about the only accesses will be by automated programs. What will make statistical studies of accesses hard to interpret is that different people will have different modes of operation. For example, I may set up my intelligent agents to scan your preprint server for articles of potential interest to me, and to download them to my machine. Just to be on the safe side, I might set the filters to pick up 5 times as much material as I really care to even browse, and do the final winnowing down to the desired 20% manually on my machine. Would you not count any of the downloads on the grounds they were done by an automated agent, or would you count all of them, even though only 20% of them lead to browsing? If you try to put in a scaling factor, would you use the 20% that applies to me, or the 50% that is appropriate for somebody else?

For truly reliable data, we will surely need what you suggest, namely a Nielsen-type system of monitoring usage patterns of a selected sample. That is what done in some earlier studies that were cited either in the [KingMR] or the [Machlup] books cited in my essay. (I don't have either one at hand to check.)

Regards,

Andrew

From harnad@ecs.southampton.ac.uk Sun Dec 11 12:47:22 1994
From: Stevan Harnad <harnad@ecs.soton.ac.uk>
To: amo@research.att.com
Subject: Re: electronic publishing pointer?
Cc: ginsparg@qfwfq.lanl.gov (Paul Ginsparg) ann@cni.org (Ann Okerson)

> From: amo@research.att.com
> Date: Sat, 10 Dec 94 17:56 EST
>
> Stevan,
>
> I am glad you found my remarks on dual publication of interest.
> It's too bad you could not come to the MSRI workshop last week.
> There were many interesting talks there that you would surely
> have enjoyed.
>
> Will Hearst (who runs the Hearst publishing empire, and has
> an honors degree in math from Harvard, so often comes to math
> meetings) said in the closing panel presentation that from
> his experience with mass market publishing, a new medium does
> not displace an old one entirely, but rather develops a new market.
> Thus, for example, radio and television did cut down the circulation
> of newspapers, but did not destroy them. Unfortunately I did
> not get to catch him afterwards to ask how he views the displacement
> of LPs by CDs, which seems to be a counterexample to his thesis.
>
> Best regards,
> Andrew

Hi Andrew, I too think that a parallel, free incarnation is fine, and would
hasten developments. On the other hand, hybrid paper/electronic
projects trying to provide the electronic version only if it piggy-backs on a
paper subscription, however (i.e., the kinds of projects most publishers
are naturally tending to think of and try at the moment), are, I believe,
regressive and doomed to fail, either because they will not have takers
who are willing to pay, or because they will be done in by the contraband
trade in the electronic version. At the same time, while they are
attempted, these hybrid projects will SLOW developments. (Readers,
authors and publishers are still confused about what there is or ought to
be, and this will compound the confusion for a bit, till it dies its natural
death.)

The open, independent, parallel path, on the other hand, has much to
recommend it. (I hope you see the subtle but essential difference.)

As to predictions based on newspapers/books vs. TV: I'm sure the analogy will hold for the commercial, entertainment and literary texts on the Net. They still have a long paper lifetime ahead of them, perhaps forever. I suspect that in the case of esoteric science/scholarship, though, the paper incarnation may well get replaced completely -- or rather as a graded function of degree of esotericity. Then the only question is: Where will the effective threshold for a continuing viable trade-model paper incarnation of texts that are freely available on the Net (or for a trade-model, subscription or access-based electronic version) fall on this continuum?

I read the Garfield/ISI statistics differently from you, I think. I still think the vast bulk of the scientific/scholarly periodical literature has no market; I don't think the citation stats for those selected journals contradict that. Besides, it's readership stats we really need, per article, comparing how many do read it under the present constrained subscription-based conditions, with how many would if it were it on the Net always, for all, for free.

I think author's end subsidy for access to the quality-validated scholarly microphone will turn out to be the uncontestably optimal solution for the work on the long end of the threshold in question.

Chrs,

Stevan

From: Stevan Harnad <harnad@ecs.soton.ac.uk>
Date: Sun, 11 Dec 94 19:56:16 GMT
To: garfield@aurora.cis.upenn.edu, amo@research.att.com
Subject: Citation stats

Hi, Gene,

Andrew branched this to me too. Could I ask a couple of follow-up questions about these stats?

Are they the average number of cites per article? What is the distribution of these cites (means and standard deviations and Ns)?

Because of course this still leaves open the possibility that a few citation classics in every volume or issue of the "core" journals are doing most of the work, still leaving most articles uncited or much less cited.

And of course self-citations would have to be subtracted from all these figures.

Best wishes, Stevan

Stevan Harnad
Professor of Psychology
Director, Cognitive Sciences Centre
Department of Psychology
University of Southampton
harnad@ecs.soton.ac.uk   harnad@princeton.edu
phone: +44 703 592582
fax: +44 703 594597

Date: Fri, 9 Dec 1994 16:40:50 -0500
From: garfield@aurora.cis.upenn.edu (E. Garfield)

Dear Andrew: As you know, David Hamilton did a disservice in _Science_ (Dec. 7, 1990, p. 1331, and Jan. 4, 1991, p. 25) by claiming that a large percentage of scholarly material is not cited, without properly distinguishing between the core journals that are regularly and consistently cited and the large numbers of small journals which are rarely cited. David Pendlebury of ISI corrected some of this information in _Science_, March 23, 1991, p. 1410.

In some recent communications on the Internet, you make some estimates about math journals. I have asked David Pendlebury at ISI to provide me with data for the past 13 years of citations to a few of the leading math journals. This report could, of course, be extended to other journals but just to give you an idea, this will tell you how often articles published in 1981 had been cited during the past 13 years.

List of papers published in 1981, and citations to these papers for the period 1981-1993

Journal	ISSN	Year	Cites/paper through 1993
ADV MATH	0001-8708	81	16.63
ANN MATH	0003-486X	81	21.98
B AM MATH S	0273-0979	81	10.70
COM PA MATH	0010-3640	81	24.67
CR AC S I	0764-4442	81	2.59
DISCR MATH	0012-365X	81	3.27

DUKE MATH J	0012-7094	81	8.33
INDI MATH J	0022-2518	81	10.23
INVENT MATH	0020-9910	81	17.67
J ALGEBRA	0021-8693	81	5.79
J DIFF EQUA	0022-0396	81	7.46
J DIFF GEOM	0022-040X	81	3.88
J FUNCT ANA	0022-1236	81	10.83
J LOND MATH	0024-6107	81	3.81
J MATH ANAL	0022-247X	81	4.93
J PURE APPL	0022-4049	81	5.38
J REIN MATH	0075-4102	81	5.95
LECT N MATH	0075-8434	81	2.00
MATH ANNAL	0025-5831	81	6.83
MATH PROC C	0305-0041	81	4.00
MATH Z	0025-5874	81	6.35
NONLIN ANAL	0362-546X	81	4.50
P AM MATH S	0002-9939	81	2.84
P LOND MATH	0024-6115	81	9.27
PAC J MATH	0030-8730	81	3.29
T AM MATH S	0002-9947	81	5.99

Papers published between 81-93, cited in the period 81-93**

Journal	ISSN	Years	Cites/Paper
ANN MATH	0003-486X	81-93	12.71
COM PA MATH	0010-3640	81-93	9.56
INVENT MATH	0020-9910	81-93	7.99
J DIFF GEOM	0022-040X	81-93	7.72
ADV MATH	0001-8708	81-93	6.71
B AM MATH S	0273-0979	81-93	6.67
P LOND MATH	0024-6115	81-93	5.14
J FUNCT ANA	0022-1236	81-93	4.86
INDI MATH J	0022-2518	81-93	4.41
J DIFF EQUA	0022-0396	81-93	4.17
DUKE MATH J	0012-7094	81-93	4.05
T AM MATH S	0002-9947	81-93	3.72
J REIN MATH	0075-4102	81-93	3.54
MATH ANNAL	0025-5831	81-93	3.46
MATH Z	0025-5874	81-93	3.07
J ALGEBRA	0021-8693	81-93	2.64
J LOND MATH	0024-6107	81-93	2.51
NONLIN ANAL	0362-546X	81-93	2.35
MATH PROC C	0305-0041	81-93	2.32
PAC J MATH	0030-8730	81-93	2.29
J PURE APPL	0022-4049	81-93	2.19

J MATH ANAL	0022-247X	81-93	2.10
CR AC S I	0764-4442	81-93	1.72
P AM MATH S	0002-9939	81-93	1.50
DISCR MATH	0012-365X	81-93	1.41
LECT N MATH	0075-8434	81-93	1.17

**It is important to realize that in the second list averages are lower, since articles published in the last year are included. Only a year by year study of cumulated cites can give a true picture. Note that the journal indicators file available from ISI also indicates percentage of uncitedness for each journal year.

For other reasons, I am interested in getting the same information on journals with a much wider readership and impact. You will be interested to know that in the same period and file, articles published in _Science_, _Nature_, etc. in 1981 have been cited on an average over 70 times each. In the list of journals that I have studied, there are only a small number of articles that are never cited.

Best wishes,
Eugene Garfield, Ph.D.
Chairman Emeritus ISI and Publisher, THE SCIENTIST
3501 Market Street
Philadelphia,PA 19104
Tel: (215)243-2205 // Fax: (215)387-1266
E-mail: garfield@aurora.cis.upenn.edu

From: amo@research.att.com
Date: Wed, 14 Dec 94 05:32 EST
To: harnad@ecs.soton.ac.uk
Cc: ann@cni.org, ginsparg@qfwfq.lanl.gov
Subject: Re: E-Pub

Stevan, Who, me? Sorry, you have the wrong guy. I certainly do not recognize anything I ever wrote as implying that "it could all be fought out by a Darwinian popularity contest among readers and commentators of the posted papers and their successive iterations." All that I every claimed (and I still claim) is that if we had a continuation of a chaotic system on the net, there would be a Darwinian evolution of some type of peer review. Moreover, given the speed with which everything moves on the Net, such Darwinian evolution would be extremely rapid. Like Paul, I am not satisfied with the present refereeing system, even though I have grown up with a much better one than he has to deal with in his field. That's why I spent so much time in my essay complaining about the inadequacies of what we have. My point is that we can do better on the Net, with improved tools.

As an example of how quickly a review system can evolve on the Net, let me cite the following story (which I also mentioned at the MSRI workshop two weeks ago). Last summer, at a cryptography conference, a bunch of us were standing around, and the conversation turned to the cypherpunks mailing list. One of my colleagues was complaining that some of the most interesting news items about security (such as about changes in government Clipper chip policy, lawsuits over basic public key cryptography patents, etc.) were showing up first on that list, but that he (let us call him X) found it much too time consuming to wade through the huge amount of stuff pouring through in order to dig up the few nuggets of interesting information. At that point one of the other chaps, call him Y, opined that it was not all that hard at all, and that he found it amusing to scan all that material. Here is roughly how it went from that point on:

X: "How much would you charge to store the valuable pieces and
        send them to me once a day for a year?"
Y: "Twenty bucks."
X: pulls out a $20 bill and hands it to Y.
Z, W: "Here is $20 for me,. How about a discount rate for our group?..."

People are resourceful, and they will find ways to cope with information overload.

Best regards, Andrew

From: Stevan Harnad <harnad@ecs.soton.ac.uk>
Date: Fri, 16 Dec 94 22:46:30 GMT
To: garfield@aurora.cis.upenn.edu (E. Garfield)
Subject: Re: Citation Stats
Cc: "amo@research.att.com (Andrew Odlyzko EJ)

> Yes, these are averages for 1981. We could also obtain separate averages
> for "cited" papers, thus omitting the small number of uncited papers.
> The second set of numbers is a cumulative average for all the
> papers published in the period 1981-93 and that is why the
> averages are lower -- less chance for more recent years to
> accumulate citations.

Hi Gene, any way to get actual DISTRIBUTIONS (average citations = 10 could happen because most papers get 10, fewer get 8 or 12, etc. all the way to the fewest getting 1 or 19; OR it could happen because most papers = 0 and a few get LOTS of citations. Which is it? Only variances and distribution statistics will tell you, not averages.

Second, self-citations must be subtracted, or you could already pump it to an average of 10 right there!

Any chance of getting data like that?

Happy Holidays!

Stevan

From: amo@research.att.com
Date: Mon, 2 Jan 95 08:40 EST
To: harnad@ecs.soton.ac.uk
Cc: 70244.1532@compuserve.com, B.Naylor@soton.ac.uk, ann@cni.org.
dpendle@isinet.com, garfield@aurora.cis.upenn.edu,
ginsparg@qfwfq.lanl.gov, lederberg@rockvax.rockefeller.edu,
quinn@math.vt.edu
Subject: citation frequency

Stevan,

At the request of Gene Garfield, David Pendlebury of ISI has provided me with some information about citation statistics, of the type we both felt would be useful to have. He wrote that generally citations to a paper peak in years 2-3 (and in years 3-5 in chemistry and applied sciences). He also provided pointers to two articles in Science, both by David Hamilton, in the Dec. 7, 1990, and Jan. 4, 1991, issues, that were based on studies carried out by Pendlebury at the request of Science. One statistic indicated that 55% of the papers in the ISI database (for the 1984 publication year) had not received a single citation in the 5 years after publication. The "uncitedness" fraction ranged from 9.2% for atomic, molecular, and chemical physics, to 47.4% for all the so-called hard sciences, to 72% for all of engineering, to 90.1% for political science, 95.5% for history (but only 29.2% for history and philosophy of science) and 99.6% for architecture. The overall figures are

  47.4% hard sciences
  72.0% engineering
  74.7% social sciences
  98.0% humanities

The March 22, 1991 issue of Science has a letter from Pendlebury mentioning a variety of caveats that have to be applied when interpreting these statistics. For example, many of the items in the ISI database that were used in compiling the statistics for the Hamilton articles were meetings abstracts, editorials, and so on, and thus would not be regarded as primary scholarly publications. Excluding just those items lowers the "uncitedness" fraction to 22.4% for the 1984 science articles, 48.0% of the social sciences, and 93.1% for the arts and humanities.

Perhaps our difference of opinion, with you feeling that the vast majority of esoteric scholarly papers are never cited, and I claiming that at least a large fraction of the papers do get cited, reflect the different fields we are in. In any case, we both get support for our opinions from the ISI data.

Best regards, and Happy New Year, Andrew

From: Stevan Harnad <harnad@ecs.soton.ac.uk>
Date: Mon, 2 Jan 95 17:33:17 GMT

Andrew, Thanks for forwarding the ISI data. There are no doubt differences between fields, and no doubt they are in the direction you note (one would also like some statistics on numbers of publications, authors and readers in each field).

You're right, that there's support there for BOTH of our (opposite) views! To sort things out one would AT LEAST have to know the following:

(1) Were self-citations (for all co-authors) systematically eliminated from this set? That's always good for a few gratuitous cites per article.

(2) Breakdowns by citation-frequency would be more informative (no doubt there were some in the articles you mention) than dichotomous cited/noncited data.

(3) Besides wanting to know (a) the absolute numbers of publications, authors and readers in the different fields, and (b) how these might be related to citation frequency, one would want to relate them to (c) the journal prestige hierarchy in each field (no doubt ISI has these figures too) and perhaps even (d) the degree of interdisciplinarity of the field.

I'm not sure the variance is accounted for entirely by the hardsci-softsci-nonsci continuum (though it might be).

Happy '95, Stevan

XIX. More on Costs -- of Digitization

Some new evidence is presented suggesting that the costs of digitization, or at least compression, may be shrinking. In order to prepare this book for publication, the editors artifically cut off a discussion that still continues at the time of final proofs (May 1995) and shows no likelihood of ending for a long time.

From: Stevan Harnad <harnad@ecs.soton.ac.uk>
Date: Thu, 19 Jan 95 09:23:53 GMT
Message-Id: <21840.9501190923@cogsci.ecs.soton.ac.uk>
To: ginsparg@qfwfq.lanl.gov
Subject: One other thing
Cc: B.Naylor@soton.ac.uk (Bernard Naylor LIB), amo@research.att.com (Andrew Odlyzko)

Hi Paul, a graduate student with many prior years in publishing just told me something interesting about the economics of electronic publishing for paper publishers that made me whack my head and say "Why didn't I think of that?" It's about the contentious issue about the true per-page costs. He said that the reason the electronic-only, nonpublishers' estimates are so much lower than the paper publishers' estimates for the same electronic page is not ONLY because of what I had said (i.e., that theirs is based on subtracting electronic savings from a production system that is still designed for paper), or rather, what I said is naive and could be said much more explicitly:

TWO THIRDS OF THEIR PER-PAGE ESTIMATE IS BASED ON THE OVERHEAD FROM THEIR PAPER OPERATIONS! That is, they are not reckoning the true saving for the electronic journal considered in isolation, but for the electronic journal within the context of the continuing costs of all the other paper journals! If the overhead were figured (as I would it think is should be) proportionately to the actual costs of the electronic journal itself, our page-cost figures would be in much closer agreement.

There may be a general economic lesson/problem in all this (though I, and I'm sure you too, would not be prepared to become an economist TOO, and not just an amateur publisher, in the service of hastening the electronic day for us all -- and for our own research lives in particular): The question is, How does one make a transition from an expensive technology to a cheap technology for accomplishing much the same thing? Railroads tried to protect the coal-stoking, IBM tried to sustain mainframes, so I suppose the advent of diesel engines and universal PCs was slowed by this economic inertial force. Maybe it's natural. Is there any benign way to help hasten things without radically jeopardizing people's livelihoods?

It's easy to mask the sympathy that I know you too feel about this side of it, with an emphasis on the stereotype of profiteering, but I wonder how fair and realistic that is, if one looks at scholarly publishing more closely. (I'm not pretending to know, just confessing ignorance, and some worries that one does not want, historically, to become a scholarly capitalist, saying "People and environment be damned, the Darwinian market forces will converge on the optimal material outcome on their own.")

Just a sample of some moral vacillation that comes over me now and again. (Ironic, considering that at the moment, it's certainly electronic publishing that is the economic underdog...)

Chrs, Stevan

From: amo@research.att.com
Date: Sun, 19 Mar 95 21:48 EST
To: ann@cni.org, ginsparg@qfwfq.lanl.gov, harnad@ecs.soton.ac.uk
Subject: conversion to electronics

Here is an interesting observation which suggests that conversion of old scholarly material to digital form may be feasible very soon, even sooner than I expected. I learned from Hal Varian, an economist from the Univ. of Michigan, that economists are setting up a project to digitize all the articles in the top half dozen or so journals in their field. Their costs (which are pretty reliable, as they are based on signed contracts) come to 40 cents per page, and "that includes scanning and OCR conversion to a very high (about 1 error/page) level of accuracy." The scanning takes place in the Dominican Republic, and involves destroying one copy of each journal issue. The scanning is done at 600 dpi, and (after application of lossless compression) leads to a file of about 40KB per journal page. If this file is kept, then as better OCR systems become available, they can be applied to obtain better text.

The cost of $0.40 per page has interesting implications. The estimates in my "Tragic loss ..." article were that the total mathematical literature consists of about 20 million pages. To digitize that would then cost $8M. This would be a one-time cost. By comparison, the total revenues of all publishers from mathematical publications are about $200M per year. Similar figures must apply to other fields. Thus all it would take to move towards converting everything to digital form is somebody to take on the task of organizing the effort. One can imagine all sorts of ways to paying for it.

One major problem in undertaking such a digitization project is the issue of copyrights. The economists do not have a problem. The journals they are digitizing are all run by learned societies, which feel that placing old issues in the public domain would be good advertising for them. What about commercial publishers? The only data point is derived from a conversation I had this past Friday with a math editor for a large commercial house. He told me that his view, which he feels others at his company share, is similar, namely that there is no money to be made on back issues, and that releasing old copies into the public domain could only be helpful. It would be nice to get more data on this topic.

Best regards,
Andrew

From: Paul Ginsparg 505-667-7353 <ginsparg@qfwfq.lanl.gov>
Date: Mon, 20 Mar 95 17:04:04 -0700
To: amo@research.att.com
Subject: Re: conversion to electronics
Cc: ann@cni.org, harnad@ecs.soton.ac.uk

andrew,

> ...40 cents per page, and "that includes scanning and OCR conversion
> to a very high (about 1 error/page) level of accuracy."

unlikely. what kind of ocr conversion are they talking about? is it to plain ascii, or does it preserve page markup and font information? (1 error/page is conceivable for single font clean text, but currently far from achievable for anything involving equations or in-line mathematics).

the only ocr i've played with that preserves page markup and font information is adobe's (the beta version of green giant), which translates to postscript (with little bitmapped inclusions of anything it can't identify) -- it does quite a good job on the overall page markup and font preservation, but reading carefully made too many errors in equations (specifically greek subscripts/superscripts, due to smaller size effectively scanned at lower resolution). but it had some tunable parameters so conceivably could be optimized better for any specifically application (e.g. not even try to identify anything smaller than a certain size, and leave instead as bitmap which still left readable sub/superscripts) on the other hand, as you point out once one has the bitmaps the ocr can be done at any later time and is relatively straightforward (perhaps involving an additional level of interaction with a system that prompts to resolve marginal cases), so the scanning alone will be a useful enterprise. (though i preferred you're alternate "suggestion" to retypset it all in tex, modulo the difficulty of getting deceased authors to correct the new proofs...)

> The scanning is done at 600 dpi, and (after application
> compression) leads to a file of about 40KB per journal page.

perhaps they have a compression algorithm optimized for bitmapped pages, standard gzip will not do nearly this well for 8.5 x 11 pages at 600dpi.

so i question some of hal varian's info, but we know he's serious (i spoke to him a bit at msri in december, and had corresponded with a few times previously and since), so we can wait and see what exactly they do, and at what functionality and cost.

> He told me that his view, which he feels others at his company
> share, is similar, namely that there is no money to be made on
> back issues,

the lack of commercial value to the copyright of the older material is of course what stevan has been harping on all along -- except they may soon find that there is significantly less money to be made on future issues as well...

pg

From: amo@research.att.com
Date: Tue, 21 Mar 95 22:45 EST
To: ginsparg@qfwfq.lanl.gov
Cc: ann@cni.org, harnad@ecs.soton.ac.uk
Subject: Re: conversion to electronics

Paul,

The quotes were for straight ascii text. I did not get the details, but I doubt there was any worry about preserving page markup. (Hal Varian was not involved in the negotiations. In fact, on some details his memory was hazy. When I checked with him on the accuracy of my message, he found that the scanning actually takes place in Barbados, not the

Dominican Republic. Also, the journals are not destroyed, only cut up and then rebound. However, the $0.40 price per page is correct, and includes the cutting up and rebinding.)

I do not know what compression algorithm is used, but 40KB per page of text at 600 dpi is reasonable, I have been assured by one of our local experts. Ordinary FAX compression (CCITT Group 4) is often superior to Lempel-Ziv, which is in gzip. It is a matter of tuning the algorithm for text.

I agree with you that it would be better to TeX all the old literature. However, that takes an order of magnitude more money. I got some precise figures from Keith Dennis, who is the new Executive Editor of Math. Rev. There are outfits in India and Poland that will do technical TeX for about $5/page. They use two typists, and have error rates of less than one error per 5 pages. (The corresponding figures for doing this in the US are around $20/page.) Thus processing the entire mathematical literature would cost around $100M. This is again a one-time cost, and is only half a year's cost of the present math journals. However, it is a large sum, and it might be hard to assemble it. On the other hand, $8M is within reach of an organization such as the AMS, and indeed I have managed to get several people there interested in trying to do this.

Basically, if you have a project costing $8M, you can think of doing it on speculation. You would only need 200 libraries to cough up $40K apiece to recover your costs. Now $40K is what a good library spends on math journals in 3-4 months, and much less than it spends annually on space for all the old journals. Thus you can easily make a compelling economic case for a library to buy the digitized version. If you increase the price by a factor of 10, though, it is a different story.

What excited me most about the information I sent out this past weekend was that we finally had reliable figures for the total cost of the entire process of taking old bound volumes, transporting them, cutting them up, scanning them, etc. The resolution of the scan, the storage requirement, and the quality of the OCR output are not as important. Those are going to improve dramatically in the next few years. If a terabyte is too expensive to store today, it will be half that price in 18 months, and a quarter in 3 years, and so on. On the other hand, the need to handle the original printed articles puts an effective floor on the cost of the project (at least until robots capable of going through books page by page are developed). To know that everything can be done for $0.40 per page is heartening.

In some cases the basic physical processes are expensive and likely to stay that way. In all the hoopla about the Information Superhighway you will sometimes see very high figures for the cost of rewiring the world with optical fiber. As it turns out, most of that cost is for general plant work. To wire up the average household in the US costs about $1,000. It does not matter much whether you use optical fiber, coax, or ordinary fiber. Of this $1,000, about $400 is for the high-tech equipment, such as the cables, the switches, etc. These costs are going down rapidly. However, the other $600 is just for the stringing or burying of the cables, and this cost is going down very slowly (as improved tools counteract increases in wages).

Best regards,
Andrew

From: amo@research.att.com
Date: Wed, 22 Mar 95 21:40 EST
To: ginsparg@qfwfq.lanl.gov
Cc: ann@cni.org, harnad@ecs.soton.ac.uk
Subject: Re: conversion to electronics

Paul,

Hal Varian checked more carefully with his sources, and it turns out that the 600 dpi scans take about 100KB per page, using standard Group 4 Fax/TIFF compression. Thus while there may be algorithms around that do get down to 40KB, they are not going to be used in this project. Sorry for the confusion.

Regards,
Andrew

Date: Thu, 23 Mar 95 01:43:28 -0700
From: Paul Ginsparg 505-667-7353 <ginsparg@qfwfq.lanl.gov>
To: amo@research.att.com
Subject: Re: conversion to electronics
Cc: ann@cni.org, harnad@ecs.soton.ac.uk

> Date: Wed, 22 Mar 95 21:40 EST
> To: ginsparg@qfwfq.lanl.gov
> Cc: ann@cni.org, harnad@ecs.soton.ac.uk
> Subject: Re: conversion to electronics
>
> Hal Varian checked more carefully with his sources, and it turns

> out that the 600 dpi scans take about 100KB per page, using standard
> Group 4 Fax/TIFF compression. Thus while there may be algorithms
> around that do get down to 40KB, they are not going to be used in
> this project. Sorry for the confusion.

that sounds more realistic, though still a tight squeeze at that resolution depending on what the pages actually look like. (as you know from a simple counting argument there is no lossless compression scheme that can guarantee to compress at all *every* file of size N bits: since $1 + 2 + 2^2 + ... + 2^{\{N-1\}} = 2^N - 1$, the total number of files of size less than N bits is less than the total number of possible N bit files. in the case of bitmapped pages, however, these are anything but generic binary files, and the compression scheme can be tuned to take maximal advantage of advance knowledge that there will be mainly whitespace. but as a simple exercise, consider a maximally idealized compression scheme that encodes only white<->black transitions, and the changes in their location from one scanned line to the next, and see a) how small a compressed file that is likely to give, and b) how its size scales with the scanning resolution)

pg

From: amo@research.att.com
Date: Sat, 25 Mar 95 19:22 EST
To: ginsparg@qfwfq.lanl.gov
Cc: ann@cni.org, b.naylor@soton.ac.uk, harnad@ecs.soton.ac.u
Subject: Re: conversion to electronics
Status: OR

Paul,

Certainly one cannot compress every file. The issue is how well can you do with standard software on printed text. The chaps who are doing the economics journal project have demonstrated 100KB per page with the usual fax algorithm at 600 dpi 1-bit per pixel (and apparently about half that at 300 dpi 1-bit per pixel). That already makes storage requirements manageable. If one is willing to give up on lossless compression, one could surely do better by applying various cleanup methods to the scanned image, but there does not seem to be any need for that.

Andrew

CONCLUSION

Ideas can change the world. Will these? The uncertainties are many. The model that Paul Ginsparg has already brought to life is one that clearly can work, at least under specific conditions. Where a well-defined group of users, all acclimated to the same kind of discourse and even familiar with standard software packages that transmit well by network, concentrate on producing rigorously analytical material, the relatively unobtrusive preprint server can be a powerful tool. Does it scale up? When the group gets larger or more diverse, when research interests start crossing disciplinary boundaries, when fundamental disagreements of method and style are a substantive part of the field itself -- does this kind of communication bog down? Are third parties needed to organize, control, and referee the conversations?

The way to find the answers to these questions is to begin to do, wherever possible, substantial projects of the kind the Ginsparg has outlined. The "hard sciences" are the obvious place to begin, for theirs is the academic culture most dependent on the journal form (to the near exclusion of the monograph) and on timely and wide distribution of resuls of their investigations. But there are areas of the social sciences and even the humanities where similar enterprises can reasonably expect to succeed. What is striking in 1995, five years after the first electronic scholarly journals came on-line, is that there has been so restrained a rush to this new medium. The growth curve has continued upwards, but considerably flatter than that for internet use among academics as a whole. If the model is so enticing, why the delay?

One reason is clearly the economic immunity of the professoriate. The "serials crisis" and the problems publishers have marketing monographs clearly have not yet had an appreciable impact on the authoring public of academe. It is not palpably difficult to "get published": rejection of a given article is taken as a personal, not an institutional, problem, and most articles in which their authors believe find homes eventually. The insulation of scholars and scientists from the economic burdens of their own publications means that they can remain content with the system as it is. A natural tendency to prefer the familiar, usually expressing itself as a concern about whether e-publication will be accepted by promotion and tenure committees, exerts its staying hand as well.

The *economic* pressure is now being felt not by faculty but by publishers and by librarians. But publishers have no desire to reposition themselves too rapidly into a market which may not be widely accepted and in which they are not sure they can recover costs of production. This leaves the librarians, guardians of the integrity of the system of scholarly communication *as a whole*. It is in fact in the library community that some of the most venturesome and at the same time pragmatic proposals have come forth. The series of symposia conducted by the Association of Research Libraries since 1992 has given stakeholders on all sides a place to express concerns and inform themselves. The Mellon Foundation published a 1992 study of the state of library budgets (noting inter alia the declining share of overall university budgets that libraries have had the last twenty years) and pointed to electronic publishing as a possible source of amelioration. (See "Hyperlinks" section at the end of this book.)

The Association of American Universities, that is to say the presidents of the leading research institutions, teamed with ARL in 1994 to write strong reports pointing a way forward through judicious use of electronic publication. In the fall of 1994, an ad hoc group of scholars, librarians, and publishers convened in the Columbia University Library to turn ideas in the atmosphere into a concrete series of proposals for ways individual institutions could begin to shift the balance towards economically more viable media. Now in 1995, other glimmers of venture are appearing, e.g., a joint project between Emory University and Scholars Press or another between the Johns Hopkins University and its own Press to put existing journals on-line. The Mellon Foundation is taking a participatory interest in several such projects, to see what the economics of the new medium are really like. It is too soon to say that this will be a groundswell, and the aggregate collection of projects proposed and under way still *feels* relatively unambitious to longtime observers of the scene. Will it take exacerbated economic crisis to impel further movement?

One of Harnad's economic points is really a sociological point and an important one. The economy of science journal publishing has been constructed so that whatever money changes hands, virtually none ever reaches the authors of the articles. They receive their compensation indirectly, from employers who value their research output. Harnad thus correctly insists that the researcher looking at the published article wants more than anything that it reach as wide an audience as possible, with as few barriers as possible. Thus in this case, traditional publishers cannot defend the need to recover costs from the end user by appealing to their need to reimburse authors. That is a real economic change whose ultimate purport we can now only surmise.

Other considerations will play a part in how this all turns out that did not arise in the course of the focused conversation here. It will not be out of place to suggest a few.

The nature of the scientific or scholarly "paper" or "article" has been shaped by the medium of publication and distribution. Each item must be an independent grain of information, linked if at all by indexes and abstracts and cross-references. There is value (for promotion and tenure) in piling up total number of such grains. We know the difference between an "article" and a "monograph" by several criteria, but a crucial one is length -- if it's too long to be an article, then it should think about becoming a monograph.

But in a world where the artifacts are distributed electronically, numerous changes are somewhere between possible and inevitable. Grains of knowledge will attract each other: if I publish a note this year and add a note next year, at the very least they will be linked to each other dynamically (whether they appear in different "journals" or not) and it may very well make more sense to replace the first note with a longer, coherent version summarizing the two stages of research. All sorts of question of version control and citation authority arise, to be sure, but as reader and as author I think my interests would be served if those can be solved and connections made stronger. Similarly, I need not worry about my article getting too long (in plain text of almost any kind, the difference for costs of storage and transmission between a two page article and a two hundred page monograph will be negligible), and so the article and the monograph may cease to be distinct categories and a new configuration emerge.

Other changes will ensue. If in a WWW document I now need to cite another WWW document, I can make the link dynamic, so that instead of a footnote that says "Smedley, op. cit. 235" I can make a link and let you *read* Smedley's page 235 if you wish, to see whether what she says corroborates what I say or not. On this principle, not only my own works will be linked to each other, but a growing body of scholarly literature may be enmeshed in a net of links and connections that multiply the value of each item appreciably. At some point when that happens, the intrinsic superiority of the electronic to the paper medium will become ineluctable and the rush to cyberspace will be on in earnest. But we still do not know for sure what it will cost. Debates such as the one included here on the percentage of costs of print publication devoted to printing, binding, and distribution (which almost always omit consideration of the costs to libraries of cataloguing, binding, shelving, circulating, and maintaining) are not well equipped to address a deeper question. How much of what we are now willing to pay for will we continue to be willing to pay for?

Harnad et al. will argue that HTML-tagged texts on the WWW are perfectly satisfactory for reading purposes, but such texts are undoubtedly problematic, not least because the author/editor cannot control *completely* the look and feel on the screen at the reader's end the way author and editor can now control it. Is that a value worth keeping? It might seem not, but recall how the first camera-ready copy for short run printing in the 1970s, based on photographed typescript, was very reluctantly received, and desktop publishing only really came into its own when the visual quality of the output was able to compete with print. Where is that threshold of acceptance in electronic audiences? It will vary from audience to audience, and for now we don't know.

We also don't know how much technology and support we will *need*. It is easy enough now to say that the traditional article will take up little or no bandwidth and so place a minimal strain on the network. But what if a scientist begins to believe she needs to give you full motion video, from six different angles, of a crucial experiment? Or if a report on an experiment conducted on the space shuttle feels it *must* be accompanied by gigabytes and gigabytes of the raw telemetry data sent back to earth? In principle (this is the power of the medium) such full presentations of data are possible and desirable, but in practice, they may begin to add costs (getting that video formatted in a standard way for transmission to all platforms) that we do not now properly anticipate.

For all these concerns, it is impossible not to have at least some guarded optimism about this future. We need not imagine substitution or totalitarian takeover by any of the players on the cyberspace frontier. What needs to be foreseen, instead, is the shift in the mixture of kinds of information available on what terms. There is already a lot of *free* information in the world (that is, information given away at no direct cost to end user): the phone book for one, all the information in the Borders or Barnes and Noble store that gets consumed by browsers who never buy -- the travel section at Borders in my neighborhood takes a pummelling in late winter as people plan their summer vacations for free, television news (paid for by soap-sellers) for another. Some information, on the other hand (stock tips from really qualified advisors), we pay for at a high price.

But life on the Internet has been marked, at least so far, by a far freer exchange of information by its producers than seems to be the case in the world of print. This "circle of gifts" culture exploits the power of the individual to multiply her words indefinitely at minimal cost of time and effort. So it is that documents which one scholar produces for more or less personal use (say for classroom distribution), or which one hobbyist produces purely for pleasure (say a Civil War hobbyist obsessed with the history of his small town in Tennessee), can now take on a utility they were denied before. Collaborations are possible, like the TOCS-IN project at the University of Toronto where a collective of classicists all over the world each take one or two scholarly journals to track, typing in the table of contents of each new issue as it appears; the whole is greater than the parts, and this easily gopherable resource is now widely used as a way of keeping current in the field, at no net cost to anyone.

It is examples like these that encourage us to dream large dreams about the free flow of information in the future, but even if those dreams fall short of realization, it must be considered likely that the *proportion* of the total information economy that will be occupied by this free exchange will be larger than is now the case. What this will mean, none can say, but it will influence the market for purchase and sale of information in many ways.

In the end, it is perhaps the word that Steven Harnad started with that begs the question: "esoteric". His idiosyncratic use of the word is meant to highlight publication with relatively few authors and readers, too negligible economically to be of interest to commercial publishers and relatively easy to redirect towards free net distribution. At some level, Harnad is undoubtedly right. Some information will move this way. But "esoteric" as he uses it is a word that defines the position of a certain sector of information as it is produced and consumed in the world of *paper* publication. When once the power of the networks has been harnessed and a substantial part of the academic population has migrated to using it, a new economy will emerge. What we cannot now predict with accuracy is what will seem "esoteric" *there* and what will be commercially viable. The lines may very well fall in *very* different places from where they fall in the world of paper publication.

The responsible course for universities and research institutions concerned about the future is to press the claims of that sector, to experiment responsibly and venture bravely, to see if those lines can be drawn in a way that favors the widest and freest flow of information of a scholarly and scientific nature. In his "Four Quartets," Eliot described the poet's mission as "to purify the dialect of the tribe"; but in a sense science and poetry work to tha tone goal from different directions, seeking by their discourse to enhance the quality of society's common discourse, by rooting out error and imprecision and finding new and true things to say and ways to say them.

To that end, we need a better word than Harnad's, for esoteric suggests something limited and restricted in scope, when what we need now is a conception that encourages us to broaden the category and make it as powerful as possible. The network is a place of dialogue, as this collection makes clear, where the best of what is thought and said enters its own world of permanent transition. It is dialogue in which only a few participate, perhaps, but which is radically open to all who meet its standards of rigor. In that spirit, perhaps we could begin to speak not of an esoteric form of publishing but of a Socratic realm of dialogue.

HYPERLINKS

ARL Publications

The Association of Research Library publishes, both in hard copy and by Internet distribution, a variety of studies and tools for the reader who wishes to become better informed about this exploding area of publishing interest. If you are interested in acquiring any ARL publications in print, please contact the ARL offices in Washington, DC.

E-Journal Directory: Since 1991, ARL has sponsored publication of the *Directory of Electronic Scholarly Journals, Newsletters, and Academic Discussion Lists*. The fifth printed edition was published in May 1995. Basic information from the directory and an abridged ASCII version appears on the ARL gopher site:

> gopher://arl.cni.org:70/11/scomm/edir

E-Publishing Symposia: Since 1991, ARL has sponsored four symposia on electronic scholarly publishing; the second through fourth symposia were published in print form, and the papers of the third will be available in June 1995 on the ARL World Wide Web sites:

> http://arl.cni.org

Andrew W. Mellon Foundation Study: In 1992, the Andrew W. Mellon Foundation prepared a study, published for the Foundation by ARL, titled University Libraries and Scholarly Communications. The full text also appears on both the ARL gopher and World Wide Web sites:

> gopher://arl.cni.org:70/11/scomm/ulsc
> http: //arl.cni.org

Since that time, the Mellon Foundation has sponsored a series of grants for electronic scholarly journal projects of varying scope and nature. A programmatic paper outlining that funding project was prepared by the Foundation and is available on the ARL gopher site:

> gopher://arl.cni.org:70/00/scomm/scalt

Association of American Universities Task Force Reports: In 1994, the Association of American Universitites organized three task forces in cooperation with ARL to examine special areas of urgent interest to libraries and scholars: (1) Acquisition of foreign materials; (2)

Scientific/technical publishing; (3) Intellectual property in research universities. The full text is available in print and also appears on both the ARL gopher and World Wide Web sites:

    gopher://arl.cni.org:70/11/scomm/aau
    http: /arl.cni.org

New Internet Journal Announcements: In 1993, ARL's ongoing Directory project was enhanced by the creation of the on-line list "NewJour," which distributes announcements of new electronic journal projects. To subscribe, send e-mail to listserv@ccat.sas.upenn.edu, place nothing on the Subject: line, and include the message SUBSCRIBE NEWJOUR. The archives of this list are available and WAIS-searchable at URL:

    gopher://ccat.sas.upenn.edu:5070/11/journals/newjour

Stevan Harnad, Related Publications

The following file is retrievable from directory pub/harnad/Harnad on host princeton.edu

ftp://princeton.edu/pub/harnad/Harnad
http://www.princeton.edu/~harnad/intpub.html
gopher://gopher.princeton.edu:9000/1

Harnad, S. (1990) Scholarly Skywriting and the Prepublication Continuum of Scientific Inquiry. Psychological Science 1: 342 - 343 (reprinted in Current Contents 45: 9-13, November 11 1991).
FILENAME: harnad90.skywriting

Harnad, S. (1991) Post-Gutenberg Galaxy: The Fourth Revolution in the Means of Production of Knowledge. Public-Access Computer Systems Review 2 (1): 39 - 53 (also reprinted in PACS Annual Review Volume 2 1992; and in R. D. Mason (ed.) Computer Conferencing: The Last Word. Beach Holme Publishers, 1992; and in A. L. Okerson (ed.) Directory of Electronic Journals, Newsletters, and Academic Discussion Lists, 2nd edition. Washington, DC, Association of Research Libraries, Office of Scientific & Academic Publishing, 1992).
FILENAME: harnad91.postgutenberg

Harnad, S. (1992) Interactive Publication: Extending the American Physical Society's Discipline-Specific Model for Electronic Publishing. Serials Review, Special Issue on Economics Models for Electronic Publishing, pp. 58 - 61.
FILENAME: harnad92.interactivpub

Harnad, S. (1994) Implementing Peer Review on the Net: Scientific Quality Control in Scholarly Electronic Journals. Proceedings of International Conference on Refereed Electronic Journals: Towards a Consortium for Networked Publications. University of Manitoba, Winnipeg 1-2 October 1993 (in press)
FILENAME: harnad95.peer.review

Paul Ginsparg: Description of Preprint Archives at LANL

Ginsparg, P. (1994) First Steps Towards Electronic Research Communication. Computers in Physics. (August, American Institute of Physics). http://xxx.lanl.gov/blurb/

Andrew Odlyzko: "Tragic Loss" Article reproduced in this Book

Odlyzko, A.M. (1995) Tragic loss or good riddance? The impending demise of traditional scholarly journals.

Available files:

file name	size	description
tragic.loss.diffs	2 KB	brief description of differences between the complete versions of Jul. 16 and Nov. 6, 1994
tragic.loss.txt	219 KB	ordinary text of both short and full versions, and the description of differences between the complete versions of Jul. 16 and Nov. 6, 1994
tragic.loss.short.ps	102 KB	PostScript of short version
tragic.loss.long.ps	387 KB	PostScript of full version

To obtain these files through email, send the message

send tragic.loss.diffs from att/math/odlyzko
send tragic.loss.txt from att/math/odlyzko
send tragic.loss.short.ps from att/math/odlyzko
send tragic.loss.long.ps from att/math/odlyzko
mailsize 200k

to netlib@research.att.com, where "mailsize 200k" is an optional command that will ensure messages are kept under 200 KB each.

These version are also available on WWW at URL

ftp://netlib.att.com/netlib/att/math/odlyzko/index.html.Z

Ftp access is available on machine netlib.att.com. After logging in as "anonymous" and giving the full email address as password, do

cd netlib/att/math/odlyzko
binary
get tragic.loss.txt.Z

to obtain a copy of the (compressed) text version, for example.

GLOSSARY OF ABBREVIATIONS AND TERMS

AAAS - American Association for the Advancement of Science, Washington, DC.

Acrobat - A program developed by Adobe Systems which allows documents to be distributed with complex formatting (fonts, spacing, graphics, etc.) to users with DOS, Macintosh, or Unix computers without their needing to have the program used to create the document in order to view it. PDF is the name of the internal format used by Acrobat, and also the extension normally used in the name of an Acrobat file.

ACS - American Chemical Society, Washington, DC.

AMS - American Mathematical Society, Providence, RI.

APA - American Psychological Association.

APS - American Physical Society, New York, NY.

Archie - A network service that allows users to find which anonymous FTP sites contain specific files of interest.

ASIS - American Society for Information Science, Silver Spring, Maryland.

Bitmap - A file format for digital images which treats the image as a two-dimensional array of pixels. This approach is distinguished from the alternate approach of describing an image as a collection of primitive shapes - lines or objects.

BITNET - Because It's Time NETwork. A network created in the 1980s by EDUCOM, connecting primarily academic and research sites. (The number of BITNET sites has remained fairly static in the last few years, as many of the sites have been able to acquire Internet connections.)

CARL - Colorado Alliance of Research Libraries. A consortium of six large research libraries in Colorado. The CARL database includes the combined holdings of these libraries and a variety of other data. CARL also operates UnCover, a document delivery system for journal articles.

CICNet - A regional Internet service for the midwestern United States, founded by the Committee on Institutional Cooperation, based in Ann Arbor, Michigan. CICNet maintains an electronic journal archive accessed by thousands of Internet users. This archive is one of the most comprehensive such sources on the network.

Client - A computer in a network which uses services, programs, or storage provided by a separate "server" computer.

ARPA - Advanced Research Projects Agency. (Also known as DARPA, the Defense Advanced Research Projects Agency.) The agency which initially sponsored the development of the ARPAnet, the forerunner of the Internet.

DECnet - A set of network protocols and programs developed by the Digital Equipment Corporation (DEC) and commonly used on DEC's computers. DECnet is a proprietary networking system distinct from TCP/IP.

Domain - A group of IP addresses corresponding to a specific site, group, university, or company, from which the IP address for a specific machine can be assigned.

EARN - European Academic and Research Network

Email - Electronic mail. Mail composed and transmitted on a computer system or network.

EU - European Union. The EU has generated a number of initiatives in telecommunications and networking as part of an overall plan for its members.

FAQ - Frequently Asked Questions. A collection of answers to the most frequently raised questions in any of a large number of different subject areas, commonly created and distributed over USENET.

Follett Report - Its full title is *Joint Funding Council's Libraries Review Group: Report*, December 1993. The report was written for the Higher Education Funding Councils of the England, Scotland, and Wales, and the Department of Education for Northern Ireland. This review of library and related issues in higher education in the UK was chaired by Professor Sir Brian Follett, Vice-Chancellor, University of Warwick. It put forward major recommendations for addressing information issues in UK universities and secured funding for a wide range of important projects as instantiations of the recommendations.

FTP - File Transfer Protocol. A standard method for sending files from one computer to another on TCP/IP networks such as the Internet. FTP is also the name of the command used to initiate transfer of files. Anonymous FTP is a common practice which permits users to access some parts of an FTP site without needing an account and password for the site. Access usually is gained by using the username "anonymous" or "ftp". By convention, the user should enter their e-mail address as the password.

ftp.uu.net - A computer on the Internet widely used as a source for publicly distributed materials, including shareware, USENET digests, and FAQs.

Gigabyte - one thousand megabytes, or approximately one billion seventy million bytes (actually 1,024 megabytes).

GNU zipped (gzipped) - GNU is an acronym for Gnu is Not Unix. The GNU project has developed and freely distributed a number of utilities which are widely used on Unix computers. One of these utilities is a compression program (gzip) which is widely used as an alternative to the standard Unix compression program. A gzipped file is normally distinguished by the extension *.gz, as opposed to the *.Z extension used by the standard Unix compression program.

Gopher - A program which uses a network of interlinked menus for accessing publicly distributed resources and documents on computers distributed across the Internet.

Gopher+ - An expanded and updated version of the original Gopher software, produced (like the original) at the University of Minnesota. Gopher+ supports a wider variety of file types and protocols. Gopher+ is not yet widely used.

Group-4-FAX - the format used by high speed Group 4 facsimile machines to transmit page images.

GUI - Graphical User Interface. A computer terminal interface, such as Windows, that is based on graphics instead of text.

HEP preprint network (HEPnet) - A "High Energy Physics" service created by Paul Ginsparg of the Los Alamos National Laboratories. It is the standard electronic networked source by which the high energy physics research community accesses preprints. Ginsparg has cloned the software for a number of other related disciplines.

HTML - HyperText Markup Language. A markup language based on but simpler than SGML used to annotate hypertext documents for publication on the World Wide Web, to take advantage of the WWW;s capacity to connect documents and sectins of documents across the Net.

HTTP - HyperText Transfer Protocol. A protocol used to transmit files over the World Wide Web.

Hytelnet - A single database providing access to Internet resources via a menu structure.

IEEE - Institute of Electrical and Electronics Engineers, New York, NY.

IETF - Internet Engineering Task Force. The IETF, a volunteer organization, develops Internet standards and discusses operational and technical problems of the Internet.

info.anu.edu.au - Address for the Gopher server at the Australian National University. The server includes a section on the electronic library, as well as information on electronic journals. (ANU gopher server)

Intellectual Property Task Force - The Association of American Universities Task Force on Intellectual Property Rights in an Electronic Environment, part of the Research Libraries Project. The Task Force worked to develop proposals for university policies on intellectual property issues. The Task Force issued a report in April, 1994. See the Hyperlinks section for the URL for the Internet version.

InterNIC - The Internet Network Information Center. Funded by the National Science Foundation, the InterNIC provides services such as access to an archive of Internet standard documents and the assignment of IP addresses for the Internet community at large.

ISO - International Standards Organization. The principal international group responsible for standards in many areas. For purposes of this discussion, the standards referenced for electronic communications.

JAMA - Journal of the American Medical Association.

JPEG - Joint Photographic Experts Group - This group developed and gave their name to a standard method for compression of digital images and a format in which to store the compressed file.

LANL - Los Alamos National Laboratory. The Department of Energy's National Laboratory at Los Alamos, New Mexico.

LaTeX - A variant of the TeX text formatting program using a set of macro commands useful for formatting mathematical manuscripts.

LISTSERV - Software which enables a distributed electronic discussion group to function. Each subscriber to a particular LISTSERV receives the submissions of all other subscribers. The electronic discussion group is itself referred to as a LISTSERV. Other softwares that perform similar functions include Listproc, Majordomo.

LOC - Library of Congress, Washington, DC.

Lynx - A program to browse the World Wide Web which works on simple text terminals, rather than requiring a graphical computer display terminal.

MacTCP - An extension to Apple's Macintosh operating system which enables Macintosh personal computers to use the TCP/IP Internet protocols, and thus to connect to the Internet.

MajorDomo - A software program for the management of electronic mailing lists and discussion groups. It provides similar functions to those of the LISTSERV and Listproc programs.

Minitel - The telecommunications software and network developed and widely used in France. Minitel was initially developed and distributed as an electronic alternative to printed telephone directories, but has evolved into a popular personal communications system.

Mirror image archives - A duplicate of a collection of files normally available from one Internet server at a different site, in order to permit users to access files from a computer closer to them, or to avoid problems caused by excessive usage at the original site.

Mosaic - See NSCA Mosaic.

MPEG - Motion Picture Experts Group. A committee of experts from the audio, video, and computer industries developing an evolving series of standards for compression of moving images. Files encoded using this standard are referred to as MPEG files. MPEG-1 is a low-resolution format currently used on the World Wide Web for short animated files. MPEG-2 is a much higher resolution format being developed for digital television and movies.

NCSA Mosaic - Mosaic is a program which permits browsing the World Wide Web with a graphical interface, which allows users to explore the Web more easily. It was developed by the National Center for

Supercomputing Applications at the University of Illinois. After the development of Mosaic, some of the NCSA team left and formed a new startup group which quickly offered another highly popular interface, Netscape, to the public.

Netscape -- See Mosaic, above.

NII - National Information Infrastructure - A set of new government funded initiatives to develop a more advanced form of national computer network, particularly as advocated by the Clinton/Gore administration.

NSF - National Science Foundation.

NSFnet - One of the Internet's backbone networks funded by the National Science Foundation. (Now discontinued, as part of the transition of the Internet from government funding to a commercial service.)

OCLC - Online Computer Library Center, Inc., Dublin, Ohio. OCLC is a major commercial provider of library cataloging services and runs the Online Union Catalog.

PostScript - A page description language developed and marketed by Adobe Systems. PostScript can be used by a wide variety of computers and printers, and is the dominant format used for desktop publishing. Documents in PostScript format are able to use the full resolution of any PostScript printer, because they describe the page to be printed in terms of primitive shapes which are interpreted by the printer's own controller. PostScript is often used to share documents on the Internet because of this ability to work on many different platforms and printers.

Red Sage - A popular Washington restaurant which gave its name to a group of publishers and librarians interested in electronic publishing which was formed at a lunch at the restaurant. The group then spawned a project by the same name. Its original parnters included an AT&T developed software called "Right Pages, the Medical School at the University of California, and several publishers of journals in radiology.

SCI - Science Citation Index. Produced by the Institute for Scientific Information, SCI indices show the pattern of citations of scientific journal articles.

SGML - Standard Generalized Markup Language. SGML is both a language and an ISO standard for describing information embedded within a document. HyperText Markup Language (HTML) is based on the SGML standard.

SIAM - Society for Industrial and Applied Mathematics, Philadelphia, PA.

SLAC - Stanford Linear Accelerator Center, Stanford University. SLAC is the site of an extensive archive of preprints for high energy physics.

Software - A program or set of instructions that controls the operation of a computer. Distinguished from the actual hardware of the computer.

src.doc.ic.ac.uk - Address for the Gopher server at the Department of Computing, Imperial College, London, UK.

TeX - A powerful text formatting program initially written by Donald Knuth. Widely used by computer scientists, mathematicians, and physicists.

TIFF - Tagged Image File Format. A file format commonly used for digital scanned images. Images saved in TIFF format can be used on most computers. Developed by Aldus and Microsoft.

TULIP - The University LIcensing Program. TULIP is a cooperative research project testing system for networked delivery and use of journals. Objectives include determining technical feasibility, developing organizational and economic models, and studying user behavior. For testing purposes, 42 materials science and engineering journals published by Elsevier and Pergamon are being used.

UNESCO - United Nations Educational, Scientific, and Cultural Organization, whose headquarters is in Paris, France.

URL - Uniform Resource Locator. A URL is the "address" for something made available through the World Wide Web. A URL consists of the access method, server name, directory, and file name. Although the URL was developed for WWW, it has become widely used to describe the location of files which may be accessed by other techniques.

USENET - An informal system of electronic bulletin boards or discussion groups commonly distributed over the Internet. USENET predates the Internet, although today most USENET material is distributed over the Internet.

Veronica - Veronica is a program to search an index to all Gopher server titles in the world. The program was developed at the University of Nevada. The initials stand for Very Easy Rodent-Oriented Net-wide Index to Computerized Archives.

VT100 - Originally, a video display terminal manufactured by the Digital Equipment Corporation. It is now the most commonly supported plain text terminal type used for network connections.

WAIS - Wide Area Information Servers. A software program originally developed by Thinking Machines Co. which permits the very rapid search of extensive indexes to find text in large documents.

World-Wide Web (WWW) - A hypertext system of cross-linked data sources, which permits easy access to or publication of complex data types, including text, graphics, sound and animation, across the Internet. Initially developed at CERN (the European Center for Nuclear Research) in Geneva, Switzerland.